BRINDA SOMAYA
WORKS & CONTINUITIES

BRINDA SOMAYA
WORKS & CONTINUITIES

AN ARCHITECTURAL MONOGRAPH

Curated by Ruturaj Parikh
Edited by Nandini Somaya Sampat

MAPIN PUBLISHING • The HECAR Foundation

First published in India in 2018 by
Mapin Publishing Pvt. Ltd
706 Kaivanna, Panchvati, Ellisbridge
Ahmedabad 380006 INDIA
T: +91 79 40 228 228 • F: +91 79 40 228 201
E: mapin@mapinpub.com • www.mapinpub.com

in association with

The HECAR Foundation
C/o Somaya and Kalappa Consultants Pvt. Ltd.
Udyog Bhavan, Ground Floor, 29 Walchand Hirachand Marg,
Ballard Estate, Fort, Mumbai 400001, India
www.thehecarfoundation.org

International Distribution
Worldwide
Prestel Publishing Ltd.
14-17 Wells Street
London W1T 3PD
T: +44 (0)20 7323 5004 • F: +44 (0)20 7323 0271
E: sales@prestel-uk.co.uk

North America
Antique Collectors' Club
T: +1 800 252 5231 • F: +1 413 529 0862
E: sales@antiquecc.com • www.accdistribution.com/us

Rest of the World
Mapin Publishing Pvt. Ltd

ISBN-13: 978-93-85360-23-7 (Mapin)
ISBN-13: 978-81-92819-01-3 (The HECAR Foundation)

Editor Nandini Somaya Sampat
Curator Ruturaj Parikh
Art Director Tina Nussirabadwalla
Research Coordinator Anthea Fernandes
Research Assistant Prerna Shetty
Photography Ishita Parikh & Noshir Gobhai

Contributors James Polshek, Jon Lang, Mary Norman Woods, Porus Olpadwala, Tod Williams and Billie Tsien, Arun Shourie, Saryu Doshi, Kamu Iyer.

The moral rights of Nandini Somaya Sampat, Ruturaj Parikh, James Polshek, Jon Lang, Mary Norman Woods, Porus Olpadwala, Tod Williams, Billie Tsien, Arun Shourie, Saryu Doshi and Kamu Iyer as authors of this work are asserted.

Copyediting: Ateendriya Gupta/Mapin Editorial
Editorial management: Neha Manke/Mapin Editorial
Production: Gopal Limbad/Mapin Design Studio
Printed at Parksons Graphics, Mumbai

To my parents Gunavati and Chinnappa, who inspired me.
To my husband Anand, who is a true partner to me as I build.
To my sister Ranjini, who mentored my thoughts and ideas.
To my son Vikram, who enlivens my thoughts and ideas.
To my daughter Nandini, without whom this book would never have happened.
I trust her with the future of our studio.

CONTENTS

9   Foreword   James Stewart Polshek

12   Preface   Ruturaj Parikh

14   Acknowledgements

17   Introduction   Nandini Somaya Sampat

25   On India
      Arun Shourie and Brinda Somaya

33   **Bhadli village and Vasant Vidyalaya**

65   **Campus for Zensar Technologies**

95   **The Cathedral & John Connon School**

133   **Tata Consultancy Services Headquarters**

153   Working from Mumbai
      Kamu Iyer, Mary N. Woods and Brinda Somaya

163   **The Street**

195   **The Community**

219   **Jubilee Church**

239   **Rajabai Clock Tower**

267   Architecture and Culture
      Saryu Doshi and Brinda Somaya

275   **St Thomas Cathedral**

301   **Nalanda International School**

331   **Houses**

373   **Club Mahindra Kumbhalgarh**

397   **Campus for Goa Institute of Management**

427   The Significance of Brinda Somaya's Work in Post-Independence India
      Jon Lang

434   Humility and Fierce Resolve: The Making of a Compleat Architect
      Porus Olpadwala

441   The Empathetic Architect
      Mary N. Woods

445   Brinda Somaya's Practice and Contemporary Architecture in India
      Ruturaj Parikh

451   Epilogue
      Tod Williams and Billie Tsien

454   Chronology

480   Biodata

489   Contributors

491   Credits

FOREWORD

JAMES STEWART POLSHEK

"Architecture and architectural freedom are above all social issues that must be seen from inside a political structure, not from outside it."

—Lina Bo Bardi, 1974

Distinguished Indian architect Brinda Somaya is both fiercely independent and profoundly idealistic, characteristics that are the foundation of her innovative conceptual approach to architecture, urbanism and preservation. I quote Bardi's words, not because both architects are women but because both, during a difficult world economy, enriched cultural history while expanding the boundaries of their professional discipline.

In 1975, Somaya opened her own studio. Her architectural practice expanded over the ensuing 40 years, the latter part of a period that critic Martin Filler characterised as being one of "all-pervasive commercialism, rampant celebrity-mongering and a dispiriting lack of social awareness". This dark observation is radically contrary to Somaya's entire belief system. Her intellect and the distinctive Indian traditions of architecture as a collaborative craft allowed her to rise above this new set of negative social and political impediments.

Notwithstanding the influence of feminism and the impact that may have had on the young Brinda Somaya, there remained almost total male domination in the domain of her chosen profession. Today, the exponential increase in the number of women students and practitioners of architecture suggests that the democratic and empathetic core of this ancient calling is alive and well. Brinda Somaya's life and practice, as comprehensively laid out in this monograph, makes clear that she is one of the models for this quiet reformation: one that celebrates service rather than power, and generosity rather than ego gratification.

This is clearly demonstrated by the typological diversity of her individual buildings and her contributions to the enlightened urbanism of modern Mumbai. These, and many more built accomplishments, attest to her firm's global reputation.

Recent major projects demonstrate her affinity for clients whose programmes contribute to the public good. These include the "Tata Consultancy Services

Campuses", which inspires an internationally recognised quality of work; "The B.D. Petit Parsee General Hospital", which represents the highest standards of healthcare service in a stimulating verdant environment; and the ongoing stabilisation and restoration of Louis I Kahn's masterpiece, "The Indian Institute of Management", in Ahmedabad, which represents the firm's contribution to education.

My acquaintance with these multifaceted achievements was not always informed by direct observation of Brinda Somaya's studio's work or from her publications, but from actual participation with her and her colleagues. In 2014, Damyanti Radheshwar, an architect who had worked with me professionally for almost 30 years, asked if I might be interested in collaborating with Somaya's studio for a competition in memory of great Indian jurist Dr Babasaheb Ambedkar, who had died in 1956. Provided with a crash course on the postcolonial history of India, I quickly came to share with my distant Indian colleagues an understanding of this man's importance. I had not been aware of Ambedkar, who had committed his life to the oppressed classes of India and was the "architect" of India's constitution. Brinda and I shared the belief that the design competition would publicly celebrate his momentous contributions and simultaneously provide an opportunity to weave together many of the beliefs that had animated our careers.

Brinda and her team convinced me that it was important to create an iconic public space that could accommodate the millions of pilgrims who would be coming twice a year to commemorate the life and accomplishments of Ambedkar.

Within days, I found myself working intimately with Somaya and members of her team. Over the weeks we worked together, I came to develop a profound understanding and respect for her anonymous but effective team. Their life-affirming social convictions encouraged both a reinforcement of Indian architectural traditions and an optimistic imagining of the future.

Brinda Somaya: Works and Continuities is a comprehensive chronicle that will influence and enhance the contributions of future architects, preservationists, designers and planners who share Brinda Somaya's convictions.

I end with a quote that befits her idealistic vision of our chosen profession.

"A historian (or an architect) ought to be exact, sincere and impartial; free from passion, unbiased by interest, fear, resentment or affection; and faithful to the truth, which is the mother of history, the preserver of great actions, the enemy of oblivion, the witness of the past and the director of the future."

—Dr Babasaheb Ambedkar

PREFACE

RUTURAJ PARIKH

A monograph may be many things: a chronicle and a record of work and the ideas behind the work; a "manifesto" of the practice through articulation of its core concerns; or a compendium of projects as a document to promote the work of the studio. When I initiated work on this book, I was overwhelmed by the quantum and variety of projects that have been produced over four decades of Brinda Somaya's consistent practice. My initial research revealed about 200 projects of varying scale and typology, encompassing an incredible range of programmes from biscuit factories to large urban interventions. How can one chronicle this unique width of the practice in reasonable depth?

Over my discussions with Brinda Somaya and Nandini Somaya Sampat, it became clear that their primary intent of publishing this book was not to produce a journal of projects; rather, this monograph was perhaps a means to evaluate their contribution within a larger framework of culture and society: a reflective document that can critically discuss the impact of Brinda Somaya's work and the validity of the intentions of Somaya and Kalappa. The ambition of this document, for me, was also to enable readers to introspect the potential of a large architecture firm in India and the impact of SNK's rigorous, pragmatic and ethical work of scale and diversity. This width and depth of work eludes "niche" firms that have largely framed the narrative of architecture of India in the past two decades.

This monograph presents a critical section of work: a thin slice through varying scales and typologies that frame the core concerns of Brinda Somaya's practice. It exemplifies their perpetual effort to have an impact that is larger than delivering on the programme or creating meaningful pieces of design. This diagonal cut through time and typology is a reflection on the struggle of a practice that resists being pushed to the periphery of the society it serves. The works presented in this monograph attempts to structure a discourse on the value of being in the mainstream while also concerning oneself with the greater agenda. The book is composed of 13 chapters—each discussing a prototype project/group of projects—that stand as a case studies in the potential of professional work to confront and resolve a specific issue or a concern that has always been a part of the "continuities" of Somaya and Kalappa.

The dialogues in the book—moderated conversations between Brinda Somaya and Mary Norman Woods, Kamu Iyer, Arun Shourie and Saryu Doshi—outline ideas that form the background narrative, engaging discussions on history, culture, arts, ethos, society, India and the profession. Essays by Mary Norman Woods, Porus Olpadwala, Jon Lang, Tod Williams, Billie Tsien and me are critical readings of this work from independent and distinct vantage points. The sections at the back of the book will enable the reader to understand the diversity of SNK's portfolio along with Brinda Somaya's professional and academic contributions.

My attempts as the curator of the book are to echo the voice of the practice that now enters its fifth decade. Reflecting on the work also meant revisiting all the buildings that were to form the chapters in this book and presenting them to the readers as they stand today: an incredibly bold path for an architect to embark upon, especially in India where the buildings are seldom maintained in their pristine original state. Ishita Parikh and Sagar Shinde of SNK revisited the projects with their cameras to represent the built environments in their honest present condition. The many traces of human occupation in the photographs of this book are a result of this wonderful exercise. This genuine portrayal of work reinforces my conviction in the values of Brinda Somaya's studio.

This book would have been an ordinary catalogue of projects without the curatorial freedom afforded to me by Mrs Somaya and Nandini, and their patience through many abstract conversations on the same. Tina Nussirabadwalla, the art director for this book, worked overtime with a deep understanding of the nature of this content to produce an unconventional design that serves the purpose of this monograph, while Prerna Shetty dug deep into the exhaustive archive of material to enable us to make sense of the great volume of architectural production. Anthea Fernandes worked on this repository of information to develop material for the design and editing of the book.

The most important and the gentlest voice in the book is that of Brinda Somaya—the protagonist of this project. For me, the authenticity of her ideas could only be validated if narrated by her directly to the audience of this publication. It would have been a disservice to her work if the observations would have been made by the eyes of an author, who could only have engaged with the work through a small sliver of the prolific practice. While this book may not follow the convention of publishing monographs, it is published with a hope that it may contribute to the discussion on architecture, landscape, urban design and conservation in India and abroad; as well as the discussion on architectural monographs, by attempting to reach beyond its purpose, true to the oeuvre of Brinda Somaya.

ACKNOWLEDGMENTS

Two years ago, upon the urging of my architectural peers and my enthusiastic family, I began on a journey. The purpose of this monograph is to share my design process with all those who are interested. Architecture has to go beyond buildings, beyond the physical and extend into the soul, without feeling that one is compromising on creativity or the thrill and excitement of design.

Working in India often makes each project feel like a completely new universe. We have to be both "barefoot architects" as well as hi-tech professionals. Every project has a distinctive client, parcel of land, climate, geography and social context, but when you put all these pieces together they form a seamless whole, much like India with its many ethnicities, languages and societies. We need to build appropriately. The 13 chapters in this book use different ways to explain this process, weaving slowly a quilt of many colors.

There are so many people who made this journey possible.

These include the architects who worked with me from the time I first set up my studio and my clients, some of whom started supporting me shortly after I began my practice: The Chauhan family, who have been my clients from the early 1970s; Vijay and the late Raj Chauhan, who believed a young sari-clad woman in her 20s could build their factories; the house of Tatas, who have enabled my studio to think big and support craftsmen and artists all over India; Mayur Patel, who gave me his carrot fields and trusted me to build the four Nalanda schools. Some good friends on my journey include Anita Garware, K.G. Premnath, Sudha Bhave, Cyrus Guzder, Meera Isaacs, T. Thomas, Peter FX D'lima and the late Gita Simoes.

Turning to the book itself, I would like to first thank Porus Olpadwala who gave me the courage and confidence to proceed with this monograph. He and my daughter, Nandini, were the driving forces that allowed me to move ever forward. I would also like to thank Mary Woods, who was always there with valuable advice whenever I needed it.

I was lucky to get Ruturaj Parikh to be the curator. It was his intellectual ability and dedication that helped me finalise the text and create the structure of the book, incorporating the dialogues and essays.

Nandini, as editor, sat for hundreds of hours with our art director, Tina Nussirabadwalla, and our research coordinator, Anthea Fernandes, to work on the narrative that had to be seamlessly intertwined with drawings and photographs. Ishita Parikh and Sagar Shinde, my "in-house" photographers, who painstakingly and over many months travelled all over India photographing the old projects. My studio, SNK, that helped me with the drawings and my staff who were there to help with a million other details connected with this book.

You all have been my foundation and my backbone.

To my friends whose essays and dialogues became part of this book, I thank you for your time.

I would like to thank four individuals whose generous donations helped The HECAR Foundation bring out this publication. N. Chandrasekaran of Tata Consultancy Services and now Chairman of Tata Sons; Deepak Parekh of H.T. Parekh Foundation; Pheroza Godrej; and the late Raj Chauhan. They have all been my friends, my clients and my support over decades of my practice.

I would like to thank Bipin Shah and Mapin Publishing, who agreed to publish this monograph at my very first meeting with them.

Finally, I have been blessed with family that have always supported me, pushed me, guided me and allowed me to reach within for peace and serenity when it was necessary. To my four grandsons—Karan, Arjun, Rohan and Varun—thank you for showing me how new life can kindle new ideas. You allow me to look ahead and know that legacy and family only strengthen one another. To my son Vikram, who has always stood on the threshold of our profession, looking in with curiosity and pleasure. Thank you for your love and your grammatical precision. To my daughter Nandini, my veritable other self. Small in stature and old in soul, she has allowed me to dream that what we build here today will not only stand tomorrow but will grow and stretch like a young banyan tree finding its way through the jungle under the warm gaze of the Indian sun. Thank you for all that you do both said and unsaid.

There is one person who has been my partner in all the aspects of my life. To my husband Anand, the big-hearted cardiac surgeon who has brought hilarity into my life with his constant wit, love into my life with his gentle soul and care, support for my choices with his constant patience. For always taking such good care of my heart, thank you always.

INTRODUCTION

NANDINI SOMAYA SAMPAT

Brinda Somaya is part of the "Bridge Generation", a term she coined to define a rarely identified generation that "bridged" the architectural space between the masters and the current generation. These are architects born after the Independence in 1947, who grew up in the wake of a free India. They had the opportunity to witness globalization and played their part in the history of Indian architecture. She is proudly one of them.

Somaya is the daughter of K.M. Chinnappa—a man that was ahead of his time and a pioneer in his profession, and Gunavati Chinnappa—a zoologist, national tennis champion, and avid mahjong player. It was inevitable with this pairing that Somaya would be special. She was exceptionally bright, an above average netball player, and one of only six girls admitted into the Cathedral & John Connon School's science programme. In 1966, her academic prowess won her the American Field Service International Scholarship to the United States, specifically to North Carolina. There, she lived in the home of Dr and Mrs Keleher and their family of six children, and so she acquired a second family who till today consider Somaya as one of their own. Her time abroad had reinforced her passion for architecture, and by 1967, she returned home to India and completed her architecture degree from Sir J.J. School of Architecture in Mumbai. She graduated in 1971 when the world was experiencing a change, primarily emanating from the United States. The age of women and recognition of people of colour, a time of the Beatles and bell bottoms, freedom of speech and in her words: "...we, as young architects, were part of a new era." Admission to Smith College, a leading liberal arts institute, gave Somaya the opportunity to learn amongst some of the brightest women in America, accompanied by a steep introduction to gender identity, leadership and empowerment of women. It gave her the chance to delve deep into the theory and practice of architecture in a superior academic setting and an environment that reinforced the incredible strength of women and their ability to change the world. Completing her Master of Arts from Smith in 1973, India called again and she returned.

With the courage kindled by a foreign education and the support of her family, Somaya began her practice in a garden shed behind her residence in Mumbai. Clients and their employees still recollect visiting her there. Being a part of her practice for over four decades, these clients are true patrons of her work and their patronage continues even today. She has always had a natural ability to connect with people, to understand their thoughts and, most importantly, to listen. The size or scale of the project was paid no heed in this regard. Being able to interpret client requirements accurately and successfully, delivering project after project, has led to the creation of an unbreakable bond between client and architect.

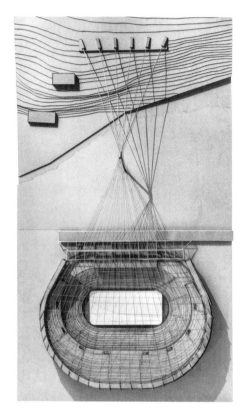

Final year model at Smith College, USA

Smith College graduation, 1973

Brinda Somaya at work, 1974

Somaya's love for her country knows no bounds. It is this love affair with India that has led her to cross the length and breadth of this great nation, to see, to understand, and to build within it—from the Himalayas to the south of India, from Bengal to Kutch and through the central plains and the heart of the country, from Ranchi to Indore and from Uttaranchal to Kodagu. She has travelled to some of the most obscure parts of the country. Her travels gave her tremendous exposure to the incredible diversity of her people and their vernacular architecture. It is this diversity, which led to a wide variety of projects, that remains constant throughout her practice. More than 200 projects built over the span of 40 years is clear evidence of the prolific practice built by Somaya. She takes great pride in this volume and diversity of practice as it is firmly rooted in her country and her people. Her ability to identify the appropriate solutions based on where she builds and to source materials locally or collaborate with vernacular artisans and craftsmen of the area has facilitated traditional know-how and techniques transcending visual form and emerging as building methodologies resulting in highly sustainable architecture. There remains a fierce activist within her to ensure that her professional skills always remain integral to the betterment of society as a whole. As such, Somaya has always voiced her strong belief:

"I am an Indian and all what I am comes from my heritage.
It is an intrinsic part of my being and will naturally reflect in my work in
many ways. The architect's role is that of a guardian, he or she is the
conscience of the built and the unbuilt environment."

Brinda Somaya on site, 2005

The language of Somaya's architecture metamorphosises based on the context in which she builds. The stark and contemporary Sanpada Church, built in the 1990s in the urban area of Navi Mumbai, is a prime example of a structure built ahead of its time while functioning exceptionally well. Fully embraced by the local residents, this building emanates a sense of spirituality through the simplicity of its architecture. As one walks through the Fort area in Mumbai, you may pass several of Somaya's restoration projects from the Cathedral schools to the magnificent Rajabai Tower. They remain iconic structures of the city that were given a second life through her sensitive and restorative care. Hover over the skies on the outskirts of the city of Indore, and there appears a magnificent form of a technology campus for over 15000 engineers. The shape of the campus from the sky reflects the sinuous Narmada river that flows nearby. The buildings commence densely as the source of the river does in Amarkantak, and then the architecture turns angular as do the jagged marble rocks of Jabalpur and the built form spreads wide and integrates within the landscape as the river exits the delta at the Gulf of Khambhat. It is also the work of the "barefoot architect" that Somaya so often references that is of great importance in India, a country steeped in complexity, tradition and culture. Somaya has worked with a great degree of sensitivity that has uncovered the importance of grassroot level interactions required for progress to be achieved and strongly advocates that small projects often have the most impact. She continues to fight for the betterment of public spaces through the Mumbai Esplanade project and contributes as a citizen by walking the streets of Mumbai documenting and identifying the old mill buildings for the Heritage Committee, for possible future rehabilitation. Her passion for her city is ever-present.

Tata Consultancy Services Campus, Indore, 2017

The presence of an incredible business sensibility is evident in Somaya and has played an important role in her ability to sustain and build a successful practice over four decades. To rise through the ranks of a profession while continuing to battle for honesty and integrity has been her journey. Somaya often talks about her isolation in her early years of practice. There was much that she experienced differently from others. Being a woman within a male-dominated fraternity meant she had to make sure her voice could be heard. Perhaps she had experienced this division during her time abroad as an Indian amongst foreigners, and was now more equipped to handle it. She was heard because of her brutal honesty and her efforts to always maintain a high standard of integrity in her professional practice. She extended the responsibility of the architect to the public and to the development of the country.

Meeting in Tashkent, former Soviet Union, 1988   Colour selection at Tata Housing, Chandivali, 2001

Forty years on, Somaya's studio is known in the industry for its values, professionalism and the core philosophies upon which it was built. Somaya's ability to command a board room is a skill that few can ever accomplish. To be able to enhance the ideating of the intellectuals, simplify the complexities of the bureaucrats, and comfort the anxieties of the financiers is the gift that Somaya possesses. The skill of a master also lies in the ability to convey to others their architecture in simple language and form, and convince them of its success as a design. To see Somaya at work is a wonderful sight and is a lesson in the art of oration and spatial thinking. She has an ability to think laterally to generate solutions while also looking at the practicality of implementation and costing implications, which are often done through incredibly complex mathematic calculations conducted with great ease in her mind. With a practice based on principles and discipline that ensures the delivery of high-quality architecture to match international standards, it has also led to her working collaboratively with acclaimed international architects.

The early years of Somaya's practice were complex and hard. Garnering clients; maintaining sites; managing an office, a home and a family... Somaya was balancing it all. It is said that much has to be given up in order for success to be achieved. Often the trade-off between family and work is the most common. Somaya is perhaps the best example of doing it all with no regrets. She has an enormous ability to work gargantuan hours, while still being able to find time for other people and interests. As her children, for us, her absence was never felt. My brother Vikram and I grew up with two working parents and knew no different. It was her strong presence that was constant. She was there for each and every elocution, debate or dramatic performance we ever participated in. She shared with us her passion for art and architecture every Saturday morning with a ritualistic walk around the Kala Ghoda galleries. For her love for food at Kailash Parbat, a sweet shop we visited after our gallery walks, we would all indulge in *paani puri* and *jalebi*s! She taught us to be good people, to value time and showed us that there was no substitute for good old-fashioned hard work. She made sure we became the best people we could be. She continues to guide us through the trials and tribulations of life, marriage and work, always encouraging our dreams while keeping us grounded. To achieve this balance, I do believe our father had an incredibly important role to play. A doctor in the Indian army, Anand Somaya found our mother and an incredible match it continues to be. A cardiac surgeon for over 40 years, this is a man of immense character and great kindness. His quick wit and good looks complemented hers, but it is his gentle nature as a husband and a father that has always been his greatest strength. They always communicated, and I do believe those conversations helped build their bond to support one another in moving ahead fearlessly. He was proud of her victories and even prouder to have her by his side. She was complete knowing she had in her husband the greatest friend and supporter through her journey of life. They completed 40 years of marriage in 2014.

Brinda Somaya and family: (left to right) Mihir, Anand, Varun, Karan, Brinda, Nandini, Arjun, Vikram and Rohan.

To build such a large volume of works is a rare achievement in the architectural profession and one Somaya has managed to do by being singularly focused. It took a tremendous amount of determination and hard work through the first 20 years to build up the practice by ensuring that every job taken on was executed. There was no time for rest. As she took on more work, she found herself delving into unknown territories of building technology, urban planning and conservation that forced her to create and develop new methodologies and path-breaking systems within which to execute such projects. The majority of Somaya's buildings continue to stand today, reinforcing the timeless nature of her architecture. Few architects would have the courage to rephotograph their buildings decades later. In this monograph, Somaya shares her work in their current form revealing their age and their use through time. She intertwines her narrative with selected works and their significance in her practice.

Recognition for her work has developed exponentially over the years, but Somaya has always viewed it simply as a process of sharing the stories of her projects with others. The accolades came in the form of several national and international awards including an Honorary Doctorate from her alma mater Smith College, USA, in 2014 and the prestigious Baburao Mhatre Gold Medal by the Indian Institute of Architects in 2015. And yet, the acknowledgment that is often most cherished by Somaya is the letters and drawings she receives from students of the Nalanda International School in Vadodara, expressing love for their school and gratitude for the buildings she has designed for them. This is perhaps the greatest compliment for an architect: the positive impact that a built form can have on the people that use it.

To have the chance to observe a successful woman at her profession is an experience that any individual is fortunate to witness. But I have seen a successful woman work, love and live. This is my fortune. Greater still, that she is my mother. The lesson that she continues to impart each day is to work with great humility, and that comes with ease when one is fiercely passionate about what they do. In her words:

"As an architect, I believe that all architectural practices that are inclusive and span our diverse population, be it economic or cultural, provide us with great satisfaction. Therefore, the motivation for inclusion and diversity should not come only from the desire to create a just society, but also because it leads to better and more powerful creative processes and solutions."

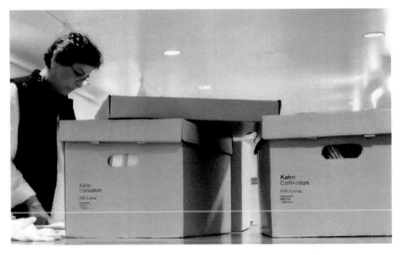

Brinda Somaya at the Architectural Archives of University of Pennsylvania, Philadelphia, 2014.

ON INDIA

Arun Shourie and Brinda Somaya

Prime Minister Jawaharlal Nehru addressing the first Constituent Assembly, India, 1946

It was at the dusk of the Nehruvian era that Brinda Somaya established her practice in Mumbai, the city she regarded as truly cosmopolitan. In that time of uncertainty, Arun Shourie returned from the United States and engaged actively with the prevalent political landscape as a journalist. While there was the promise of the developing country, there was still a very strong connection to one's roots. A discussion ensues of the diverse nation and how one's origins influenced and determined, in many ways, the trajectory.

India has come a very long way in the six decades after Independence, but we continue to battle with fundamental issues. Today, what do we find meaningful in the trajectory of our nation? What are the things that we value and what are our values as we deal with abundance?

RUTURAJ PARIKH   I want to begin by asking you both about the time of the new and modern India, when the influence of Nehru was waning and this new idea of industrial India was poised against of an agrarian India. Mrs Somaya, you were setting up an architectural practice, and as a journalist Mr Shourie, you returned to India and became politically very active. What are your views of this time?

ARUN SHOURIE First, there was a glow of the Independence Movement. We had a much deeper rootedness in our country and its ancient culture. At that time, the work of Sri Aurobindo, Lokmanya Tilak, Gandhiji's own interpretations of the Indian culture, Swami Vivekananda, the long-lasting influences of Sri Ramakrishna, and Sri Ramana Maharshi were discussed. People would not just say "we have an ancient culture"; they were truly in a sense rooted in that culture. That is one great difference between then and now. I think the second was that in the political leadership, the quality of persons in the public domain was very high. They had been through the crucible of the Independence Movement; they spent 14 years in prison. They therefore got to reflect a lot on what India means. If you see Panditji, for instance, speaking of urbanisation and industrialisation, you realise that he was deeply aware of our culture. There were some essential aspects about India that he would have wanted preserved. The third aspect of that generation, especially in the case of Panditji, was a profound respect for institutions. Today, institutions are seen as just instruments. But at that time... in the case of Panditji, I remember as a child we were usually taken from our school to see the Parliament. We were sitting in the galleries and some fool was speaking. Panditji was meticulously taking down notes.

RUTURAJ PARIKH Mrs Somaya, since Mr Shourie brought up this entire idea of modernity being a very strong influence and with the coming of somebody like Le Corbusier, Chandigarh almost became a laboratory to train architects and engineers. Here begins this understanding of the idea of modernism in architecture. I want to ask you, what was modernity like for you as somebody who has grown up in Bombay, witnessing the kind of work done by Corbusier and eventually Louis I Kahn?

BRINDA SOMAYA Well, I think looking back, one is able to analyse situations and understand things that have gone before. But when you are in that time yourself, you don't have the ability to do that. When I first started my practice, it was the late seventies and modernity was becoming more apparent to us. But my childhood in many ways was very different. I was influenced by what India offered culturally and historically at that time. I was being taken by my parents to Nalanda; to the temples of Konark and Khajuraho, to the wonderful temples of the South, to the Taj and to Hampi. We were taken to different parts of our own country, and we didn't separate architecture from art or music from history. It all seemed so well integrated. There were no computers, no internet and no Google; things took a long time to come to India. We had limited exposure to the rest of the world. India was the biggest thing in our imagination. In architecture school, people like Corbusier and Nehru were like gods in a way for us. We never wondered how we would play a role in this history. Of course, the influences came, but I don't think I have ever borrowed literally from traditional Indian architecture or modern works. I believe it is ideas that have to be translated, and that is what I believe modernity is. Modernity is not necessarily an architectural definition. I think it is understanding everything that has gone before to the best of your own capability and seeing how it is right for the time and for the future.

AS   You know, quite a wonderful sentence, Brinda. At that time, and actually throughout our own history, music, art, visual imagery, sculpture and architecture were not separate things. This has to be an essential feature of the Indian culture. Today, everything is a separate profession so there is no integral principle. I am not very aware of architecture, but certainly, if we saw the musicians of that age—M.S. Subbulakshmi, Mallikarjun Mansur, Bhimsen Joshi—were not just professionals. For them, the way they would organise their homes would be quite integral to the way they conceived of music or prayer.

A young Brinda Somaya (centre) with her parents and sister at the Nalanda ruins

RP   I am shifting in time to a phase after Nehru. There was an entire restructuring of the nation. I want to bring back the time of the Emergency, a difficult time as a professional to work with people being constantly under a sense of fear of the state. What was it like to be a professional then, especially as somebody involved in culture and production of creative work in India?

AS   I think this is where the change of perspective came. Indira Gandhi was not a person of great reading or reflection. Her view of individuals and her view of institutions was utilising them as instruments. The state became dominant. Panditji's ideas of secularism and socialism lost ground and became ossified. Indian socialism meant the utilisation of everything: it meant the Licence Raj, which meant everything in the hands of the state. And thus, a great fear of the state started to emerge. And therefore, the institutions of the state became vicious instruments, while the common man became docile.

RP   As an architect, did you feel the same, working during that time?

BS   Well that was the seventies, and I had just begun my practice. As young architects living in Bombay, we knew that there was no patronage from Delhi. The state and government were building much more, and it was out of bounds for us. We were isolated, unlike the first-generation architects in India. We felt that we will not have the same stake in the architectural history of our country as they did. There was a sense of diminished value. But one managed, right Arun? We lived through those times.

AS   Architecture may be, in that sense, was also insulated as a profession. But if you were in journalism, law or civil service, you were in the direct line of fire. Even the judiciary was in the direct visual field of the rulers. During the Emergency, very few professionals stood up and many leaders of these professions became lackeys of the rulers. That diminished the Indian academia. It almost destroyed Indian journalism. It destroyed the independence of mind of the entrepreneurial class. So that diminishing of values that Brinda talks about started in public life and slowly seeped into professions.

BS   And that sense of diminished value has remained.

AS   Yes. And now it has become habitual.

RP   After Indira Gandhi and the Emergency, there was an attempt to quickly reorganise and find new ways of framing what India was. Maybe because the idea was almost lost. Was that the time you, Mrs Somaya, would term as the "Bridge Generation"? Between 1975 and 1990? A period of uncertainty but also a period when practices were being built. Being a journalist Mr Shourie and an architect Mrs Somaya, your activism was closely related with urban events like the issue of the mills in Bombay. How do you see that period?

BS   One of the most important thoughts of this time was that, as an architect, I never saw my role as just building structures. I think, right from the beginning, it was always to go beyond buildings and that is what has given me the greatest satisfaction. In the India of the eighties and nineties, the population was growing, and the economy was not at its best. There were shortages of everything; there was poor quality of cement and steel; there was adulteration; and there was rationing. There was so much to be done for so many people. When I talk about the role of the architect, I talk about what we did at the time. I looked around, and whatever need existed, and I felt I could be a part of, was what I wanted to do. Whether it was a village or a tribal area or whether it was something in the big cities like Bombay or Bangalore, I took it on. I believe that gave me the diversity of practice, and a sense of justice. I guess a sense of patriotism as well in some way. A sense of India wanting to develop prevailed, and we wanted to be a part of that growth, to be a part of something good. It was a country that we felt proud to belong to.

AS   In case of journalism and writing, activism was a part of the job. So, there was no conscious effort to do it. The state was assaulting us at *The Indian Express*, so, naturally, one puts up a fight. This, in somebody else's eyes, must seem like activism. This is one aspect, but there were many who stood up because of their commitment to values. I remember L.K. Advani's sentence during the Emergency: that while the rulers asked the press to bend, it chose to crawl! There were two papers that fought: *The Indian Express* and *The Statesman*. Some magazines resisted. There was Raj Mohan Gandhi's *Himmat* and Ramesh Thapar's *Seminar*. They had a huge impact with the limited circulation they had. So, we had to resist. It was the duty of the professionals committed to liberal values to stand up and look beyond the profession, as Brinda said, "not just building a building".

BS   There must be many factors that make us the individuals that we are today. What motivates one to grow and challenge one's boundaries may be seen as one's commitment, interest or courage. I never saw all these aspects as being disconnected. If our city was to survive, then we had to work on so many aspects of it, and I perhaps tried to do it in different ways. I worked independently, but I also got invited to the committees for protection of heritage and public spaces. I felt I could work here without compromising my values. I always say your ethics, your integrity and the systems you believe in prevail. A lot of people will like you for who you are, and many will not like you for the same reasons. And then you find like-minded clients and institutions that believe you can contribute. My mother was a very active social worker and my father was a power engineer, so they brought to me a combination of being professional and yet having a commitment to society at large.

AS   I want to make an important observation. A lot of good work was also begun and done by the civic society. Let's take the position of differently-able children today as compared to 30 years ago. A positive change has been brought about by organisations such as the Spastics Society in Mumbai and spastics schools and societies elsewhere. Similarly, we can see Dastkar working for handicrafts in India. This was the time when a lot of good work had been initiated, which has borne great fruit now.

RP Thinking of the liberalisation of the nineties, when in one quick shift, everything was opened up. India was now open to new capital, promise of money and investment to come. Globalisation was coming through the door, and in a very short time of just 10 years, land had become a commodity and the markets had opened. What do you think of this sudden change?

AS The fact was that socialism and the socialist economy had ossified. It was a desiccated tree. It had to be replaced, and it was the far-sightedness of Narsimha Rao that enabled him to keep talking the old language but change the course completely. The Indian middle class had attained a huge mass and by enabling them to access opportunities, the economy was changed. You saw Indian writers writing in English and matching world standards. The design of newspapers, the typography and the layouts changed. Yet another change had come through: the internet. The middle class was well prepared to take advantage of all this. Even though Narsimha Rao embodied the ideals of the old socialist period, he was intellectually honest enough to see that we must change course. But many professions also saw a general decline in values. Suddenly, money became important. Globalisation is not to be blamed, but it is the deterioration of public persons in public life along with an increase in powers of the state.

BS Yes, liberalisation was a great intervention, and it has changed the way we operate. But I also see it as one of the biggest problems for architects, as we have not had the courage or the persistence to be able to successfully interact with the state. If there is no political and bureaucratic will, then no really meaningful projects can happen. I know with my personal experience how hard I have tried to work on certain projects, which were for the public good, but I was unable to convince city administrators of the importance of the same. Whether it is a restoration project or the Mumbai Esplanade project, efforts were made, and we must continue to do so. Until architects are able to implement such projects successfully, we will always be peripheral to society, and we are never going to have a real impact on what is to come up in the next 30 years.

AS As professionals, we should also have more self-confidence. Professor Paul Samuelson, a very witty columnist, concluded his address to the American Economic Association saying, "We should write for our own applause."

BS   We should fight?

AS   You know, write.

BS   Write for our own applause!

AS   As professionals, we need to acquire more self-confidence and look not for admiration but for appreciation from our own small community. There will be in time a general debasement of standards and values, and this would be a way of preserving the oasis.

BS   Do you think the oasis will spread? It could.

AS   Yes, at least it will survive. Sometimes in a period of drought, all you can do is to keep some saplings alive for when the rain comes, so we can sow.

BS   I am an optimist. I always believe that if we nurture the seeds, they will grow. But I do believe we live in significant times and that we must rise up to it.

Brinda Somaya in conversation with Arun Shourie at Lavasa.

Recorded on 27th January, 2016. Moderated by Ruturaj Parikh.

BHADLI VILLAGE AND VASANT VIDYALAYA

For Sunil Dalal and the People of Bhadli

MASTER PLANNING, REHABILITATION AND ARCHITECTURE

Gujarat, India [2001–2003]

Architecture becomes a vehicle for hope and reconciliation as a settlement is rebuilt through a deep dialogue with the village and the villagers following a devastating catastrophe.

Fig 1

I was at home in Mumbai with my 86-year-old father in 2001 when the Gujarat earthquake struck. We were far from the epicentre, and yet, I remember the panic in which my father and I ran down nine storeys; quite the opposite of what we were taught to do! Eventually, the trembling of the earth stopped and news came of the epicentre being in Gujarat (a neighbouring state), where the quake had struck the heart of the region and there had been incalculable devastation.

We had just completed some projects for a remarkable man, Sunil Dalal, in 2001. He was young and carried out inspirational pro-bono work with his trust. He was a silent patron and never sought acknowledgement or visibility for his charitable works. We received a call from Sunil Dalal, and there was a grave sense of urgency in his voice. "We need to do something; we need to do something in Kutch, which has been devastated." He was incredibly motivated as this was a region in Gujarat that was most affected and where his family had connections with the Shrujan Trust. "We have got to find a village that has been devastated and we have to rehabilitate it," he said. A large amount of aid flowed into the region; the government stepped in, as did many non-governmental organisations (NGOs), who involved themselves with the herculean task of rebuilding a region with huge populations suddenly rendered homeless and vulnerable. We were committed to finding a village that had not been identified for assistance, and it was at this juncture that Chandaben Shroff of the Shrujan Trust helped us identify Bhadli village for the intervention.

Fig 2

Fig 1. The damaged wall of the Bhadli village school that was destroyed in the 2001 earthquake.

Fig 2. The devastation in the village reduced the settlement to rubble.

Bhadli is located about 40 km northwest of Bhuj. To reach the village, we drove through the devastation unleashed by the earthquake, which measured 6.9 on the Richter scale. It was winter, it was cold, and all we could see through the haze was rubble. Bhadli was a village composed of both Hindu and Muslim communities. Made up of about 325 households and about 1500 people, a major part of the village, including the school, had been completely destroyed. When we reached, everybody was sleeping near the remains of what used to be their houses. There was debris everywhere. In the cold winter air, a veil of sadness had descended.

We found ourselves in a daze, overcome physically and emotionally by the impact that this natural disaster had brought on this rural settlement. Talking to the people, we learnt that not just had the houses been destroyed, the people too had been uprooted from their homes. They did not want to be dislocated to some empty piece of land in houses built on a grid worked out mechanically: the only

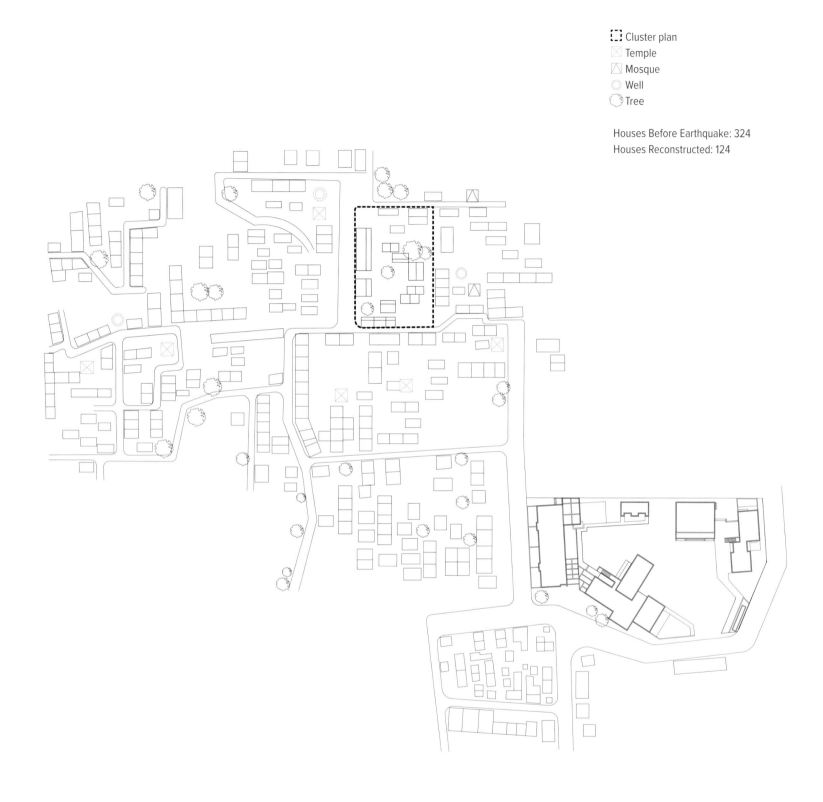

Cluster plan
Temple
Mosque
Well
Tree

Houses Before Earthquake: 324
Houses Reconstructed: 124

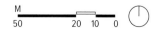

M
50   20 10 0

Fig 3

alternative that was offered by the government. We had to push beyond the idea of simply providing them with shelter. We needed to assist them in reconstructing their lives. To commence this process, it was imperative to preserve the familiar: their neighbourhood and its footprint.

The first critical decision was to relocate them all to the original parcels of their land. To be able to do this, we initiated a very thorough and detailed process of mapping the village: who lived next to whom, who was whose neighbour, which community resided next to which community, how many were joint families and so on. In hindsight, this was one of the most important exercises of the rehabilitation process. We realised the importance of social and religious patterns and that we had to respect them to be successful in our endeavour. By reinstating the people to the places from where they had been uprooted, the layer of existing socio-cultural fabric of the village could be retained. We also believed that by providing everybody with an equal opportunity in housing, education and support facilities, we were inadvertently strengthening the entire village.

This meant that it would take much longer for the villagers to get their final homes. It was winter, and I was worried about the people sleeping out in the cold, but there was no hesitation in their minds as to the direction they wanted us to proceed in. Some had even stacked their old doors and *jaali*s (grills), and when we told them we would use these items in their new homes, smiles appeared on their worried faces.

Fig 4

Bhadli village was then led by a Hindu woman *sarpanch* (the village head). She was in charge and was a feisty woman. The Panchayat (village committee) meetings were conducted with all of us seated on *charpoy*s (a traditional woven bed) laden with metal plates containing peanuts and cut raw mango pieces. The *sarpanch* kept a watch and her gaze ensured that everyone partook of the hospitality extended. All the key decisions about relocation, sizes and types of houses were jointly taken with the consent and participation of the local leadership. She ensured that all the stakeholders were consulted. She brought everyone in: the Muslim families who worked on intricate *bandhani* (tie and dye) fabric work and were an intrinsic part of the village; Patelbhai, who was interested in the ecology of the village, its water sources and the trees; skilled engineers who spearheaded a project to create a reservoir for water, saving any rainwater they received (since the groundwater had become saline) and were eventually involved in creation of toilets, drainage systems, septic tanks and building infrastructure for the place. Each stakeholder brought their individual skill-set and knowledge. There was an instance where the *sarpanch* pointed out that sloping roof asymmetry was considered unlucky. As we worked on the plan, we received varied inputs, such as these, that we believe had to be carefully heard, considered and integrated in the design.

Our design process was primarily concerned with incorporating details that would assist in healthier living environments, such as designing the kitchens with *jaali*s to ventilate and remove the smoke emitted by the *chulha*s (coal/wood stoves)

Fig 5. Panchayat (village committee) meeting with the various stakeholders to discuss and strategise the way forward.

Fig 6. Cluster plan of the new houses within the existing village footprint reinforces the importance of rehabilitating the villagers in their original parcels of land.

Fig 5

used by the women. The houses had to combat dust and intense heat of the desert-plains of Kutch. We accomplished this by minimising openings and using concrete *jaali*s, thereby allowing exchange of air through very small apertures. Recycling materials was also essential, and so it was decided to use the debris from the collapsed structures and to retain the doors and windows (which were largely intact after the earthquake) to continue to render an identity and restore the unique character of the village. Courtyards were planned to avoid direct sunlight as verandas and raised plinths or *otla*s (raised thresholds) were oriented in clusters of five to six houses to retain a sense of a close-knit community. Space was made for their livestock and other precious possessions.

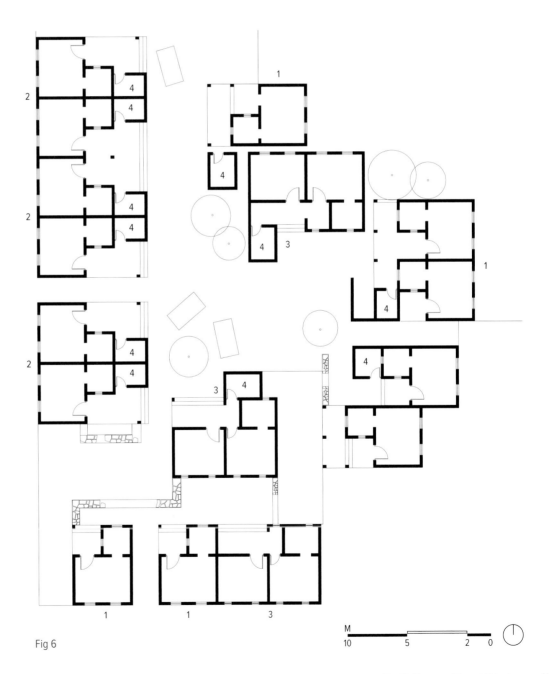

1. Type 'A' module
2. Type 'B' module
3. Type 'C' module
4. Toilets

Fig 6

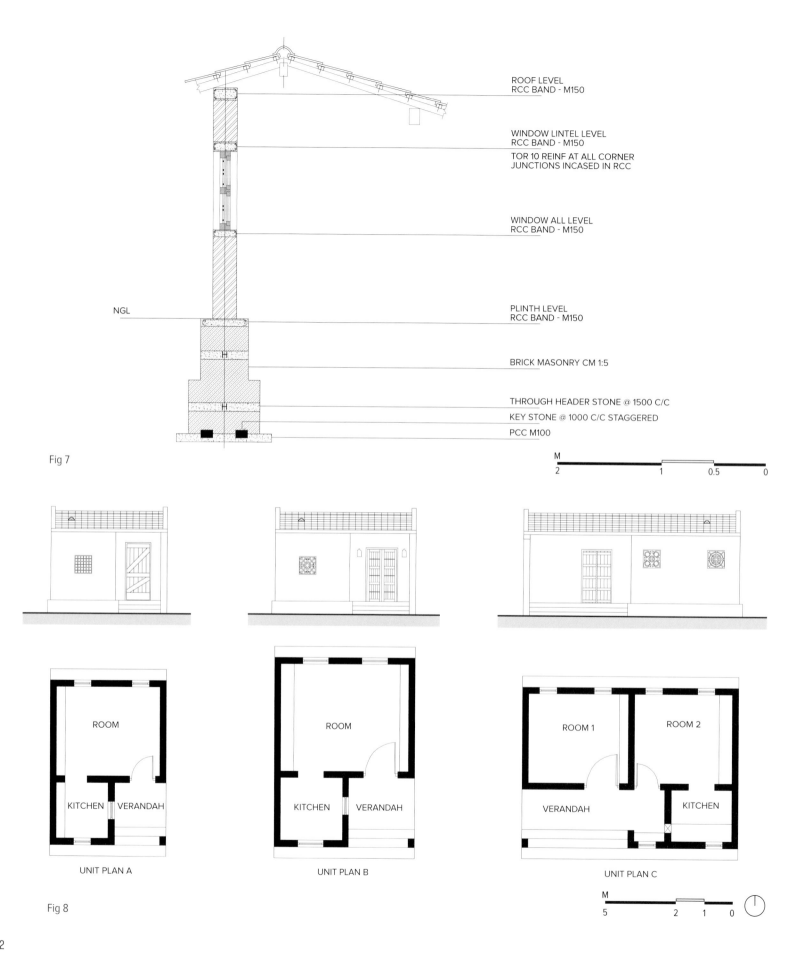

ROOF LEVEL
RCC BAND - M150

WINDOW LINTEL LEVEL
RCC BAND - M150

TOR 10 REINF AT ALL CORNER
JUNCTIONS INCASED IN RCC

WINDOW ALL LEVEL
RCC BAND - M150

PLINTH LEVEL
RCC BAND - M150

BRICK MASONRY CM 1:5

THROUGH HEADER STONE @ 1500 C/C

KEY STONE @ 1000 C/C STAGGERED

PCC M100

NGL

Fig 7

M
2   1   0.5   0

ROOM

KITCHEN | VERANDAH

UNIT PLAN A

ROOM

KITCHEN | VERANDAH

UNIT PLAN B

ROOM 1 | ROOM 2

VERANDAH | KITCHEN

UNIT PLAN C

Fig 8

M
5   2   1   0

Fig 7. Detailed wall section
strengthening the load bearing
structures.

Fig 8. Unit plans and elevations of
Type A, B and C.

Fig 9. Process of reconstruction of the
houses by the villagers themselves.

For the houses, it was important for us to play a catalytic role rather than to force a top-down design approach. The most evident aftermath of the trauma was insecurity and fear and restoring confidence became central to all our endeavours. Some principles were laid out to ensure that the rebuilt houses perform well in the eventuality of another earthquake. The plinths were composed of random rubble and lined with an RCC plinth beam. The rubble mostly came from the debris. Three tie-beams were placed: one each at the sill, the lintel and the roof-base. The RCC members were braced with vertical steel bars in concrete at L and T junctions. All fenestrations were lined with RCC on top and bottom to avoid cracks in case of movement in the base. Sheer keys at critical junctions prevented displacement.

We encouraged the villagers to rebuild their own homes. To support this venture, the village reached an agreement with Sunil Dalal's trust: The Pentagon Charitable Foundation. The trust would only procure and supply materials and the villages would provide the labour. Our reasons for advocating this methodology were two-fold. The first being to counteract the depression and listlessness that sets in after a major disaster. By helping the villagers to build for themselves, we were able to mobilise them for an occupation, which gave them a sense of purpose. The second was the lack of paid work available to the

Fig 9

villagers at the time. By paying wages to the villagers and by disaggregating the process of building, we were able to motivate many to engage in the process of reconstruction. While this process was slow and tedious at the onset, the pace soon started to build, and the village was consumed in the building activity.

Sanitation was also a central issue that we had to address. Not all the houses in Bhadli had toilets. We studied the eco-friendly neem-lined lavatories that already existed and upgraded them. It was a very successful experiment. The government took notice and eventually contributed to the effort, but only after the completion of the rehabilitation work. As the houses neared completion, the incredible artistic wealth of the village was revealed to us. The original houses in the village were always decorated, and embellishment was natural to them. We encouraged the villagers to use lime, clay and mirrors—the materials familiar to them—to adorn the houses. They made niches for oil lamps on the sides of the entrance door and decorated the walls in great detail. There was a sense of nostalgia.

To achieve this level of participation was a difficult task for us. There was a sense of despondency in the village, but it was the initiative of one man that made a difference. He decided to start the construction of his own house, even if no one was willing to help him. We gave him the construction materials, and he began.

Fig 10. Patterns and design details implemented in the process of rehabilitation.

Fig 11. The people of Bhadli.

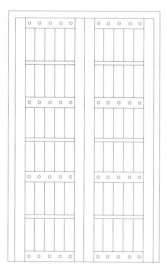
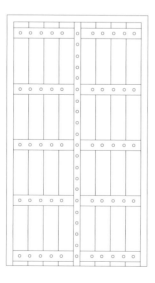

Fig 10

Fig 11

Others watched and soon realised that a door had opened for them. Not long after, he had a group of villagers helping him. They then went on to the next house and the next and a momentum was created. We heaved a sigh of relief: the reconstruction of the village was well on its way.

While the process of rebuilding had begun, a group of villagers approached me with a grave concern. The village school had been completely destroyed and people were very worried about losing the teaching staff to other schools. More importantly, they were afraid they would lose the children to agricultural work in fields. We thus created a school for the children with basic facilities and then moved on to the new construction. I agreed to rebuild the school on the condition that the new facility would have a crèche and a women's centre to enable the mothers of the village to work and support one another. Many women in the village were engaged in embroidery and home industries, and they no longer had a space for these activities, resulting in the loss of that meagre but most vital source of additional income. The allotted village land was not big enough for all the anticipated facilities, but we soon received a generous donation in the form of an invaluable piece of land from the neighbouring farmer, which led us to build the larger programme of requirements.

The initial design of this complex 'Vasant Vidyalaya' had sloping roofs and two levels: ground floor and first floor. The Panchayat requested us to design a school with a flat roof and a structure that could support future expansion. The complex was redesigned to accommodate this eventual growth to enable the village to have a secondary school so that one day the children would not have to travel to the neighbouring villages for further education. I am now working on raising funds for that second floor.

Fig 12. The temporary school that enabled the village children to continue their education, after the earthquake.

Fig 13. Brinda Somaya with the team of women that led and participated in the project.

Fig 14. Ground floor plan of Vasant Vidyalaya.

Fig 15. First floor plan of Vasant Vidyalaya.

Fig 12

Fig 13

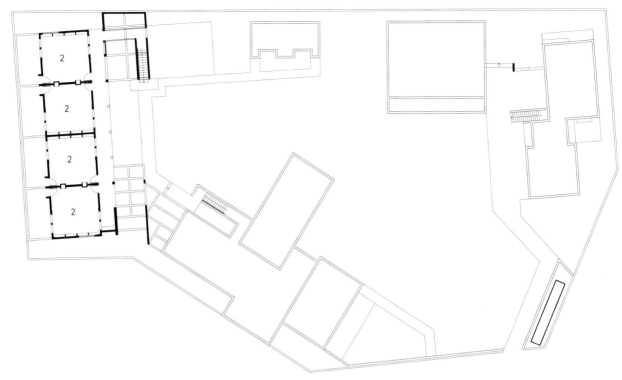

Fig 15

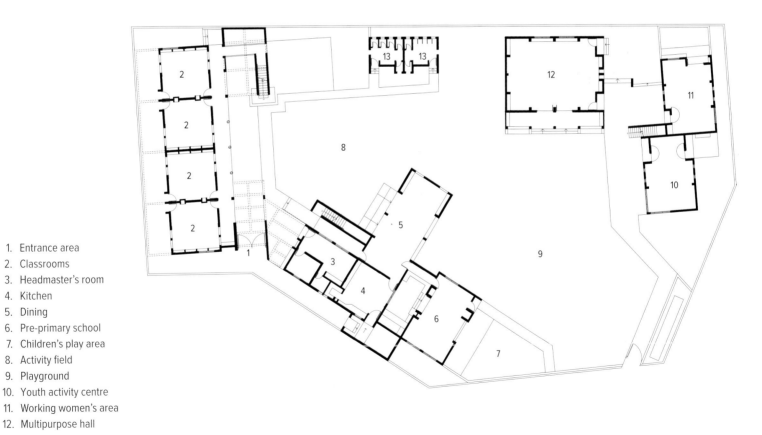

1. Entrance area
2. Classrooms
3. Headmaster's room
4. Kitchen
5. Dining
6. Pre-primary school
7. Children's play area
8. Activity field
9. Playground
10. Youth activity centre
11. Working women's area
12. Multipurpose hall
13. Toilets

Fig 14

M
20   10   5   0

The architecture of the school follows the principles that all my buildings follow at the very core. The plan is legible and becomes the point of departure for the scheme. A courtyard helps create a secure enclosure, thus creating a microclimate for the building. The court is crucial. In many of my works, the location and scale of the court follows the understanding of the land, the climate and the nature of the activity it contains. While the school has rooms as the primary functional space, it is a series of intermediate and hierarchical open and semi-open spaces that contribute to the architecture: the corridors, the covered corridors, the pergolas (sun-breakers), the *otla*s and the staircases that connect the rooms with the open-to-sky spaces. The staircases are special and a lot of emphasis is dedicated to their design and situation. Not only do they create connections and transitions, but they act as spaces to gather, sit, to lean over the parapet and to look at life and time move by.

Fig 16. Construction of Vasant Vidyalaya, the new village school complex designed as a community space for Bhadli.

Fig 17. East elevation of the school complex.

Fig 18. North elevation of the school complex.

Fig 19. Isometric view of the school complex.

Fig 16

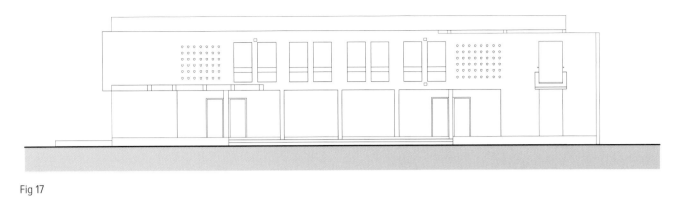

Fig 17

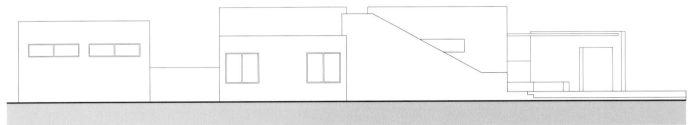

Fig 18

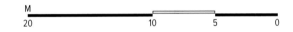

M
20   10   5   0

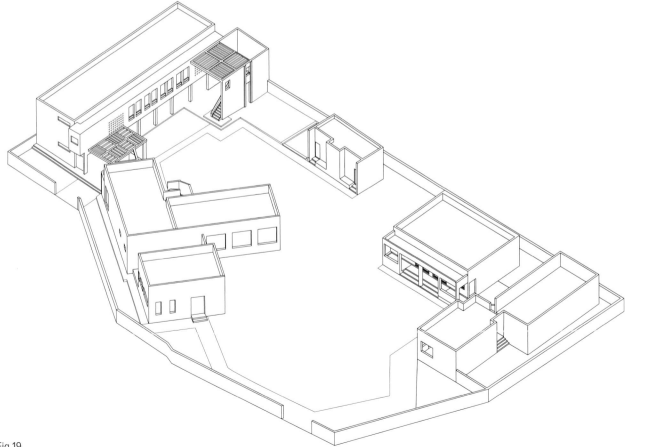

Fig 19

Kutch is a desert with particularly sharp sunlight. The landscape is constrained and bright colours have naturally become an important part of the visual palette as the arid land becomes a backdrop to receive this colour. Even as we were building the school, we decided to bring in colour and the elements of the desert in many inexpensive ways, involving the children of the school in the process. We painted the doors and windows the way the villagers wanted, and they helped us design the kitchens and the community spaces that became the essence of their life and of our collective architecture.

The school was not built by the villagers but a small contractor on a shoestring budget. The school was also envisioned to be a vital village centre, a place that the community can use for many purposes in addition to learning. It forms a public space. Later, I received an invitation to attend the opening ceremony of the school. There was much fanfare and celebration, and the villagers gifted me the most beautifully embroidered sari. I wore that sari for my daughter's engagement in Mumbai. It remains one of my most prized possessions and brings back many memories. A local village girl who was very young when we started our work in the village grew up to be an important citizen of the village, because she now found an opportunity to study in her own village. This is a privilege afforded to very few girls in India. Her name is Mehazabeen. From a small school that had classes for children between 5 and 14 years of age, Vasant Vidyalaya has become a small campus with multiple classrooms, library and dining facilities, a crèche and a community centre with a multipurpose hall filled with women working on their craft.

Fig 20. Mehazabeen, a resident of Bhadli, through the decades. She got the opportunity to study at the newly-constructed Vasant Vidyalaya.

Fig 21. Invitation for the opening of Vasant Vidyalaya in 2002.

Fig 22. Archival photograph of Bhadli village.

Fig 20

Fig 21

Fig 22

The communities of the village got together to repair and rebuild damaged parts of a temple and a *dargah* (mausoleum of a saint), to plant trees and create a reservoir tank for water. There was a group of about ten houses belonging to the Dalit families who were poor people from the backward caste. The tragedy for the residents of these houses located on the periphery of the village was that they were not registered, as they were not considered *pukka* (permanent structures). This was the irony of the situation: the poorest of the poor would be left without aid just because they did not qualify in the first place to be registered. We decided to raise the funds for these houses to be reconstructed in their original locations.

It is critical for us architects to understand the village to be able to rebuild it in a way that addresses the social, economic and cultural landscape of the place. While it is natural to resist change, in many ways, change operates silently and a remarkable transformation has come to this village in the form of better living conditions, sanitation, education and entrepreneurship over the years since we have been engaged.

Fig 23

Fig 23. By 2016, Vasant Vidyalaya had integrated into the village with the local artwork adorning the walls and the architecture connecting seamlessly with the landscape.

In 2006, we went back to the project and saw the transformation the houses have gone through. Many had expanded their homes by covering parts of terraces and domestic courtyards while the kernel of the original community spaces has remained integral to their life. By enabling the community to contribute to the rebuilding of their own spaces, we ensured that the community is empowered in the process. We visited the village again in 2016. It has now been more than a decade and a half since the project has been completed, and as I look at recent photographs from the village, my faith in this collective approach is reinforced. The village received an award for the way they have managed their green cover. Bhadli today exports *bandhani* fabric. One can see dish antennas, cars and communication systems, including the internet. The village is now connected to the world.

While we have done several community projects before and after Bhadli, some core concerns raised here remain persistent in my practice. From designing for the city in Colaba Woods to rebuilding shops for the flowersellers in the Nityanand Ashram Temple Complex, from a centre for VOICE to an Anganwadi in a slum in Worli; there is an engaging process that shapes my social projects and the conversations enrich the architecture. In all our projects, we insist on sanitation and fundamental human facilities for all the migrant workers who stay on-site, and I think these projects enable me to be aware of and sympathetic to those we are building for and those we are building with.

In my work, I don't think images of inspirational views of the finished buildings appear in my mind when I look at the site. I work within the story that unfolds. A logical and sequential process follows involving understanding of context and the challenges of each project on one hand, and working on architecture that is contemporary and unique to the situation on the other. While there may be no apparent similarities in my projects, a hidden thread that binds all of them is this process. I realise that in projects such as Bhadli, which involve many stakeholders, the best solutions are brought about where we, as architects, planners, designers and professionals, approach the project as catalysts and not as brokers of change.

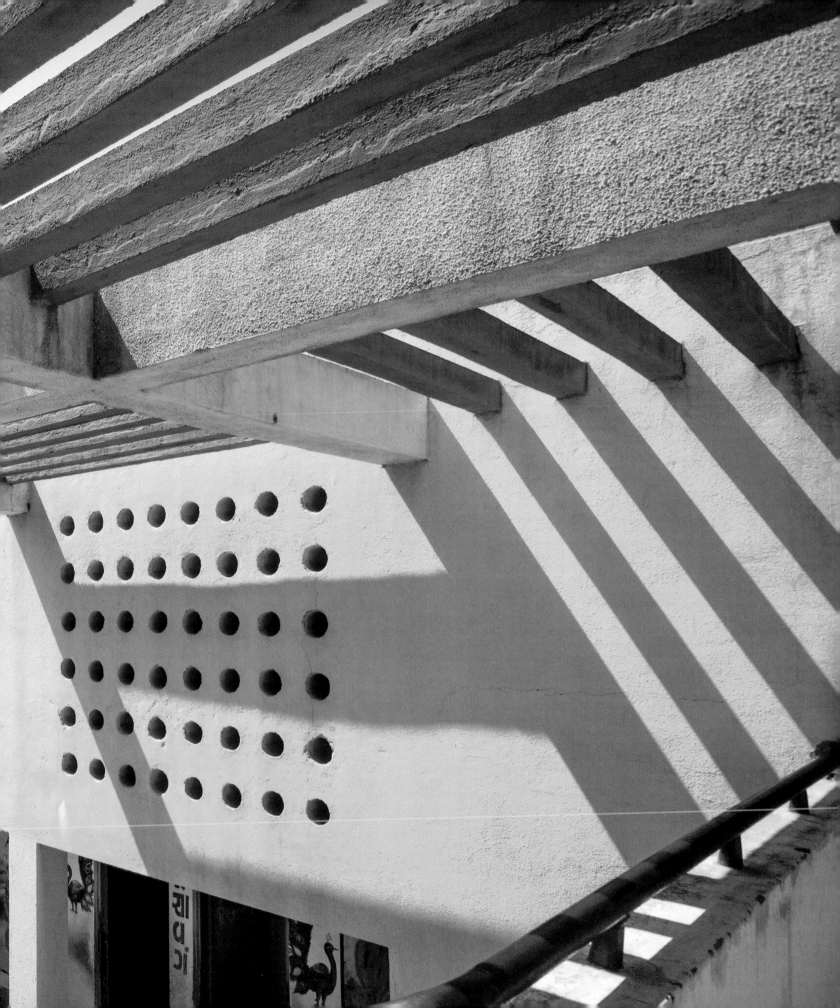

CAMPUS FOR ZENSAR TECHNOLOGIES

For Zensar Technologies Limited

MASTER PLANNING AND ARCHITECTURE

Pune, India [2003–2010]

Architecture that uses institutional language for a corporate campus in order to generate a pattern that enables creation of humane and interactive spaces.

My first office was located in the National Insurance Building near the famous Sterling Cinema in Fort, Mumbai. The basalt-stone colonial building had towering ceiling heights, magnificent jack-arches and a grand wooden central staircase. The structure inherited typical issues faced by old colonial buildings in Mumbai: exposed electrical wiring, haphazard extensions, lack of an elevator and so on. I do believe that climbing three storeys several times a day kept me fairly light on my feet through the years. One morning, I received a call from two gentlemen, referencing a publication on my work. They wanted to share their plan to build a campus in Pune for their information technology company. We met at a coffee shop near Sterling Cinema to discuss their vision of the IT campus. There was much excitement, as it was the first IT campus I would design, and it has remained one of our most important projects. Decades later, our portfolio has built to include many technology and educational campuses, but to trace back the origins of these works to a coffee shop near Sterling cinema is special to me.

Fig 1

Fig 1. SNK office at the National Insurance Building near Sterling Cinema in Fort, Mumbai.

Fig 2. The site for Zensar Technologies campus.

I have always held a conviction that architecture has a profound connection with the land on which it stands. It is, therefore, significant to me to understand the lay of the land for any project: to walk it and to understand the nature of its composition. This piece of land for the campus in Kharadi was largely featureless. It had a gentle slope with an occasional tree. There were no vantage points or views to be captured. The eventual campus thus had to create an internal environment and work cohesively as a microclimate. A conceptual approach began to

Fig 2

develop when I thought of the word "Zensar", derived from the Japanese Zen philosophy with harmony and balance as its key concepts. A vocabulary began to develop in my mind for the campus that had to accommodate 3,500 engineers in an environment of peace and tranquillity. Unlike an "IT Park", designed to be mechanically efficient, I wanted a campus that would not only lend itself to state-of-the-art technology operations but also focus on place-making for the human resource that is at the core of IT operations.

We began our work on a masterplan, which according to me is the most important document if one is dealing with a large site and a complex programme. The masterplan helps in assimilating stages of growth and plays an instrumental role in reconciling the architecture with the site. The campus had to incrementally accommodate a large number of engineers. We were conscious that it was a greenfield project, and there were challenges in generating a controlled ecosystem with the desired densities on the site. We located the buildings in close proximity

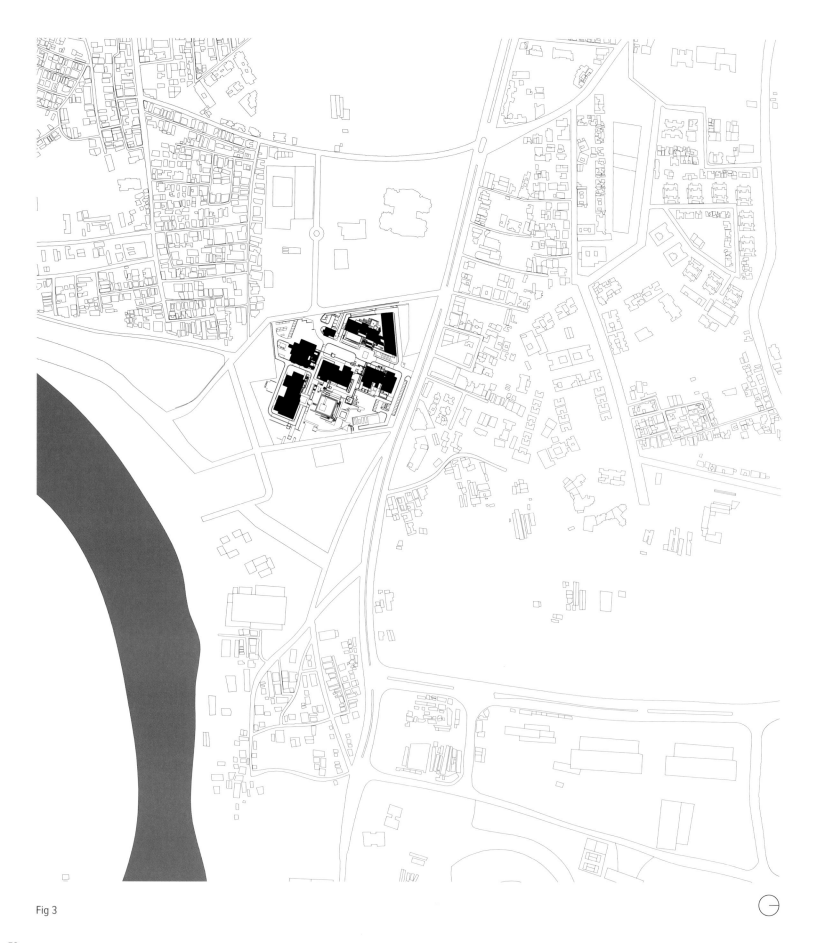

Fig 3

Fig 3. Context plan.

Fig 4. Site plan.

in the plan, while ensuring that they did not overwhelm the scheme. By integrating the built forms into open spaces and landscaped areas, a natural rhythm was created as we began to develop a complex programme that was implemented in three phases. As we worked on the design of the buildings for the campus, we ensured that the integrity of the masterplan remained uncompromised.

While designing in India, one must be consistently conscious of the project budget. There cannot be any justification for excesses, and in this context, unused and under-used spaces in any building burden the working costs of a project. We wanted the Zensar buildings to take advantage of the sun and the wind, thereby minimising air-conditioning and mechanical support systems. We designed the campus to protect the inhabitants from the harsh Pune sun, to harness the breeze, and to harvest rainwater on the site by creating sumps with zero discharge. I think that the architecture of a building plays a pivotal role in its sustainability and resource-management: critical and fundamental ideas that cannot be left merely to the domain of instrumentation and technology. The Zensar campus, like many of our projects, is consciously and sensitively designed to respond to the forces of context.

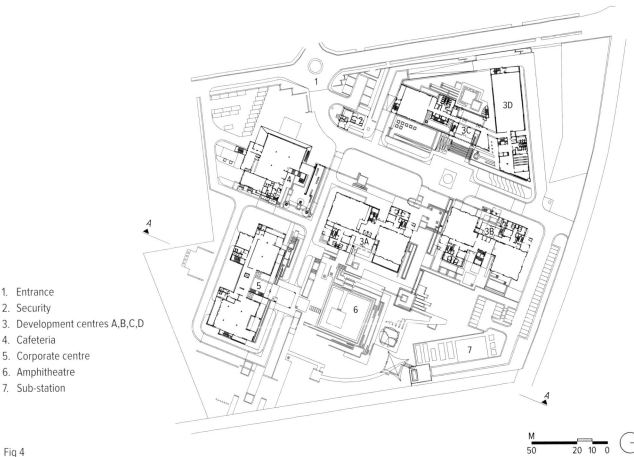

1. Entrance
2. Security
3. Development centres A,B,C,D
4. Cafeteria
5. Corporate centre
6. Amphitheatre
7. Sub-station

Fig 4

M
50   20 10 0

Another interesting aspect of IT campuses, which we discovered in the process of design, is that the average age of the user is 24 years. Working on computers in a sedentary posture is an indispensable part of their work culture. We were conscious of the implications of this aspect in our design, and we paid significant attention to the way in which young people relate to spaces. Zensar has spaces for them to take breaks, get fresh air, interact, eat, sit in groups and think. Open-to-sky spaces and outdoor spaces with varying protection were woven in the design and landscape of the campus. The need to create an architectural element that binds the various buildings together and connects the built forms to the landscape became more pressing.

We designed a meandering stone wall. This wall runs through the entire campus as it divides and unites, changes scale, creates areas of seclusion and areas of congregation, organises movement, provides opportunities to find shade and comfort and, by using simple gestures, binds the campus in a thematic whole. Composed monolithically of the local Nevasa stone, it zig-zags around sunken courtyards, amphitheatres, water bodies, trees and plantations, steps and sit-outs, where the young find value in interaction and reflection. We worked closely with the landscape architects to understand nuances of the material: the way it interacts with light; the detail and the finishes; the patterns of shadows; the texture; the very simple ideas that anchor the buildings to the land.

Open spaces of various scales designed in a hierarchy fortify the campus in a cohesive complex. With the water bodies and the greenery, these spaces help create a micro-climate that is contained in the voids. This progression leads one to the large amphitheatre, a congregation space where a banyan tree, which symbolises knowledge in the Indian culture, was planted and has grown tall and wide over the past 12 years. This space is central to the effectiveness of the masterplan and has a wonderful sense of enclosure with the surrounding buildings and the sky.

Fig 5. A landscape section of the stone walls that meander through the campus.

Fig 6. Brinda Somaya at the Zensar site (below left) and the stone walls that shaped the landscape (below right).

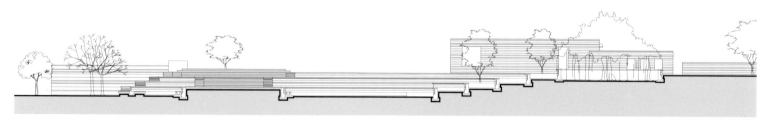

Fig 5

Fig 6

Campus for Zensar Technologies · 73

The design work for the Zensar campus began in 2003. The campus was built over three major phases. Phase 1 consisted of the two main development centres. As the client wished to name all the buildings after mountains and mountain ranges, these were called Alps and Himalayas. These two buildings with the amphitheatre and the banyan tree, when completed, became the core of the campus. A strong north–south and east–west axis ties up the walls, plazas and water bodies with the two buildings. These buildings were designed to ensure a sustainable architecture, as were the buildings that followed. Only the development centres were air-conditioned, and all the common and breakout spaces and corridors were open, hugely reducing air-conditioning costs.

The volumes from within and massing from outside was broken down by punctures, overhangs and recesses, cantilevers, steps, lines and planes. This is the vocabulary that we used for all the buildings, adding walled gardens, pergolas (concrete and timber) and canopies. Thus, although the six buildings were built in phases and with different functions, they came together in perfect harmony. This phase was completed in 2004.

The next phase entailed design and execution of two buildings but with very different functions. One was the cafeteria for the workforce and the other, the corporate head office of the company. We positioned them on the southern side of the site, completing the strong L-formation of the campus. At the same time,

Fig 7. The development centre and the amphitheatre under construction.

Fig 8. East elevation and ground floor plan of development centres A and B.

Fig 7

74

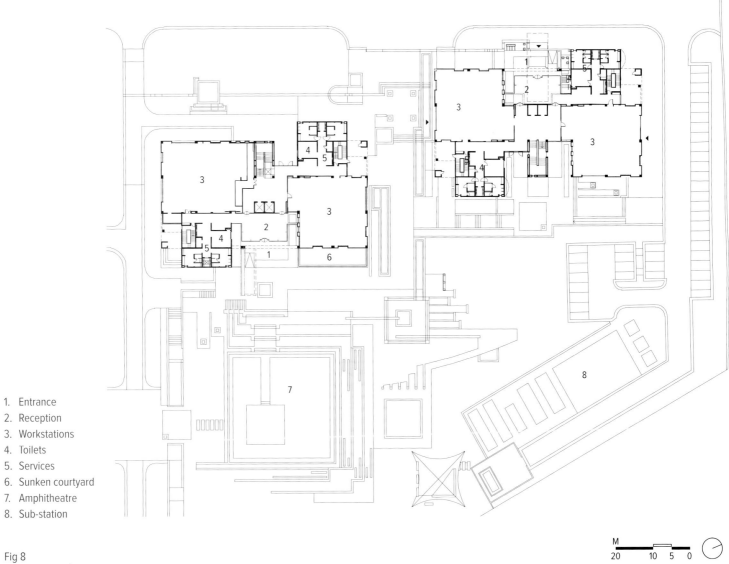

1. Entrance
2. Reception
3. Workstations
4. Toilets
5. Services
6. Sunken courtyard
7. Amphitheatre
8. Sub-station

Fig 8

M
20   10 5 0

these buildings needed to have their own identity. They differed considerably in volume from the four-storeyed development centre blocks as they comprised only the ground and first floors.

To cater to the young employees and ensure their movement across the campus, it was important that the cafeteria building was designed independently and not within their development centres. This circulation enabled employees to interact with one another and develop a sense of community beyond their individual workspaces. This would bring them out into the beautiful green space as they walked to their lunch, tea or dinner. The cafeteria building has an evocative high-roofed dining space, a crèche for working parents and, of course, all supporting services. A large canopy creates a covered plaza, which provides shade for the engineers after their meal to catch up with friends. Finding a personal space on a large campus may not be easy, but is essential for young people.

Positioning of the corporate building was debated, and we finally decided to close the L as outlined earlier. The corporate building is much more transparent with the use of larger expanses of glass. It has a central core with two wings, while the details and materials have been changed. We had connected this building to the wall using Nevasa stones. The pergolas were made of timber and the canopy served as a porch for parking cars. The chairman of the company, being a collector of art and sculpture, shared his collection with us generously, and, therefore, sculptures and paintings are displayed in the spaces within all the buildings.

These two buildings were completed by 2007.

Fig 9. The process of construction of Phase 2 of the project.

Fig 10. North elevation and ground floor plan of the corporate and cafeteria block.

Fig 11. Views of the completed Zensar campus.

Fig 12. The levels of the site complement the situations of the buildings as the landscape becomes the moderator.

Fig 9

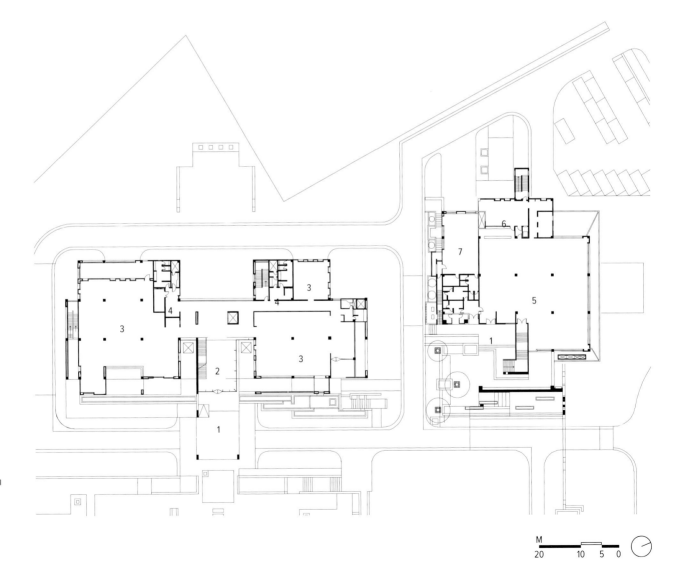

1. Entrance
2. Reception
3. Workspace
4. Toilets
5. Dining room
6. Kitchen
7. Creche

Fig 10

Fig 11

Fig 12

Campuses are living and evolving pieces of work. When we build in phases, we incrementally add to this history. The last two development centres, Rockies and Fuji, were built to accommodate the additional workforce requirement set out by the client. Pressure on the land with its escalating cost played a role in increasing the density of the built form in this part of the campus. While the Rockies was designed in continuity with the architectural vocabulary of the larger campus, Fuji was a new challenge. It needed to accommodate a large number of engineers and would therefore be a much taller building. To prevent it from overshadowing all that had gone before, I decided to fragment it into two parts: a rectangular workstation block and an elliptical block for the conference facility. This fragmentation brought dynamism to the built form.

The final phase of this campus was completed in 2009. Thus, our six-year involvement with the site came to an end, or so we thought. Recently, we were contacted by Zensar about the possibility of adding a third floor to the corporate building. So, it never ends. Meanwhile, the trees have grown, especially the two

Fig 13. The process of construction of Phase 3 of the project with its dynamic edge of juxtaposed ellipses.

Fig 14. North elevation and ground floor plan of the development centres C and D.

Fig 13

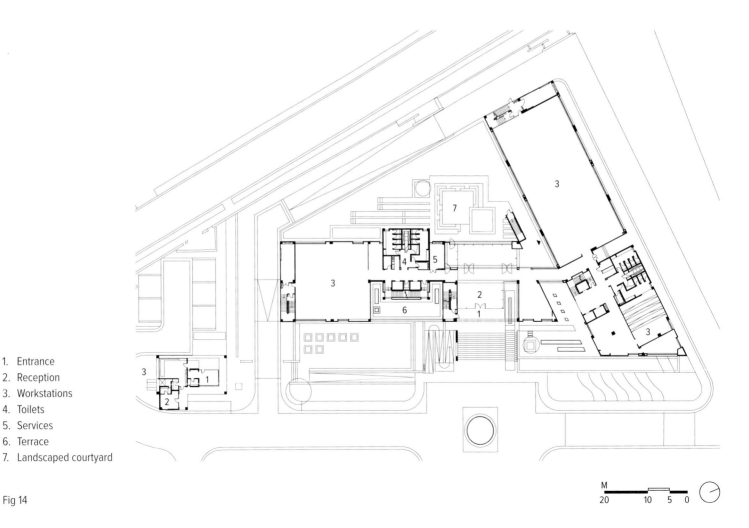

1. Entrance
2. Reception
3. Workstations
4. Toilets
5. Services
6. Terrace
7. Landscaped courtyard

Fig 14

M
20   10 5 0

Fig 15

Fig 15. Elements and critical ideas that shape a cohesive campus.

trees of "learning and wisdom". The landscape continues to evolve and integrate with the built form.

Zensar is a contemporary campus with an architectural vocabulary that belongs to the present. The buildings are a composition of solids and voids, and there is a visual balance in these compositions. The geometry of the buildings enables architecture and the land to interact and coexist in a fine balance. My work, however, is primarily informed by the land, and the formal considerations of geometry follow without overpowering and taking over the site. The design process is thus often reversed, and this idea of a practice that employs architecture to find equilibrium rather than making a statement has been an unfailing conviction of mine as made evident in the Zensar campus.

While a set of few fundamental ideas and elements form the foundation of our work at SNK, the design process enriches the architecture and ensures that no two responses are alike. For instance, the Nalanda school courtyards are very different in their scale, composition, proportion, materiality and surface articulations as compared to the courtyards at the Goa Institute of Management and at the Zensar campus. In hindsight, I think these patterns are subtle and readable in my work, but they are not obvious. I do really enjoy working with these elements, and I focus on them as they become a part of the design vocabulary that has evolved over the last few decades of my practice. While I don't subscribe to ideas of style, this foundation has given my work a sense of identity and uniqueness. If one looks at our projects carefully, one can decipher a strong thread that exists and underlines my belief in these core elements and ideas.

After 12 years, the Zensar campus has seen three complete phases of development and an ongoing fourth phase. I feel privileged that the client returned to us as the campus grew. The trees have grown. The landscape has mellowed. Spaces have integrated. When I went back to the campus, many people expressed how much they enjoy the spaces and the deep connection of the landscape with the buildings. It is essential to understand that the campuses of today are second homes for thousands of people who work in the IT and outsourcing industries. I believe that these "campuses" are institutions and have a role that goes much beyond the production cubicles of a corporate office space. The setting must stimulate the young inhabitants, offering them a creative atmosphere. Campuses cannot be viewed, approached and designed as sculptural design objects. They must be living, cohesive and enriching environments.

THE CATHEDRAL & JOHN CONNON SCHOOL
For The Anglo Scottish Education Society

CONSERVATION, RESTORATION AND REJUVENATION

Mumbai, India [1994-2001]

The conservation process becomes instrumental in revival of heritage buildings as design negotiates a sympathetic relationship between the old and the new for a fine balance of continuity and change.

I believe individuals derive a sense of stability and continuity from their physical environment. There are some buildings that connect us to our past and represent an essential part of our identity. The Cathedral school buildings are one such group in the colonial city of Mumbai. This is one of the most important projects of my studio and the one that has impacted our work and thinking a great deal. The Cathedral and John Connon School buildings form a cluster of historic structures that are known and revered not only for their presence in the district but also for the institution they represent within and beyond Mumbai. I have a personal connection to the school as an alumnus and so do my children and grandchildren. I had joined Cathedral school when my parents moved from Kolkata to Mumbai in 1959. I was then in the sixth grade, and I recall my first day at the current Middle School building that functioned as the Girls' Middle and Senior School at the time. We were a single section of 30 girls; only six of us chose science. As a result, we attended the "Boys' School" for physics and chemistry. And so, in different ways, all three school buildings are deeply embedded in my memory.

Fig 1

Fig 2

Fig 1. Archival photograph of the Cathedral High School for Girls designed by John Adams.

Fig 2. Archival photograph of Brinda Somaya (left) from her schooldays at Cathedral.

Fig 3. Archival photograph of the boarding establishment impacted by wartime austerities.

Back in 1991, when the conversation for restoration of the three school buildings was in the nascent stage, there were very few precedents for the kind of programme we were working on. The Trust approached us for a limited competition that involved restoring, upgrading and expanding the heritage buildings. There were certain individuals who were instrumental in the process of this work. I am incredibly grateful to the Chairman of the Board, T. Thomas; the Principal Desmond Shaw; and subsequently Principal Meera Isaacs, for their steadfast support through the years to my approach, which was quite distinct from the convention.

It was a very challenging project. The schools were running to full capacity, and there was not a single empty, unused or underutilised space that we could identify to sequence the process of refurbishment. Every nook and every corner was occupied, and the entire project had to be executed without disturbing the school schedules. The logistics were very complicated. A system was developed by which the schools would function on different shifts for the children, enabling us to work on the empty sections of the buildings. A primary concern was for the safety and security of the students and serious measures had to be put in place. What worked in our favour was the considerable support and accommodation that we received from all involved in and affected by the project: the trustees, the teachers, the staff, the students and, of course, the parents.

Fig 3

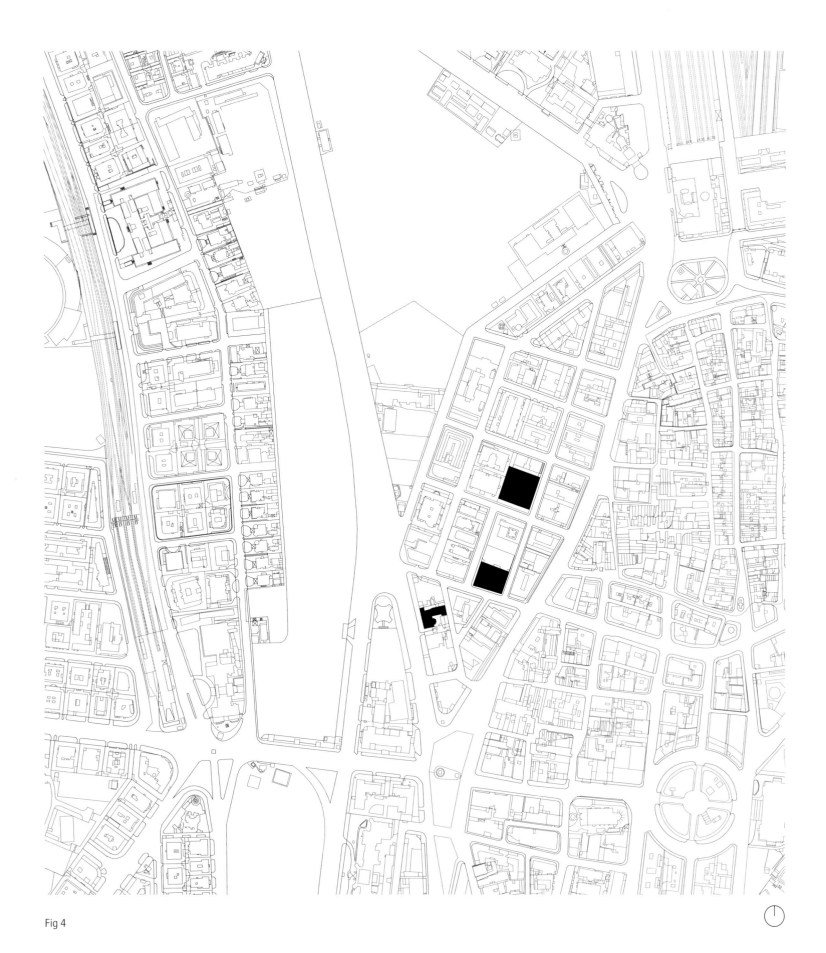

Fig 4

Fig 4. Context plan of the Cathedral &
John Connon School within the historic
Fort precinct in Mumbai.

The technical challenge lay in seamlessly introducing the modern requirements of the school without disturbing the original design. It meant rehabilitating the building while maintaining a balance between preserving the character and heritage of the building and creating a contiguous construction of the modern extensions required. We had to achieve this through sympathetic massing, design and materials that would ultimately lead to a single unified statement. As architects and conservationists, the essence of the process means interpreting the past the way we see best and providing for the future without losing the spirit of the place.

The Junior, Middle, and Senior schools were originally built at the turn of the 19th century. The first three were built by John Adams (the then Architectural Executive Engineer to the Bombay Government) in Victorian Gothic style and the Infant School was built in the 1960s by Indian architects. The three heritage buildings had extensions that were constructed in the 1970s and, unfortunately, owing to the prevalent adulteration and substandard quality of building materials during the "Licence Raj", the structures were constructed with many crucial compromises. On the other hand, the century-old historic parts of the buildings were in a much better condition. We then decided to demolish and remove the RCC additions made in the 1970s that were compromised due to quality and poor construction. There was a requirement for an additional 30 per cent area increase in each building, within the existing footprint, and if this requirement could not be accommodated, the exercise of conducting the restoration of the buildings would be futile. We also took a decision to carefully insert an additional floor within the existing frame of the buildings in a non-obtrusive way, keeping the final heights of the buildings constant. This was an innovative solution for introduction of additional area without altering the final heights of the buildings, an alteration not permitted due to the heritage regulations. In addition, I was not in favour of increasing the floor space on the ground, in the interest of the already sparse play area.

Before we could begin the major restoration work, we needed to remove all earlier interventions. We had to sensitively re-plan the buildings and revert to the original plans, which had the classrooms in the centre surrounded by the colonial corridors. The school buildings were not air-conditioned, and the corridors served as a climatic buffer, protecting the classrooms from heat and rain. They were also wonderful breakout spaces that I vividly remember from my childhood. The problem of multiple levels connected by intermittent flights of staircases was tackled by introducing a central staircase that serviced all levels.

We began designing the Middle School in 1991, and the work started in 1993. It was the first building we restored and expanded. We then began the Senior School in 1995 and completed it in 1998. In 1999, work began on the Junior School, which in my opinion was in many ways the most beautiful of the three. We completed it in 2001. From initiation to completion, the restoration and retrofitting of the school buildings spanned a decade. As conservation architects, we were very aware of the visual presence and significance of the three buildings in the urban context. There has been an overall urban revival (perhaps building-by-building) in the vicinity of the schools that has even prompted shops and art galleries to open in the neighbourhood. The ability of this cluster of buildings becoming the single source of change that affected a precinct always fascinated me, and I kept this lesson in mind for all projects thereafter.

As we began work on the Middle School building, upon documenting, we found that all the corridors had been encroached upon by cabins and washrooms. There were some very damaging water leaks and seepages, owing to the random running of service lines throughout the building. The issue of adding a floor was first addressed by casting a ring-beam along the periphery of the building, followed by columns cast from this beam. We had developed this solution as we had discovered four-feet wide and six-feet deep stone walls below the plinth. This necessitated casting of a plinth beam that carried the floating columns for the four floors above. All masonry arches with their keystones were left undisturbed by adjusting the new floor height accordingly. The asbestos sheet roofing and wooden add-on canopies were removed completely, exposing the grand arches and openings.

Rooms and cabins in the corridors were demolished, enabling unrestricted and efficient access throughout the building, without cutting through classrooms. This intervention greatly increased the light and ventilation. All toilets were relocated in a central block, eliminating sewage lines cutting through corridors. Contemporary materials such as glass blocks and anodised steel sections were introduced, while a feeling of continuity was maintained by matching the colour of the anodised steel sections to the stone. The glass blocks tied into the white marble mosaic flooring, which extended from the RCC structure to the old stone building. Colour was introduced to the buildings by using ceramic tiles for the flooring pattern, also representing the colours of the school. A similar theme was carried onto the door frames, light fittings, and the furniture. To achieve a colour balance, tones of grey were introduced on the shutters and wooden rafters.

The façade of the old stone building was left untouched, except for the removal of some asbestos sheet roofing and wooden add-on canopies that were in a state of

Fig 5. Archival drawings of the plans of the Middle School building pre and post restoration.

Fig 6. Archival drawings of the elevations of the Middle School building post restoration.

near collapse. Structural steel members that cut across old arches were removed and the holes were filled with "maladcrete". The stone effect was achieved by pressing actual stone in the plaster while the cement was still wet to achieve the desired texture. The original entrance in the south had to be changed because of a change in traffic circulation. The new entry to the building was accentuated by introducing an entrance canopy and porch, with the school crest boldly displayed in front. We requested the famous cartoonist and painter Mario Miranda to fill the three arches in the porch with his dynamic art; this continues to welcome children into the school each morning.

The Middle School was my first building for the Cathedral school and, for that reason, remains very special. It raised a plethora of challenges ranging from expansion and restoration, to instilling a sense of identity for the school. However, I do believe that it is buildings such as these that gave me the confidence and know-how to successfully carry out such work at a time where we were in the nascent stages of applying our skills in restoring and caring for older buildings.

Fig 7. The Middle School building undergoing the process of restoration.

Fig 8. Views of the restored Middle School building reveal the concordant coexistence of the old and the new.

Fig 7

106

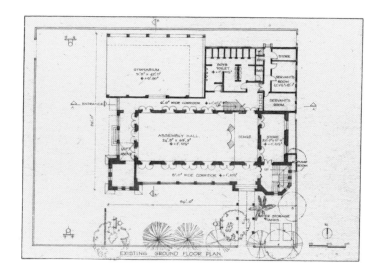

EXISTING GROUND FLOOR PLAN

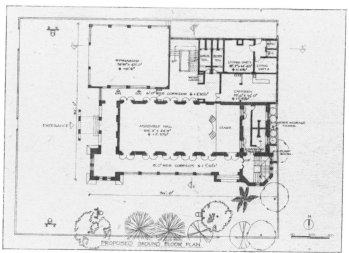

PROPOSED GROUND FLOOR PLAN

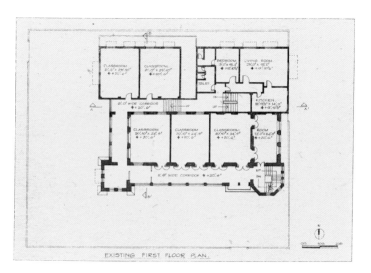

EXISTING FIRST FLOOR PLAN.

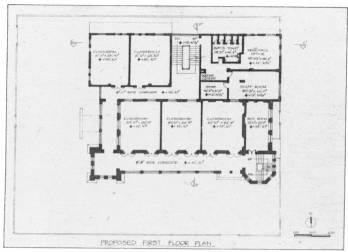

PROPOSED FIRST FLOOR PLAN.

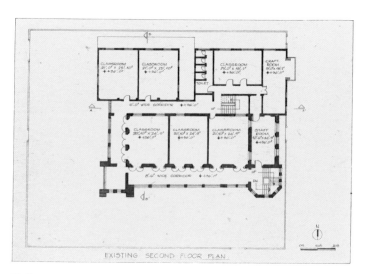

EXISTING SECOND FLOOR PLAN.

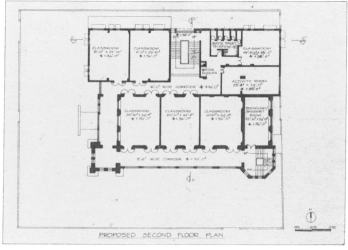

PROPOSED SECOND FLOOR PLAN.

Fig 5

PROPOSED WEST ELEVATION.

0ft   10ft   20ft

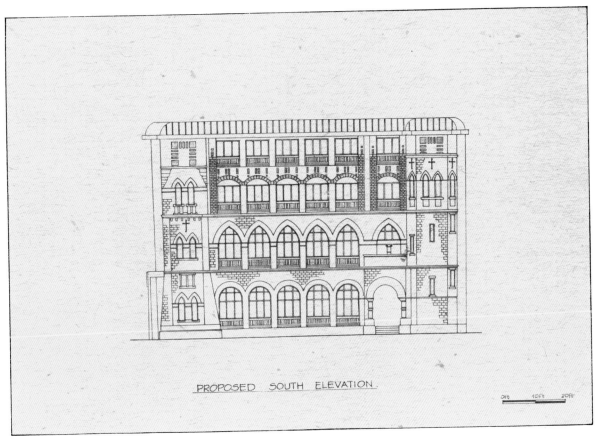

PROPOSED SOUTH ELEVATION.

0ft   10ft   20ft

Fig 6

Fig 8

The Senior School was an old load-bearing structure with RCC extensions added in the 1970s that consisted of stilts and three floors, with staircases connecting different levels and toilets randomly inserted into corridors, resulting in extremely poor circulation. Water percolated into mortar joints as well as into external walls, resulting in weakening of the walls. Due to various ad hoc extensions, existing masonry openings in stone were punctured and spanned by steel sections as and when required, without any thought for aesthetics. The existing roof consisted of wooden trusses and Mangalore tiles covering the old building, and steel trusses with AC sheeting and RCC flat roofs covering the extensions. The random insertion of cabins and toilets in corridors had caused major circulation and service issues, a recurring problem in most of the buildings.

Keeping in mind the municipal regulations for maintaining the existing plinth and height of the building intact, we began the work in phases. The first phase included the expansion, renovation and upgrade of the previous RCC extension by jacketing existing RCC columns and footings, and introducing steel portals to support the roof, which would accommodate column-free spaces for the gymnasium. New facilities were also introduced, including modern laboratories, computer and audio-visual rooms, and additional classrooms. It was in the second phase that we began restoring and expanding the old stone building.

Fig 9. The central courtyard of the Senior School bustling with activity.

Fig 10. Archival drawings of the plans, elevations and sections of the Senior School building pre and post restoration.

Fig 9

The first unique challenge we faced was with the existing roof over the main staircase, which was supported by eight embellished wooden trusses housed into a wooden finial. The new RCC roof had to be cast 18 inches above this finial. As the trusses were over a hundred years old, there was a strong possibility of the joints snapping if they were separated. Realigning and fixing them once again would most likely prove more problematic. To tackle this issue, we decided to brace all the eight trusses and anchor them to each other with a steel frame. The legs of the trusses were then cut and the whole unit was lowered with a gantry to its new height. The existing blue paint was burnt out and the trusses were polished to bring out the richness and fine grain of the wood. To ensure homogeneity between the RCC and wooden staircase, great care was taken of all elements, from the balusters to the handrails. On-site conditions often reveal problems in old buildings that must be individually and innovatively addressed each time. This, perhaps, is the distinct issue that a conservation architect has to regularly face, enabling one to generate creative and unique solutions.

Fig 11. The complex restoration and repositioning of the roof truss over the central staircase in the Senior School.

Fig 12. The discovery of a quaint chapel during the restoration process.

Fig 11

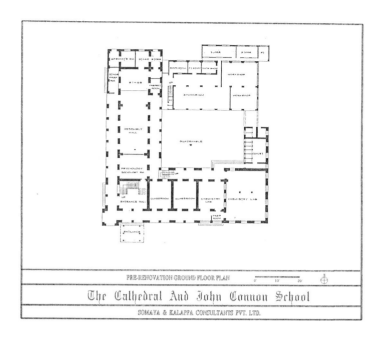

PRE-RENOVATION GROUND FLOOR PLAN

The Cathedral And John Connon School

SOMAYA & KALAPPA CONSULTANTS PVT. LTD.

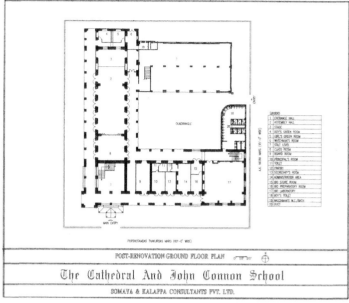

POST-RENOVATION GROUND FLOOR PLAN

The Cathedral And John Connon School

SOMAYA & KALAPPA CONSULTANTS PVT. LTD.

POST-RENOVATION SOUTH SIDE ELEVATION

The Cathedral And John Connon School

SOMAYA & KALAPPA CONSULTANTS PVT. LTD.

Fig 10

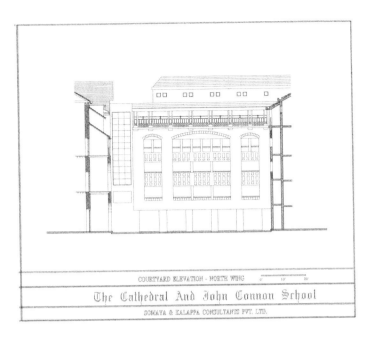

COURTYARD ELEVATION - NORTH WING   0'   10'   20'

The Cathedral And John Connon School

SOMAYA & KALAPPA CONSULTANTS PVT. LTD.

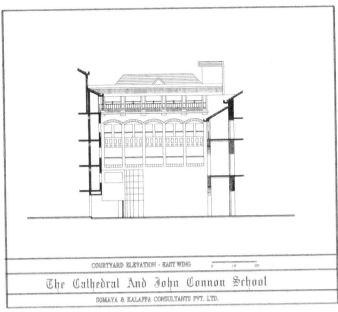

COURTYARD ELEVATION - EAST WING   0'   10'   20'

The Cathedral And John Connon School

SOMAYA & KALAPPA CONSULTANTS PVT. LTD.

POST-RENOVATION EAST SIDE ELEVATION   0'   10'   20'

The Cathedral And John Connon School

SOMAYA & KALAPPA CONSULTANTS PVT. LTD.

Fig 12

Old buildings also reveal to us the most wonderful surprises. In this school, we came across one such wonder while re-planning an access corridor. We discovered a wall that was part solid and part stained glass. The stained glass lured us to delve further, and the space we always thought to be a classroom revealed itself to be a chapel as per the original intent. We initiated the cleaning of walls and took apart the additional layers to find stained glass windows, a timber ceiling and wonderful timber floors. The process entailed scraping off years of paint and insensitive veneering. The space was restored to be the chapel it was always meant to be. The removal of the layers had now revealed windows, niches and some treasures of the original structure and its patina. This chapel of the school today serves as a small sanctuary for children during stressful times. Other interventions included connecting all buildings with a common staircase

Fig 13

on all levels and moving the washrooms to one central block, eliminating the plumbing lines cutting through corridors. Electrical wiring was completely changed and redone with casting strips fixed to the stone wall by drilling only at the joints, and we ensured that all cables and wires with floor distribution boards were located in the specially created electrical ducts. The *chajja*s (weather shades) were replaced by tile cladding on the arches to highlight the Porbandar and Basalt stone walls, thereby restoring the beauty of the external facade of the building.

Fig 13. Views of the Senior School
building post restoration.

Fig 14. Cathedral Junior School building
before restoration.

The Junior School building had been subject to insensitive interventions over decades and suffered from structural deterioration. In the corridors, we came across the repetitive issues of toilets causing extensive leakage and the open spaces being encroached by storage. Further investigation revealed severe rotting of wooden joists, damaged stone work, cornices and column capitals, and deterioration of the roof members and the spire over the staircase block. Restoration, expansion and upgrade began initially with the heritage building and was followed by the addition of a fourth floor within the existing height and footprint. An independent RCC framework from within the building supports the additional floor load. The columns along the verandah were embellished with foliage and

Fig 14

animal icons in a delightful touch of the whimsical. Rabbits, eagles, squirrels and tortoises were delicately restored and, where necessary, reconstructed using stone masons and craftsmen rather than machines. Teak louvered doors with the trefoil motif, a John Adam's signature, were also restored where damaged, and created anew. Expansion facilitated more classrooms, both airier and larger, and additional space such as a magnificent library and an art room flooded with natural light. For those with a scientific bent of mind, a laboratory with an unconventional conical ceiling and the two original, imposing and extraordinary teak-wood staircases, facing the Mahatma Gandhi Road, were also restored. The restoration work enabled us to reinstate the dignified presence of such buildings in their precincts and on the streets. The restored edifices also helped us in catalysing the upgrade of other buildings on the street. Working on a very restrictive urban site also posed difficulties.

Fig 15. The process of restoration and construction of the Junior School building.

Fig 16. Archival drawing of the pre and post renovation plans and south elevation.

Fig 17. Archival drawing of the pre and post renovation west elevation and east elevation.

Fig 15

Fig 19

Fig 20

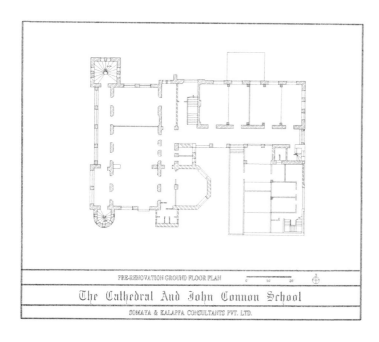

PRE-RENOVATION GROUND FLOOR PLAN

The Cathedral And John Connon School

SOMAYA & KALAPPA CONSULTANTS PVT. LTD.

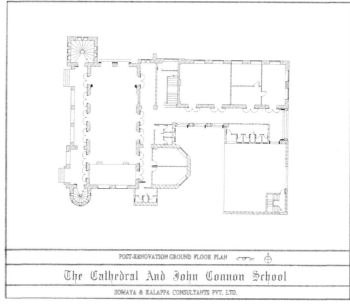

POST-RENOVATION GROUND FLOOR PLAN

The Cathedral And John Connon School

SOMAYA & KALAPPA CONSULTANTS PVT. LTD.

Fig 16

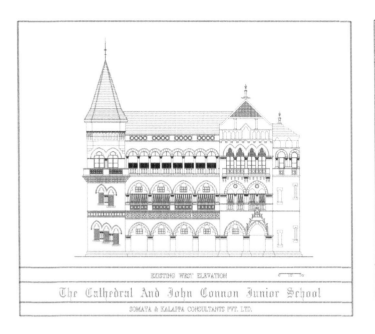

EXISTING WEST ELEVATION

The Cathedral And John Connon Junior School

SOMAYA & KALAPPA CONSULTANTS PVT. LTD.

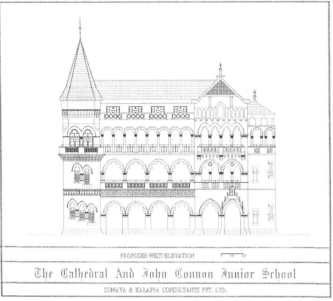

PROPOSED WEST ELEVATION

The Cathedral And John Connon Junior School

SOMAYA & KALAPPA CONSULTANTS PVT. LTD.

Fig 17

Fig 18

Fig 18. The Junior School building in its restored condition unveiling the process of reconciliation of the old and the new.

Fig 19. Brinda Somaya (left) on the site during the construction process for conservation and restoration of the Cathedral & John Connon School.

Fig 20. The mural by Mario Miranda at the Middle School entrance.

There is a distinction, in my opinion, between restoring buildings as monuments and restoring buildings meant for active use. In the Cathedral and John Connon School, we were very aware of the vocabulary of the old and the new. While we preserved the specific character of the buildings, we were able to introduce contemporary programmes and design modern extensions that are sympathetic and responsive to the old but do not in any way try and mimic the old. While a unified statement is important, I do not subscribe to the idea of conservation in which the new additions are designed to be caricaturised versions of the old. It is an act of fine balance. Conservation is not an elitist engagement reserved for the few. Rather, the conservation movement must work in the larger scheme of urban design, planning, and development strategies. The owners of heritage sites and structures must be incentivised to preserve their buildings and precincts. Lower taxes, transferable floor area ratio (FAR), and special planning authorities to decide on the regulations can instil a sense of stability and continuity for these projects.

We were intensely involved with the project in all aspects and stages, from the formulation of the programme of requirements to the detailed design. In a way, I think we stand at the beginning and at an end of a tradition as we deal with the new and the old. We have inherited many legacies from the British, from the cultural and intangible heritage including language, social norms, administrative and judicial systems to the infrastructure and physical heritage that deals with the railway lines, the colonial urban structures and buildings. The Bombay Fort is an important image-centre for the city of Greater Mumbai. Being the focus of the urban and economic growth of the city for over a century, its cityscape is composed of remarkable landmarks and ordinary buildings on the historic layout that is organised in avenues, streets, colonnades, squares and waterfronts. Long after we have completed the project, we are frequently approached by the staff, parents and students, who come up to me to express how much they have enjoyed studying in the school and how the buildings have played a role in their lives. We went on to become the architects for the Tata Consultancy Services building in the neighbourhood and are appointed again by the Cathedral school to restore another building in the vicinity that they have acquired for their International Baccalaureate School. This constant engagement with the client and the project reaffirms my belief that in an unconventional way, I have managed to retain the legacy of the buildings and their patrons while continuing to play a role in their growth and expansion over the decades.

TATA CONSULTANCY SERVICES HEADQUARTERS

For Tata Consultancy Services

CONSERVATION, RESTORATION AND REJUVENATION

Mumbai, India [2005–2007]

A complex project to preserve the historic façade of a dilapidated structure entails its resurrection and transformation into global headquarters of a corporate through a unique architectural process.

The "Ralli House" was built in 1922. I knew the building as I had studied in the neighbouring Cathedral school building, and I was aware that the building held a very important place in the central district of the Fort area. It stood between the Tata Palace and the Esplanade building, which was once home to the Tata family. Apart from its historic significance, the building has a presence on an imposing corner site in the district. The external walls of this building compose its most iconic face. Mr Subramanian Ramadorai, the then CEO of Tata Consultancy Services, was aware of our reputation for new work as well as sensitivity towards restoration. He expressed that Tata Consultancy Services (TCS) wanted to have their headquarters in this building.

Fig 1

We had already started restoration work on the Cathedral and John Connon School. The gentrification of the district had begun, and so it was extremely important to restore and upgrade this building and ensure its value was preserved. I was convinced that it was necessary to preserve the important attributes of this building so that it continued being a significant part of the urban fabric of this area.

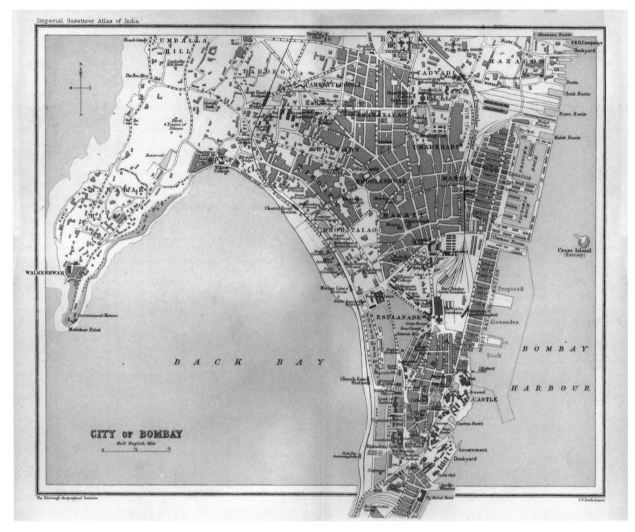

Fig 2

Fig 1. Archival photograph of the Ralli House built in 1922 and renovated in 1966.

Fig 2. Archival map of the city of Bombay (1909) that depicts the historic context of Ralli House in the Fort precinct of Mumbai.

When we started work on the project, the building was in a very poor condition and the entire interior space had imploded. We had worked with Malad stone while we were designing the Erangal House, at a beach near Mumbai. I was aware that the quarries had since closed, so it was impossible to procure a stone of the same beauty and size that was used in the building. In the 1980s and 1990s, I had witnessed a transformation in London, particularly while visiting Victoria House in Bloomsbury. It stood as a majestic example of a historic building that was retrofitted with present-day services and spaces that worked for the demands of the 21st century. Inspired by this approach, my instinct guided me to keep the skin and the walls of the original structure intact while dealing with challenges of the imploded interior spaces of the building. When we presented the plan to the clients, they were supportive of my ideas. They understood the broader vision for the building and the value in preserving the heritage aspects of Ralli House. We had previously adopted a similar approach in the Banyan Park campus for TCS, and they trusted our judgement.

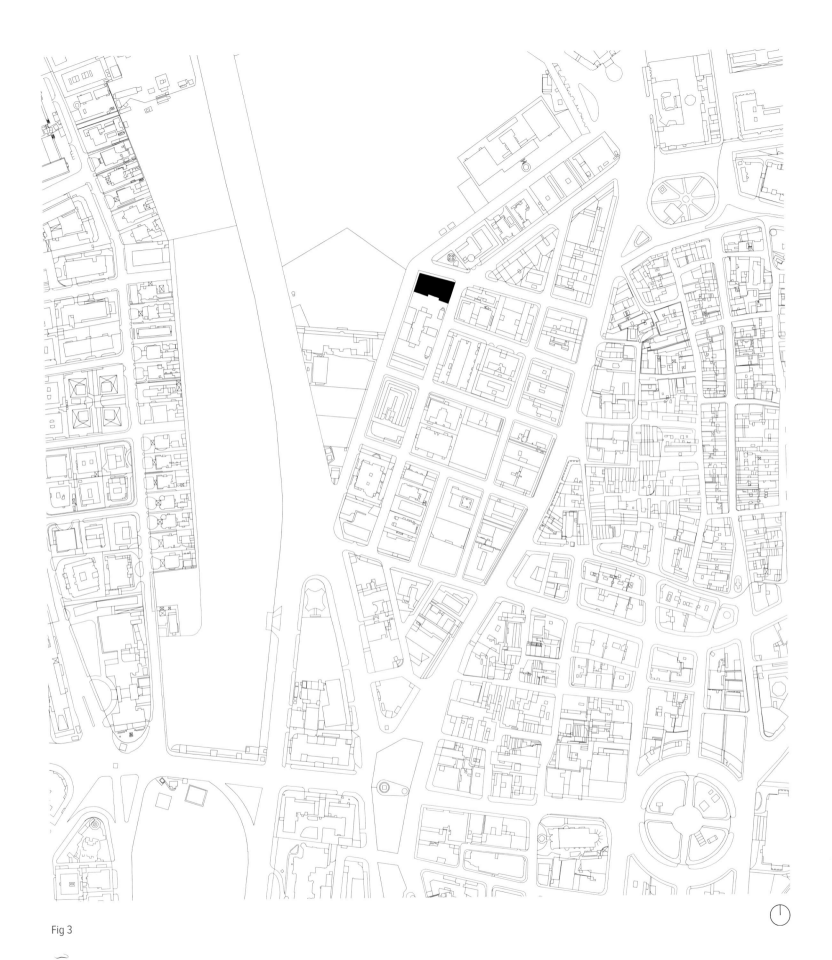

Fig 3

Fig 3. Context plan of the Fort precinct
in Mumbai.

Fig 4. Aerial view of TCS House and
surrounding buildings that overlook the
Cross Maidan in Mumbai.

The real challenge was presented by the Mumbai Heritage Conservation Committee. For the particular process that we wanted to follow, there was no precedent in Mumbai. While restoration and adaptive reuse was common to many old structures in Fort, an intervention of this scale and type was unique to the TCS House. We had to communicate the complete process and intent to the committee. The heritage committee is composed of a combination of public servants and private citizens: an eclectic mix of state government representatives, municipality employees, historians, architects and activists. Their thinking spans from being very conservative to being broad-minded and pragmatic. We presented to them the case where the new building would retain the shell of the old. We also presented to them the process by which the interventions would take place. The vision and the intent of essentially reinstating the beauty of the heritage structure beyond the mere preservation of the streetscape was communicated to them. The structure, being a Grade-II heritage building, enabled us to make changes and remove certain insensitive additions.

In India, we have a huge stock of built space in our cities. A few buildings are special, but most of our urban architecture is composed of ordinary buildings. While the conservation movement continues to save those earmarked for their historic significance or architectural heritage value, I believe that by recycling ordinary buildings, we can tap into the immense embodied energy that is consumed by the construction process. Our effort as architects is not just directed

Fig 4

towards converting these old structures into extraordinary buildings; there is a conscious thought to make them more relevant for our times. This is the architectural challenge and the central question. We are not a wealthy nation, and we cannot afford to demolish and rebuild everything. In my view, this is the essence of conservation: a process not limited to saving beautiful objects and prolonging their life, but one that uses architectural thinking to recycle and reuse buildings, with an ability to accommodate continuity while thinking of change.

Coming back to the TCS House, an analysis of the condition assessment report of the existing structure was made. Taking into account the existing dark and dingy interior spaces, we decided to utilise the western facade of the building to bring in natural light. Insertion of a light and transparent staircase block on the west side assisted efficient vertical circulation and moderated the intensity of light within the building. Retaining the fenestrations on the stone walls on three sides that flanked the street was also critical. Being the headquarters of India's largest IT company, the technical and service requirements were very complex and sophisticated and had to be integrated seamlessly into the building. New systems to manage air-conditioning, electricity, water and data were introduced. The primary directive was to design the building to function as a hi-tech working space.

Fig 5. The deteriorating condition of the facade of TCS House prior to the retrofitting and restoration process.

Fig 6. Section A through the new staircase block.

Fig 7. Ground floor plan post restoration.

Fig 8. Ground floor plan pre restoration.

Fig 5

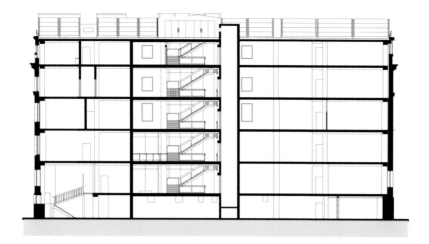

Fig 6

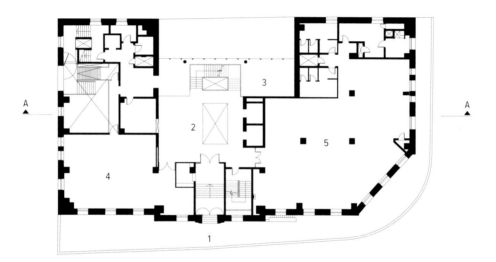

Fig 7

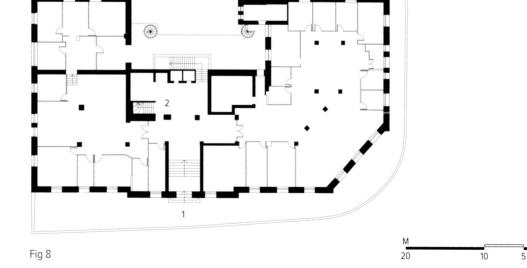

1. Main entrance
2. Receptions
3. Waiting area
4. Multipurpose room
5. Experience zone

Fig 8

M
20   10   5   0

With a construction process that was technically complicated, having the support of a strong and committed team of architects, specialists and skilled workforce was integral to the success of this project. It was challenging to build within the existing envelope on a very restrictive urban site. The old building was a load-bearing masonry structure with an internal framework of RCC and steel. However, it had deteriorated considerably over the years and the Malad stones of the external composite walls had delaminated from the brickwork. The distressed internal structure had exposed reinforcement at places and the deterioration had rendered the structure weak and unsafe. A decision was taken to gut the entire internal structure and reconstruct new slabs and frame. The new frame was erected while sequentially removing the earlier support system. Care was taken to ensure that the unsupported height of the external wall did not exceed safe parameters during construction.

Fig 9. Brinda Somaya at the TCS House construction site.

Fig 10. The complex and simultaneous processes of demolition and construction.

Fig 11. The systematic process of deconstruction that involved bracing the stone walls of the heritage structure in order to erect the new framework from within, while simultaneously dismantling the old support system.

Fig 9

Fig 10

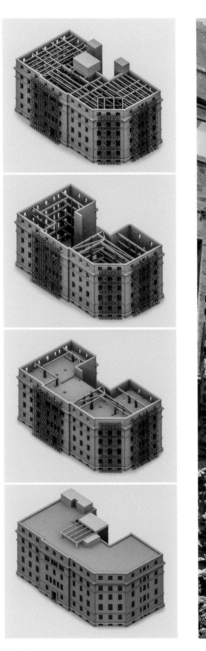

Fig 11

A specialised team demolished the structure carefully and with precision to avoid any damage to the stone façade due to the vibration. Tedious work by handheld chippers was required, as a diamond saw would have invariably damaged the wall. One of the biggest challenges of the site was a complete lack of storage space. The heavy Mumbai monsoon also posed many difficulties. The four Malad stone walls were supported independently as the interior structure was being deconstructed and rebuilt. I recall spending many a day and night in grave concern, while still convinced that they would stand strong through the torrential rains. They did.

Fig 12

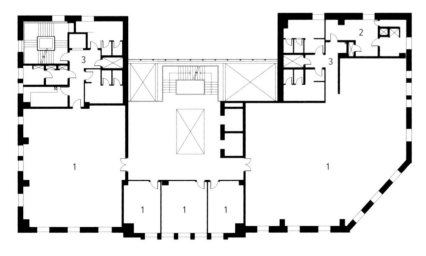

1. Workstations
2. Pantry
3. Toliet

Fig 13

M
20   10   5   0

144

It was very logical for us to create a public space on the terrace of the new structure: a space that opens up to the vistas of the historic Fort district. The landscaped terrace became a community space. It enabled the people at TCS to organise music concerts, dinners and informal gatherings, thus carving out an additional open-to-sky space on a site that otherwise renders no opportunity to have one.

I think that one of the most significant ideas to have emerged from the experience of the TCS House project deals with an architectural approach that bridges the reverential connection we have with our past with our aspirations of the future. A feedback from the UNESCO Asia-Pacific Heritage Award jury, for which the building was then nominated, surprised me. While commending the conservation effort, they questioned the contemporary design intent of the interior spaces with respect to the historic shell. I have a fundamental difference of opinion in this regard. While we did, as we do often, reuse and refurbish some of the artefacts and furniture we found on site. I insist on the new structure to have my contemporary voice as the author of such architecture. In trying to imitate the past to create a stylised version of a period, we lose the authenticity of what was unique to that time and what is possible today. One of the key markers of success in the TCS House project is the fact that the clients continue to utilise this building as their headquarters and the building responds to the demands of their lives in the present day.

Conservation is an act of fine balance. We are currently restoring Louis I Kahn's Indian Institute of Management, in Ahmedabad, where I find myself having to respond to a very powerful and authoritative modern architecture. If the process of reuse and conservation responds to the specific history it deals with while eloquently and genuinely accounting for the future aspirations of the users of the conserved space, the architect's work is done.

WORKING FROM MUMBAI

Mary Norman Woods, Kamu Iyer and Brinda Somaya

The house of Brinda Somaya's childhood designed by Claude Batley

Kamu Iyer and Brinda Somaya initiated their practice in Mumbai. The city is both a laboratory and a backdrop for their work. They have witnessed the fabric of the urban landscape change over the years from what was primarily a network of precincts and neighbourhoods to a dense metropolitan agglomeration. While Mumbai became the source of their endeavours, the city influenced their ideas on architecture and urbanism and captured their imagination in many forms: from the houses they grew up in to the professional responsibility they assume in the interest of a larger agenda.

So, how does Mumbai influence their thoughts? How does the city feature in their practices? What are their concerns about the practice itself? Mary Norman Woods, who has sharply observed their practices, discussed their ideas and written about their work, moderates the dialogue.

MARY WOODS You both grew up in buildings by two important Bombay architects, one Indian and the other British. You spent your lives in wonderful architecture. Kamu grew up in a G.B. Mhatre building that has, sadly, now come down, and Brinda, you grew up in a Claude Batley house. So, you both intimately knew another kind of modernism apart from the modernism that was brought from the West to Ahmedabad and Chandigarh. Did this particular "other modernism" of Bombay shape your ideas and design practice?

KAMU IYER Chronologically, Batley preceded Mhatre. In fact, Batley was older than him and brought in a kind of a modernism that, I would say, is still not really truly modern but it was in transition. Batley was a great admirer of traditional Indian architecture and was very keen on transiting to modernism through a deep study of the traditional. In fact, he brought out this book on design development of Indian architecture, where he got his students to make measured drawings because he believed that it was important. Great examples of traditional architecture were already recorded in the *Archaeological Survey*, in the *Jeypore Portfolio* and others. But there was no recording of any of the domestic architecture and the lesser of the smaller buildings, which is why he took up this whole exercise of documenting. He believed in tradition. Batley was also very English in the design of his buildings and even in the layout of the rooms, and there was a lack of colour... his buildings totally lacked colour. Yet, I would say that they still rank better than most buildings. G.B. Mhatre was quite different, eclectic in a way. The bulk of his practice was actually residential buildings. It was not a transplant of Western ideas. If you see G.B. Mhatre's art deco, his usage of art deco features, he yet adopted a lot of Indian features too, like the necessity of weather shades. You know, in the West they called it *eyebrows*. They called *chajja*s an eyebrow! So, he brought that in. There was a lot of colour and a lot of flair, the use of mosaic tiles and the use of new materials in his work.

BRINDA SOMAYA I was just eight years old when my parents moved from Calcutta to Bombay, and we moved into this house. I hadn't heard of Claude Batley or Mhatre or anybody else. I just remember growing up in this wonderfully designed apartment. What was different looking back at those days was that either people lived in step-up apartment buildings or they lived in individual houses. And this was very different, because it was just a four-storied building, but each floor was one apartment. So, it was sort of a mixture of a house and an apartment. I remember going as a child to the third floor and Batley always had these wonderful sloping roofs, which he believed were very important in our weather. I recall looking up at the dark stained wood on the third floor and seeing that great space and height that he created, the multiple roofs, his joinery, the marble mosaic floor. I remember some of these things as a child, and it is only later when I studied about all these people did I realise the importance. But certainly, looking back, I definitely feel that growing up in a house like that left on me an impact about space, light, woodwork, connections and angles.

MW   Of course.

BS   And I recall so clearly my journey to school on the bus via the Rajabai Clock Tower, the University buildings and the High Court building. Only school buses were allowed on Cuffe Parade and not public buses. We had the elevated walkway and then the broad road with no divider. Then studying in the Cathedral school, which were also in colonial buildings, was also important. We had a lot of friends in central and north Bombay in the Parsi colony and the Hindu colony. Marble Arch, right next door to where I stay now, is one of Mhatre's projects... beautiful buildings! So, I was very aware, and it was not just one architect—Corbusier or Kahn—that one talked about.

KI   In fact, we didn't know these architects!

BS   Yes! We didn't even know, exactly! We didn't even know much about good architecture but it was around us, it was part of us... and I think a part of growing up in Bombay was the privilege of being surrounded by all this. To me, this was as important as or even more important than just seeing one famous house built by one person or one public building built by another. These were our surroundings, we were breathing it. We were part of it.

KI   Yes. You will know, Brinda, that the thing that was common between them is that both Batley and Mhatre were sensitive architects aware of their context. Since both of us have grown in beautiful buildings designed by good architects, I am quite sure that our sensibilities would have been very different had we been raised in ordinary buildings. I actually took to studying architecture only because of the building I lived in. We always thought of the building as part of a bigger scene.

BS   Yes! Exactly!

KI   Not a standalone object.

BS   It was part of the city. Of course, we enjoyed growing up in that building, in that space, in that apartment. But, as Kamu says, what's important and different about this city is that you are often a part of something that is a part of something much bigger, and for which you have a responsibility too.

MW What I think is so distinctive about both of you as individuals, as designers, as citizens, is that it is about entering into dialogue and listening to people. So, could you talk about that in terms of your relationship with your clients? And clients being not just those who pay the fees but a kind of larger clientele, a community?

BS Well, you know about my practice and how diverse it has been, and I think that is really what led to clients that were also very different. The Bhadli village, where the village was the client and the villagers were the users… how to interact with them, as against a big corporate IT campus, where the client is a big corporation, and we may not even know all the users. It is that wide expanse of work that has been the richness of the profession that I belong to and that I have enjoyed so much.

KI But tell me about your experience when you started with factories.

BS It was for the Chauhan family who own the Parle Products Pvt. Ltd. They gave me my first real job, which enabled me to set up my practice. I have built many factories for them over the years: in Bengaluru, Lonavala and Mumbai. The first job they gave me was a small-time office and extension to a wheat storage godown. It was followed by many other factories and their homes. They have been my clients now for 40 years! So, for me, industrial work and patronage from an industrial family like theirs was only possible in a city like Mumbai. In those days, who would give a young woman an industrial project?

Brinda Somaya (second from left) with Raj Chauhan (left) of Parle Products Pvt. Ltd.

MW I read a statistic that 98 per cent of Indian businesses from the tea stalls to these huge industrial groups are family-owned. Brinda, but isn't it because you're really dealing with individuals within a family as opposed to a kind of corporate entity where the executive staff may change over time. So, because of the "Great Indian Family", again, it's possible to build over time a dialogue with the client. And I think of the clients that Frank Lloyd Wright had, like Edgar Kauffman or CF Johnson. Again, they were family businesses, and they were dealing directly with them. So, have we sort of lost that with our impersonal corporate structures in the West? And so, you really do have a particular advantage that has continued over time.

BS   Absolutely. Even with our corporate clients, we have always been very involved in the conversations about the projects. If I consider any one of my corporate buildings, they have been commissions for people who have believed in us and therefore have come to us. There may have been many other architects who perhaps would build for them quicker and maybe in a more "Alucobond way", much faster.

KI   Alucobond architecture!

BS   Exactly! We have built all types of corporate buildings. For instance, Gokaldas Images for an individual who owned this company, and he was very involved with the building. It was built in 1990, almost 25 years ago. Same thing with Parle. Then we have Zensar Technologies, the campus I built in Pune. As Kamu said, we had a few people at the top who were involved with the project from the beginning to the end, and they very much wanted the campus, and they often told me that this was going to be their first campus. It was so important for the company to send out its message of its beliefs through the way we built this campus. Same thing with the Nalanda school in Vadodara... Mayur Patel was always involved. So, I don't think scale necessarily means that you are not in close contact with your client. It depends on who they are, why they have come to you and what they believe in.

KI   So it's the same story. It reminds me of my own practice. I have not had such a huge roster of clients, but my clients have given me work for 25–30 years!

BS   Yes!

KI   That is exactly the same case with Brinda.

BS   Absolutely. My repeat clients and different types of buildings have sustained me.

KI   One of the nice things in India is the relationship between a professional and the client. These are personal relations. I am sure that clients who I have worked for say that this Kamu is a lousy architect, but he's been with us so long so let's give him work!

MW   So you're part of the family!

BS   You become part of the family.

KI   It makes for inefficiency, but it makes for good human relations! It is such an important factor but one that is disappearing fast. It has now become so very impersonal.

MW   Years ago, when I first met you, you were very philosophical. I mean your sister had left and you had such an important bond with her, she was the person you really could dialogue with, and you spurred each other on. But she left, and you had to build the practice. Do you feel that your daughter's presence now makes this a more hopeful situation than perhaps Kamu is indicating? That she will bring clients of her generation into the practice, who might be from the same families with whose older generation you interacted?

BS   Well, it is a combination of that. For instance, an old client came to us for their daughter's house recently. Nandini was involved, but she is also building her identity independently. She has her own connections who know her and her work. So, she has brought in clients of her generation. I think it was very important that she shadowed me for a while. Now she is her own person. She understands very well the values this design firm has been built upon. Many clients that I had earlier are still with us. I think that it is a combination. There is change.

MW   In a way, it circles back to the beginning of our conversation, Kamu, which you so aptly put in terms of Batley and Mhatre… that there was a way to approach modernism, but it was through tradition and it was through certain values. In the same way, I am very cognizant when I talk to her that Nandini is very much aware of the traditions and history of a practice and she very much values that. There is a sense of tradition here, but it is a tradition that can also project me into the future. They can root me in some way, which I think is something precious and remarkable that I have seen in the Indian practices that I have had the privilege to study and learn about.

BS   I hope so, because we cannot be around forever, and we hope that some of the reasonably good things we have believed in and tried to do or contribute to in our own small ways will be continued.

KI   I am sure this will be true of the people who have worked with her, whether they continue with her or they go out on their own. They would've imbibed some of the values. Those values are very important.

BS   Absolutely.

MW   Kamu, you have produced four publications and your last one, *Boombay*, was this wonderful kind of intertwining of the history of the city with your own personal history as an architect and as a citizen of the city. Brinda, you've been involved with many publications through your foundation HECAR, and now you are going to produce a monograph. You both have a voice and a presence outside of your practice, and so, I wonder if you could reflect a bit on the point at which you felt that it was important... to have that voice? What was your entry point?

BS   My entry point was very much connected with women. The "Women in Architecture" conference that I chaired, followed by the exhibition and the document that I brought out, was my first real interaction with publications and something outside the profession that I was involved in. In 1990, I had started building up my body of work, and I found that I was very isolated. There were only male clients and architects, and I never ever came across any women who were running their own practices. There were problems that I wanted to talk about and issues I wanted to share. That is when I identified and wrote to women architects, but I got very poor response. But 10 years later, in 2000, things had changed a lot, and that is when I brought out the first publication. I think it was a seminal exhibition. It was not an exhibition of complaints; it was a celebration of women's work. I believe that it led to various other interests of mine being translated into publications.

Books as discourse on architecture: *An Emancipated Place—Women in Architecture* (2001) by Brinda Somaya and Urvashi Mehta (published by The HECAR Foundation) and *Boombay* (2016) by Kamu Iyer.

MW   It inspired me, and I think it was important because, as you say, it was not just about "women" architects, which many women object to, being defined by their gender. It was the diversity of practices and of interests that were of significance.

BS   And it was all of South Asia.

MW   Yes, it wasn't just India.

BS   There were architects from Pakistan, Sri Lanka and Bangladesh.

KI   There were very few women architects those days.

BS   Very few.

MW   So, Kamu, when did you feel the desire to begin writing?

KI   Actually, I never really thought of writing specifically, but I used to spend a lot of time talking to people and, you know, sharing experiences, most of all with Charles Correa. We used to travel together, and Charles talked about Bombay. He loved Bombay, and I knew a lot about Bombay, so I would keep telling him about the city. He and many others began telling me to write and put it all down in a book. Then one day, Charles told me, "Look, I'll tell you what, I'll interview you." So, then I said, "I tend to ramble on," and he said, "don't worry we'll edit it." But then afterwards, I thought to myself, if Charles interviews me, he will ask a question and he will give the answers, and so it seemed simpler if I wrote a book. That's how I wrote the book!

MW   That's wonderful! So, to conclude, Kamu, you said that one important thing is to pose a question. For you and Brinda, what questions about working from Mumbai would you pose?

BS   It is a difficult question. I think what we have to worry about is the future of the practice of architecture. What is going to be an architect's role in the city of Mumbai, and what do they see as their responsibility to the city, as architects? How are they going to be able to handle this responsibility? As Kamu said, groups of people getting together, discussing ideas, thoughts that are good for the city ... how will they be able to convert that into reality? That is what is really important. I always say that even the smallest project, if completed, can have a much greater impact than the biggest idea. I also think a lot about urbanisation and the process of building a city. Growth is inevitable, and we are looking at decades of rapid growth to come, so the core question perhaps is: What kind of development is it that we want to see?

KI   Also, the real question for architects today is: How are you going to cope with the onslaught of the real-estate lobby and those people who have a vested interest in the most important resource of the city, i.e. the land? Will architects abandon their roles as professionals, or are they going to really toe the line?

BS   And we need to begin talking about the protagonist of the space! Nobody talks about *man*, the person who is living in the city, and that is really where we need to begin.

Kamu Iyer, Brinda Somaya and Mary Norman Woods at SNK office, Mumbai.

Recorded on 22nd December, 2015. Moderated by Prof. Mary Norman Woods.

THE STREET

Mumbai, India [1989 to Present]

Architecture of four buildings built on brownfield industrial sites of the erstwhile Mill lands in Mumbai reveals patterns of growth and urban aspirations of the city in distinct slices of time.

NRK HOUSE

Adaptive reuse for an office and showroom.
For Naveen Kapur [1989–1990]

BRADY GLADYS PLAZA

Architecture of a corporate office building of five independent firms.
For Naveen Kapur [1996–1998]

EMPIRE INSTITUTE OF LEARNING

Revitalisation and adaptive reuse of an old mill shed.
For Satish Malhotra [2000–2002]

THE WORLD TOWERS

Urban design, architecture and infrastructure design.
For Lodha Group in collaboration with Pei Cobb Freed & Partners [2014 to Present]

I have always held a belief that conservation and heritage is not limited to a discussion on listed buildings and grand edifices in a country like India. We are a nation with limited resources and we cannot afford to ignore the vast number of ordinary buildings that exist in our city. We must recycle, renew and retrofit these buildings to enable them to be relevant today. The process of re-architecture also deals with the embodied energy of the building stock that exists.

I talk about this stretch of the Tulsi Pipe Road, locally referred to as Lower Parel, as a case study and how the city of Mumbai has changed over time. My studio has been engaged with the development on this street since the 1980s when we started work on the NRK House, a small revitalisation project to the World Towers skyscrapers that we are building today. The Brady Gladys building and the Empire Institute were two critical interventions that served the low-rise and high-density character of the precinct. These four projects highlight the various approaches of urban design used to sensitively respond to the built form and density. Over the years that I have been involved with these projects, my understanding of urban recycling of land has changed, and I have begun to appreciate the coexistence of many typologies in a very small precinct of Lower Parel in Mumbai. The history of the city, in many ways, lies in its urban fabric, and in these layers, we find a critical mass of structures that we can save for the future as continuities in change. Thus, we must add a critical mass for the demands of the future. Our contribution in these layers speaks for our time and adds to the collective history of the place.

Fig 1. Sketch of 'The Street' of Tulsi Pipe Road in Lower Parel, with all four projects on a contiguous parcel of land.

Fig 2. Context plan.

Fig 1

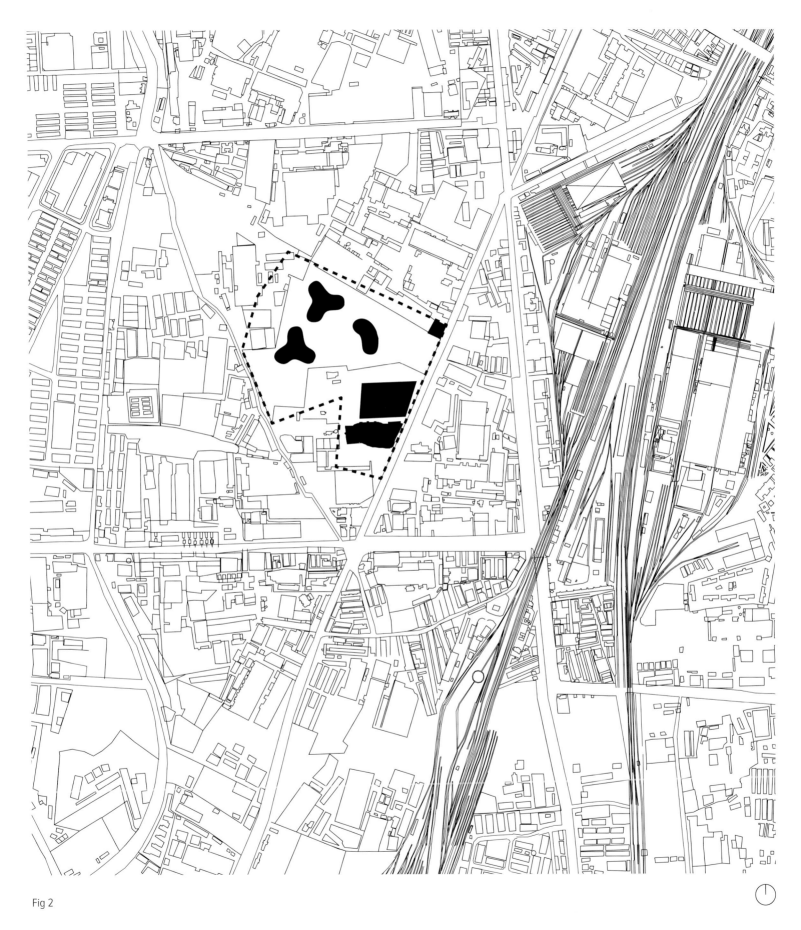

Fig 2

The Street · 167

NRK House

I would like to begin with the NRK House. In the 1980s, the words recycling and restoration were not often used in the context of industrial architecture. In an interview with journalists after the project, Naveen Kapur, the owner–proprietor of the NRK House, said that he strongly believed the 3–4 million sq. ft of land attached to the failing mills in Mumbai must not be sold in the free market to the highest bidder. In fact, he was keen to propose to the government a plan to reconvert the land into non-polluting industries and make Lower Parel a free-trade zone. This area would guarantee employment to many, and we could retain the beautiful stone buildings of our shared heritage. The NRK House somehow became an experiment and almost a prototype for this thinking. My thinking had always echoed this view.

Fig 3

Kapur had the imagination and foresight to purchase this group of derelict little sheds. When we visited the buildings, we found them in ill repair, but they had a presence in the precinct, and we were determined to maintain the scale and relevance of these structures on the street. The buildings included a crèche for Kamala Mills, a wheat-storage unit, a small kitchen and some service areas, which needed to be converted into the office space for NRK, who was primarily a garment exporter. The visual significance of these buildings in their context was also an important aspect of preservation, and I did not want to disturb the street line. The design process entailed converting the kitchen into the office space and the service areas into the office of the secretary. We planned the conversion

Fig 3. Archival photograph of the original structure at Kamala Mills that was later restored as the NRK House.

Fig 4. Ground floor plan.

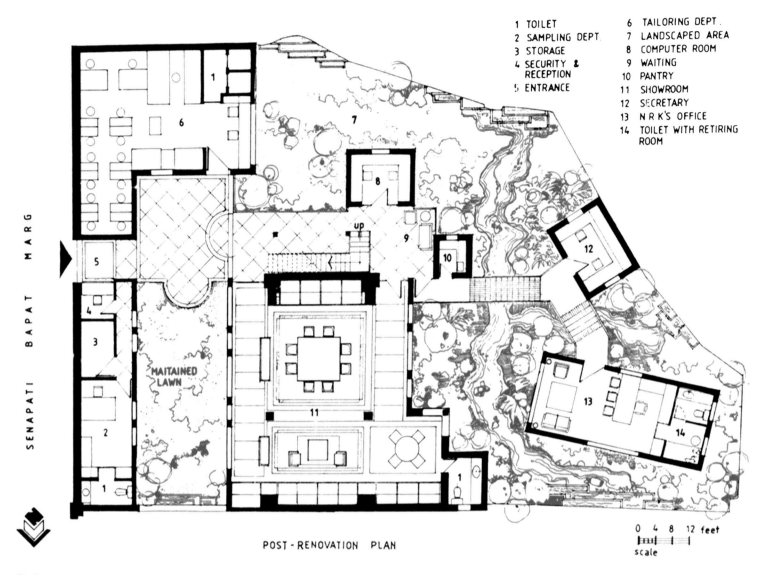

Fig 4

1 TOILET
2 SAMPLING DEPT.
3 STORAGE
4 SECURITY &
   RECEPTION
5 ENTRANCE

6 TAILORING DEPT.
7 LANDSCAPED AREA
8 COMPUTER ROOM
9 WAITING
10 PANTRY
11 SHOWROOM
12 SECRETARY
13 N R K'S OFFICE
14 TOILET WITH RETIRING
    ROOM

SENAPATI   BAPAT   MARG

MAITAINED LAWN

up

POST-RENOVATION PLAN

0 4 8 12 feet
scale

of the defunct crèche building into a showroom for the brand and the run-down storage shed into the back-office areas. Thus, there was a metamorphosis of the old buildings into four elegant and contemporary pavilions. We ensured a continuity of design in the interiors as well, through the choice of furniture, detailing and the artwork lining the staircase. Restraint was essential as the client was insistent that nothing should detract from the garments being shown. Black, white and grey were the chosen colours for us to work with. Natural light pouring in from the large semicircular windows and views to the lush greenery in the small courts outside completed the picture. We designed a rich landscape between the buildings and created a homogenous space that binds all these structures. The set of buildings could be accessed from the street through this green urban relief in the heart of the concrete jungle!

Fig 5. The NRK House takes form within the skeleton of the old building.

Fig 6. The NRK House building post restoration.

Fig 5

Beyond the significance of the project typology and approach, I was very glad that the NRK House became known in the neighbourhood, and as a consequence, the building catalysed the adaptive reuse of many other structures on the street. The NRK House continues to have its cultural significance in Lower Parel as one of the first buildings to have undergone an adaptive reuse and retrofitting process in shells of the old. When we received the Urban Heritage Award from the Indian Heritage Society for progressive conservation, I remember thinking about the value this design approach had brought. This project encouraged the upgrade of other buildings on the street, which ultimately transformed Lower Parel into an acceptable corporate address.

Fig 6

Brady Gladys Plaza

In 1996, we received a call from the same client informing us of another purchase, this time a completely derelict shed, very close to NRK House, in a condition impossible to salvage. The land was purchased in partnership and the programme entailed designing five corporate offices with an equal distribution of area.

Fig 7

Fig 7. The urban site for the Brady Gladys Plaza with a narrow frontage towards the Tulsi Pipe Road in Lower Parel.

Fig 8. Stilt, first and second floor plans of Brady Gladys Plaza.

The concept behind the design of the building was to provide privacy to individual clients while integrating them into a single building. To extend the connectivity to the outside, stepped terraces were introduced, enabling employees to engage with one another in a green outdoor garden space, beyond the constraints of four walls. The buildings were terraced to create these green outdoor spaces at all three receding levels. The roofscape and the scale of the building reflected the surrounding buildings in all their nuances and relationships to the street. When we observed the trusses and chimneys of the industrial buildings that surrounded us, we were convinced of not creating a flat terrace and a box for a building. We combined the requirements of all five independent owners in a 6,000 sq. m cascading structure. The single-plane north façade contrasted sharply with the stepped terraces on the south that have now grown into a lush urban garden.

By dividing the requirements vertically, we ensured an independent entry on the ground floor to the five major offices, giving them their own identity. The building form took a stepped design, resulting in the creation of gardens and green spaces on all floors. The design challenge was to combine the different requirements for a varied user group into a single building. On the southern side,

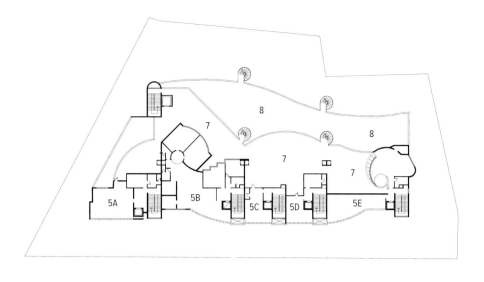

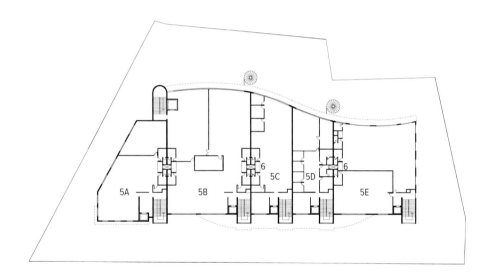

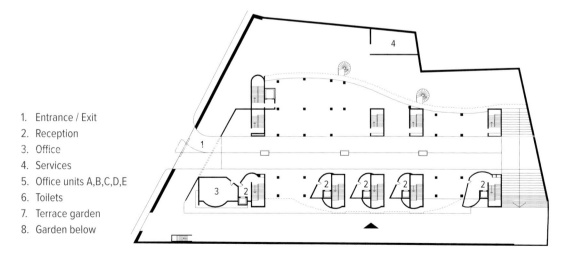

1. Entrance / Exit
2. Reception
3. Office
4. Services
5. Office units A,B,C,D,E
6. Toilets
7. Terrace garden
8. Garden below

Fig 8

M
10   10 5 0

Fig 9

Fig 9. Views of the Brady Gladys building under construction.

Fig 10. The receding terraces of the building that transformed into a community space for the employees of the office.

every office opens onto its own landscaped terrace, which with the greenery provides protection and shade from the sharp sun. The third floor, along the entire length of the building, houses the management offices. Sculptural forms echoing the chimneys of the surrounding mills were introduced and brought a similar fragmented feel to the profile of the building as seen from its surroundings. In a simple and elegant unfolding of spaces, we ensured that each owner had an independent access to their office, enabling them to use the floors and gardens at all levels—a privilege for people who work in the dense suburbs of Mumbai. As our second project on the street, the Brady Gladys Plaza became a much-discussed piece of architecture that continues to retain a combination of pristine white buildings and lush green sky gardens.

Brady Gladys proved that a low-rise large footprint could result in a considerable built-up area. Once the permissible floor space index was raised in these areas the value of land increased phenomenally and, with it, the density of the built form. When land was not so expensive, owners did not feel that they needed to consume every inch of permissible space, giving architects greater opportunities to design buildings that had context and worth.

Fig 10

Fig 11

Fig 11. Views of the completed Brady Gladys building.

Fig 12. Archival photographs of the original Empire Mill shed that was a voluminous space used for the storage.

Empire Institute of Learning

When Satish Malhotra took me around to see the Empire Mills compound, I encountered this luminous empty shed full of cement bags. The condition of this shed was such that the structure could be salvaged, and it had a robust architectural character that came from the very rational steel-truss structures that served the efficient processes of the mills. The new programme for this site was supposed to be for a design institute, and while this was not one of the handsome stone buildings from the industrial heritage of central Mumbai, it had an amazing sense of space owing to the great height, the north lights and some wonderful timber trusses that existed within the space. The old structure enveloped a volume that would have been too expensive to build today.

Fig 12

The shed covered about 20,000 sq. ft of space. We had to structurally evaluate the existing building in terms of its stability and its capacity to be reinterpreted into a new building with a much longer lifespan. There were certain elements that I wanted to retain, which included the cast-iron columns, the wonderful north-light trusses and the wooden posts, reminiscent of the time when these buildings anchored the economy of a booming city. Using these elements as the starting point of our design, we worked on introducing the idea of a street within the structure.

The multiple requirements of the institute grew from and were distributed around this street. This included a library and several training rooms for stitching, sewing and other garment processes. We added an elliptical design studio to the plan, and the language of the new structures within the shed was decided by the usage of contemporary materials. This juxtaposition created the potential of a modern space. All existing cast-iron columns were retained. We cleaned and brushed them with anti-rust additives, and we painted them in red to highlight these unique elements of the bygone era. The unusually high ceiling was left undisturbed in order to ensure that the character of the original building was preserved. The Indian Patent Stone flooring was in a very bad condition and was replaced with Kota stone. Owing to the particular volume of the shed, some select areas were carpeted for acoustic reasons. When the interiors were completed and the building became functional, it was enthusiastically received by the students and faculty. The facility was bustling with young students, and it also became a very popular location for TV commercials and advertising firms, providing a backdrop that depicts the spirit of Mumbai.

Fig 13. Ground floor plan of the Empire Institute of Learning.

Fig 14. A new built environment in the skin of the industrial heritage structure.

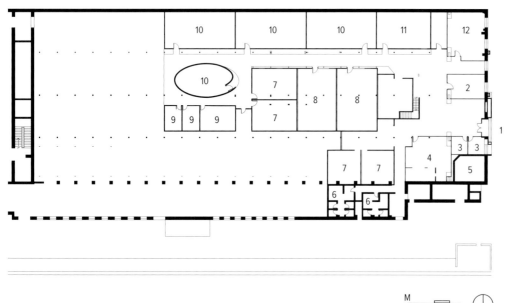

1. Entrance
2. Administration
3. Meeting room
4. Canteen
5. Temple
6. Toilet
7. Classroom
8. Computer lab
9. Photography studio
10. Design studio
11. Library
12. Faculty room

Fig 13

Fig 14

The World Towers

Our fourth project on the street is a set of three residential skyscrapers, christened the World Towers. This project is as interesting as it is complex. When we were approached by Pei Cobb Freed and Partners, a New York-based architecture firm, to be associate architects on the project with Abhishek Lodha as the client, I was faced with a very difficult decision. The towers are supposed to be the tallest in Mumbai and, in the initial days, it felt like a complete contradiction in many ways to our approach in the three earlier buildings on the street. Many thoughts went through my mind. I decided to take it up after discussing it extensively with the architects in my studio. They wanted to work on the project as a learning experience in the design and architecture of a skyscraper and in the complexity of scale, structure and programme that follows this process. We have many young people working with us. Their aspirations are high and often very different from perhaps what mine were. I believe one must listen to their thoughts as well, and understand how India is changing and what pressures exist in our urban areas. This led to the commencement of the fourth project on "The Street".

Fig 15. Site plan of the World Towers with a public street that connects the two vehicular streets on either side of the development.

Fig 16. Digital rendering of the World Towers.

1. World One
2. World Crest
3. Trinity
4. Clubhouse

Fig 15

M
100   50   20 0

Fig 16

The masterplan established a link connecting the east and the west by providing public access across the site. Also included are public amenities with a small museum and civic facilities. A part of the site, returned to the Municipal Corporation, is to be developed into a public garden. The towers in themselves are elegant, and Pei Cobb Freed and Partners have done a very sensitive sculpting of the same. They are light. They almost float. They have dynamic conversations with one another as they are viewed from afar.

The association with a firm that had designed many towers in New York and across the world is very rewarding, and our understanding of the building processes in India and the city of Mumbai lies at the core of this collaboration. The elegance and simplicity of the three towers stands out in stark contrast to some of the massive floor plates around. Building in a seismic zone, with an asymmetrical plan and such great heights, was challenging. The towers had to be designed with structural tube system with moment-resisting frames at the periphery of the building. Deep raft foundation on piles, transfer girders at various levels, tuned sloshed dampers to limit the sway of the building due to wind velocity are part of these unique skyscrapers. The lateral deflection due to the asymmetrical shape of the building and the self-load were carefully mitigated by constructing upper floors that were marginally leaning. The MEP systems adopted in this building, too, had challenging strategies, specifically with regards to mechanical ventilation, lightning protection and sewage disposal. Presentations and workshops were organised within the studio as work progressed. The studio drawing management was taken to a different level altogether. This taught all of us new ways of coordinating drawings and utilising international systems that we later integrated into our other projects as

Fig 17. A project in collaboration between SNK and Pie Cobb Freed and Partners.

Fig 18. The towers as they take shape in the heart of the city.

Fig 17

Fig 18

well. In a way, we leapfrogged into a different technological level and hopefully will now be a part of the high-tech decades ahead of us.

I am often asked about the difference in a collaborative project compared to our very own projects and whether we should do them at all. I strongly believe that these global collaborations are crucial. They could be with different specialties for large urban and planning projects or they could be for a singular architectural building. As long as the various professionals work together as equals and learn from each other, I think it is beneficial for all concerned. After all, did not Doshi and Raje collaborate with Louis I Kahn for the IIM-A design, in which we are now emerging as the fourth collaborator as we restore this landmark project?

The significance of including stakeholders in the discussions on the value and purpose of heritage in a city has always been essential. When we were discussing the issue in the late 1990s, we were architects, planners and conservationists in the committee that shared a common vision. So long as architects and conservationists

Fig 19. Aerial view of 'The Street' in the city of Mumbai, 2017.

Fig 19

do not work with bureaucrats and developers, we will always seem to be on one side of the issue and largely incapable in generating a solution for everybody. I do believe that in large re-developments of the likes of Lower Parel and the Eastern Seaboard, there is very little to be gained if the vision for the schemes is unilateral from any side. A debate enriches urban decision-making.

In the 1990s, I remember going early one morning to a mill to inspect it as a part of the Mumbai Heritage Conservation Committee listing, and we found that the previous night bulldozers had broken into the building. It was a sight I will never forget. It broke my heart. This conflict of attitude between the conservationist point of view and the development narrative can only be resolved if there is a dialogue between the two. Living in cocoons and feeling despondent will only demoralise our resolve for a better and more equitable city. With land becoming the most valuable asset in a city, the urge to squeeze the maximum out of it will always exist. In Lower Parel, a lot of valuable heritage and landscape that were once essential to the very existence of Mumbai was lost. The Supreme Court ruling went against the city and the very effective suggestions by Charles Correa were not followed. The city, in turn, lost acres of open space and space for public amenities. If we had the opportunity to work on a holistic masterplan for Lower Parel, we would have had one of the most beautiful industrial heritage areas in the world. We have an opportunity with the Eastern Seaboard, one that we that we must not lose. There are many facets of dealing with history, especially when one works on brownfield sites of urban significance. From the early works of restoration involving the Yacht Club and the St Thomas Cathedral that deal with colonial heritage to the restoration works of IIM Ahmedabad building of Louis I Kahn, our works that deal with history and heritage have always informed our practice. In many ways, our achievement as architects is in finding a middle ground that often accommodates opposing points of view. Urban transformation will never yield a single image or a solution that everyone will subscribe to completely. The question, then, is what is valuable, especially in a case where the contemporary replaces the old in a process of constant renewal. If a consensus is to be reached, urban design can lead to a middle ground by addressing the past and the future in a cohesive whole.

THE COMMUNITY

Four projects in the public domain outline the central concerns of our work as architects and professionals in India, as they act as hinges for discussions on the human condition in the country.

COLABA WOODS

Redevelopment of a refuse dump and transformation into a green public park for the citizens of Mumbai.
Mumbai, India [1989]

NITYANAND ASHRAM

Design intervention in the premises of a temple complex with the Nityanand Ashram Temple Trust.
Ganeshpuri, India [1995]

VOICE

Architecture of a rural residential school campus for girls with an NGO that works with street children to give them an opportunity for a better future.
Vasai, India [2006]

MUMBAI ESPLANADE PROJECT

Urban design proposal for the core business and heritage district in the heart of Mumbai with Apostrophe A+uD.
Mumbai, India [2011]

In 2000, the late Prof. P.G. Raman wrote a piece for the Italian magazine *Space and Society* on a few of my projects that dealt with the public domain titled "On the Precious work of Brinda Somaya". This chapter is a reflection of these "precious" projects that Prof. Raman rightly and sharply singled out from my body of work as an important discussion of the larger role of architecture in India. Designed at different times, there is a conceptual thread that connects these projects, and they continue to serve as models of the impact of architecture that I am deeply interested in: a pragmatic capacity to address critical problems.

Pro-bono public projects, often initiated by my office, have been the most significant learning experiences. There is generally no plan or a conscious effort to find public projects. Often, these projects are initiated through a personal interest in an issue or a situation that we think we can better through architectural or design thinking. Many public projects pose demands on one's professional ability owing to the complex and often exhaustive process of public discourse and consultation that one must work with. Constant negotiations, deep dialogues with the stakeholders, and a water-tight budget are often important parts of the project process. After much effort, there is very little promise of execution. The projects of my office that fall in the domain of the public realm demand much patience and perseverance.

With the nature of projects, scale and impact, the challenges of working in urban situations often have no precedent. Working with administration, citizens' groups and NGOs requires a continuous pursuit, knowing that some of the projects may never really materialise. More importantly, when we engage with the city and groups of citizens for a positive impact, they too recognise us as people who are willing to work in these spheres and soon, you have aware and active citizens who approach you for public projects. It is important to recognise that not all public projects demand pro-bono work. Sometimes, as architects, we can judge the nature of a project, where architecture can make a substantial difference, but the budgets do not permit conventional architectural fees. Many public projects are thus subsidised by the practice, but I have always taken up work on which we can deliver professionally. In public works, once we decide to engage, fees do not dictate the time and effort invested.

Colaba Woods

Colaba Woods was perhaps my first realised public project. It was an incredible learning experience, and it was the beginning of my understanding of the complexities of working on a civic issue. I grew up in a house on Cuffe Parade that, at some point, faced the sea. In the 1980s, the seafront was reclaimed and the mangroves were replaced by a refuse dump, in turn replacing the crabs and the fish with red earth that was alien to the landscape. This dump was eventually built over with years of informal encroachment and a few quarters for Public Works Department employees. The small piece of land where Colaba Woods now stands was the only piece of open land left from the original reclamation. A few citizens and I were quite apprehensive that this last remaining open space would be encroached upon or grabbed by a developer, and we would lose a crucial opportunity. We wanted a green lung in the area, and my father, who was then in his 80s, requested the Tata Electric Companies to fund the conversion of this eight-acre piece of land into a public park.

Fig 1

We were able to relocate the PWD quarters and initiate a lengthy and considered process of converting this place into a people's park. One of the most significant aspects of the project was that it was one of the first public–private partnerships where private citizens partnered with the Municipal Corporation of Greater Mumbai to design a citizens' public space. The government reduced the water and electrical charges and we were able to use the treated grey-water from the housing complexes around for irrigation. It was decided that we would not plant

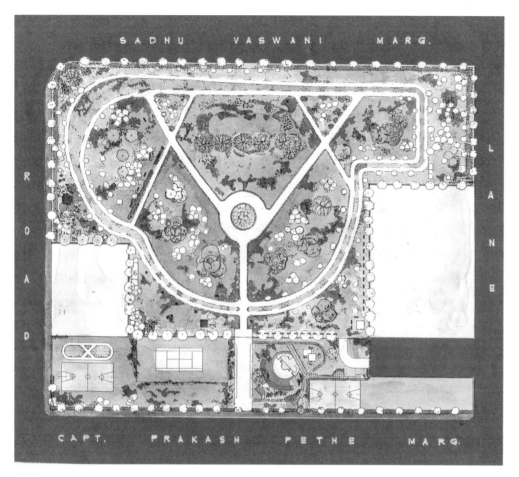

Fig 2

Fig 2. Archival drawing of the
Colaba Woods.

Fig 3. A neighbourhood landmark that
provided a greenscape in the heart of
South Mumbai.

decorative plants but native trees instead. We had, in our time, been witness to the chopping-off of ancient trees of our city in a relentless pursuit for 'development', driven by irrational infrastructure. Presently, there are more than 200 species of plants and shrubs in the park, some of them are rare varieties of flora!

We designed paths for senior citizens with benches for them to sit and a playground where children could play football. We designed a lit gazebo for the slum children to study at night. An amphitheatre enabled public meetings and events to happen. The park connected the upmarket housing on one side with one of the largest informal settlements on the other. Indian cities are different from the West where there is high degree of segregation. In our cities, the rich live in close quarters with the poor, as the joggers with their fancy sneakers and the fisherwomen with their nine-yard saris share the same urban space. We also stood against the decision of the municipal corporation to charge a meagre sum as an entry fee as we felt that any amount, no matter how small, will deter the poorest of our city from enjoying the beautiful canopies of the Colaba Woods. It was truly a democratic space and continues to be so in our increasingly exclusive city.

Fig 3

"This project points the way to the sort of initiatives that are necessary in many large cities in India. Rather than wait for the bureaucratic inertia to be overcome, the citizens of Cuffe Parade, Colaba in collaboration with the Tata Electric Companies and the local Lions Club transformed 8 acres of Municipal land into a green forest amidst the concrete desert of the neighbourhood."

—Professor P.G. Raman

Nityanand Ashram

Ganeshpuri is a small temple-town on the peripheries of Mumbai and the Nityanand Ashram is a religious hermitage with a temple as the centre of the complex. The temple and its environs were in a constant state of deterioration, and there were encroachments by the flower sellers and small shops. The plaza of the temple was disorganised, and the board of temple trustees were keen on revamping this plaza. In the process, they relocated the shops at some distance from the temple in contemporary facilities. When the shops were complete, the shop owners declined to move. I was then involved in a project for Captain Nair, who was the Chairman of the board of trustees at the ashram. In one of our meetings, he shared with me the concern and asked me if I would be willing to look into it.

As I visited the temple complex in the following week with some of my colleagues from the studio, I asked the flower sellers about the reason for their resistance to move into new and well-built shops. We then realised their needs for the project. One of the sellers said, "*Nobody asked us what we wanted. They have built the shops far away from the temple. We have to be located on the way to the temple so that devotees stop and buy our flowers. We don't sell all our flowers every day, and we can't afford to throw them away in the evening! We have to have a raised platform, below which we can keep our flowers overnight. We also need a place to display and hang our wares on posts outside. How do people know what we have and what we are selling: the types of flowers and lengths of malas (garlands)?*" The enthusiasm and interest that the shopkeepers and their families showed in the discussion amazed me. This made me determined more than ever to give them a solution that I felt would be appropriate for them.

Fig 4

Fig 4. Archival photographs of the Nityanand Ashram temple complex in its original state.

Fig 5. Archival drawing of the temple complex.

Fig 6. Elevation and section of the proposed line of shops.

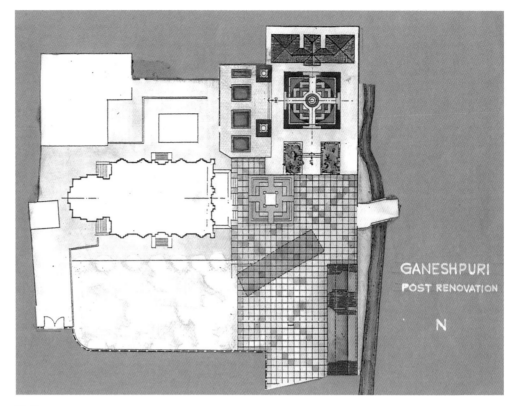

Fig 5

I asked Captain Nair to allow us to redesign the plaza in a way that would enable the flower sellers to relocate without losing their precious business. We worked with them to understand their special requirements and designed simple stalls on the way to the temple. Every one of them moved to their new premises, and we could then redesign the temple plaza, repave it, and reorganise it. This project enabled me to understand the significance of some fundamental questions that architects often don't ask: What is our role? Whom are we building for? What are their needs? What are their dreams and aspirations? After all, we are not building for ourselves.

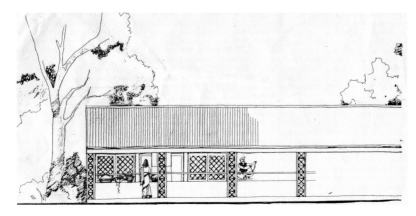
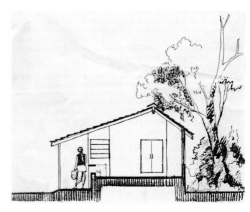

Fig 6

Fig 7

"In this project, too, the Geddesian notion of conservation surgery is put into practice in a rigorous way. As population increases, pressures on religious buildings by devotees as well as by those who provide commercial support become intense.

"Kenneth Galbraith once remarked that India is a living example of anarchy. He certainly meant this as a compliment. The vast crowds that pour into religious buildings and the complex rituals that take place inside may appeal as being chaos to the casual observer."

—Professor P.G. Raman

Fig 7. The re-designed plaza and shops within the temple complex that caters to a large number of pilgrims.

Fig 8. Ground and first floor plans of VOICE.

VOICE

Voluntary Organisation in Community Enterprise (VOICE) is an NGO that works towards the education of children whose parents cannot afford to raise them. Gita Simoes, an acclaimed designer and a close friend, was a trustee on the board of VOICE, and they wanted me to design a residential school with classrooms and dormitories for 80 children, a cafeteria, a kitchen, a library, a small administrative facility and ancillary services on a piece of land in Vasai, a satellite town in north Mumbai. The children for whom this facility was to be planned generally lived on the streets of the city, begging at the railway stations and under the flyovers. Being girls, they were particularly, and often, vulnerable. VOICE was instrumental in taking them off the streets and into a home by convincing their parents of their

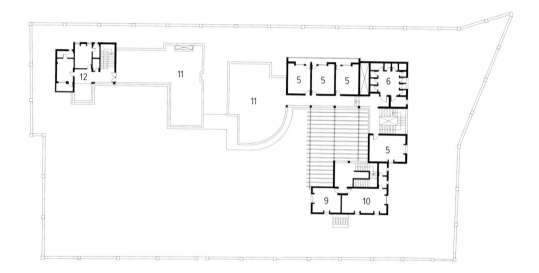

1. Entrance
2. Administration
3. Vocational training room
4. Store room
5. Classroom
6. Toilets
7. Kitchen
8. Staff quarters
9. Computer room
10. Library
11. Terrace
12. Warden's room

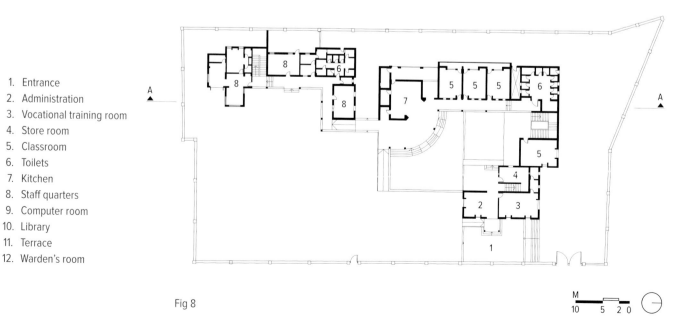

Fig 8

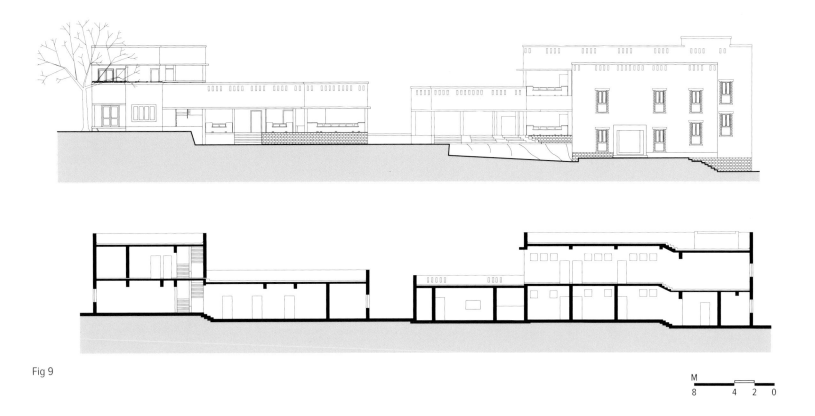

Fig 9

M
8   4   2   0

better future. In this campus, they would be educated and trained in certain skills that would enable them to regain their self-confidence to go back to the world to find a dignified life. This project was critical as it was not just for children, but the girl child.

We had to build on a very limited budget and in a design vocabulary that was appropriate for a rural campus in the context of a village. As I have stressed before, we place a great emphasis on understanding the user in our projects. We have to build for the emotional and physical relationship the users have with our buildings, and this means that we design with a humane ambition. I wanted the VOICE buildings to be a protective environment, with an enclosure and a sense of safety. The cafeteria and the dormitory blocks envelop the play areas with simple and familiar materials: brick and paint. While all architecture can be made by brick and stone, I believe in architecture that enables the users to transcend the boundaries that bind them and elevate their spirit to a higher plane through the spatial experience. This is perhaps the distinction between building and making architecture. While the merits of its architecture can be discussed, the purpose that this building fulfils is much higher and perhaps closer to the very idea of architecture that I practice.

Fig 9. North-east elevation and Section A of VOICE.

Fig 10. A vibrant space for education, creativity and interaction for the young children living here.

Fig 10

"Likewise, nuances in her community work too should be noted. Aldo van Eyck once wrote that it is devilishly hard to combine, let alone reconcile, the task of an architect with his involvement in the socio-political sphere, and what it means to be loyal to both at once; loyal in such a way that the one sustains the other, instead of thwarting or distorting it. Acute social awareness of this kind—direct engagement—very easily tends to dislocate—surreptitiously, in fact—a meaningful thought structure; certainly, when that thought structure concerns architecture and one fails to resist its subordination. I have known quite a few architects thus doubly dedicated, but only very few have managed to play the game intelligently and gracefully."

—Professor P.G. Raman

Fig 11. Masterplan of the Mumbai
Esplanade project in the Fort precinct
of Mumbai.

Mumbai Esplanade Project

The Mumbai Esplanade project is the only unrealised project that I have included in this book. This project is personally important to me as it deals with core issues of the city I love. This urban design proposal was drafted by Apostrophe A+uD with Somaya and Kalappa Consultants, in an attempt to design a continuous and uninterrupted pedestrian realm in the Fort precinct. Connecting Churchgate Station to the Chhatrapati Shivaji Terminus—the two major suburban rail terminals—this stretch of Fort expands to assimilate about 7 million people traversing these points to get to work. There are major junctions of conflict between pedestrians and vehicular movement. Subterranean connections for pedestrians exist, but the abysmal standard of maintenance ensures that it is the least popular choice with the commuters. Impossible to use if one is old or differently-abled, the subways are out of bounds for many who feel vulnerable and exposed to unsafe situations at night.

The Mumbai Esplanade project plans to connect 102 acres of currently independent open spaces or *maidan*s (playgrounds) by adding another 63 acres of new pedestrian open spaces. The Azad, Cross and Oval *maidan*s can be seamlessly connected by a short east-west vehicular underpass, a design that has successful global precedents. Working for months, we prepared many detailed drawings and visualisations to make presentations to stakeholders and get the citizens excited about the idea. Large panels that explained the project in detail were generated for an exhibition at the Horniman Circle, and the project was presented to the press and interested people through public meetings. The media coverage was very positive, and many understood the project to be feasible and desirable to improve the quality of urban space by prioritising the right-of-way for the pedestrians in the Fort.

However, even after much effort and public discourse, we were not able to excite the city administration and generate the necessary political will for this project. It continues to be one of those projects that I truly believe has immense potential. Time has come for some radical yet implementable proposal to revitalise Mumbai's core. The creation of an open, publicly accessible and pedestrian-friendly urban space is one of the key ingredients of this proposal. The Esplanade project, once completed, will be a gateway for Mumbaikars commuting by train to South Mumbai and will serve as an integral link element for the area's historic architecture. Our sense of place and belonging will be reinforced.

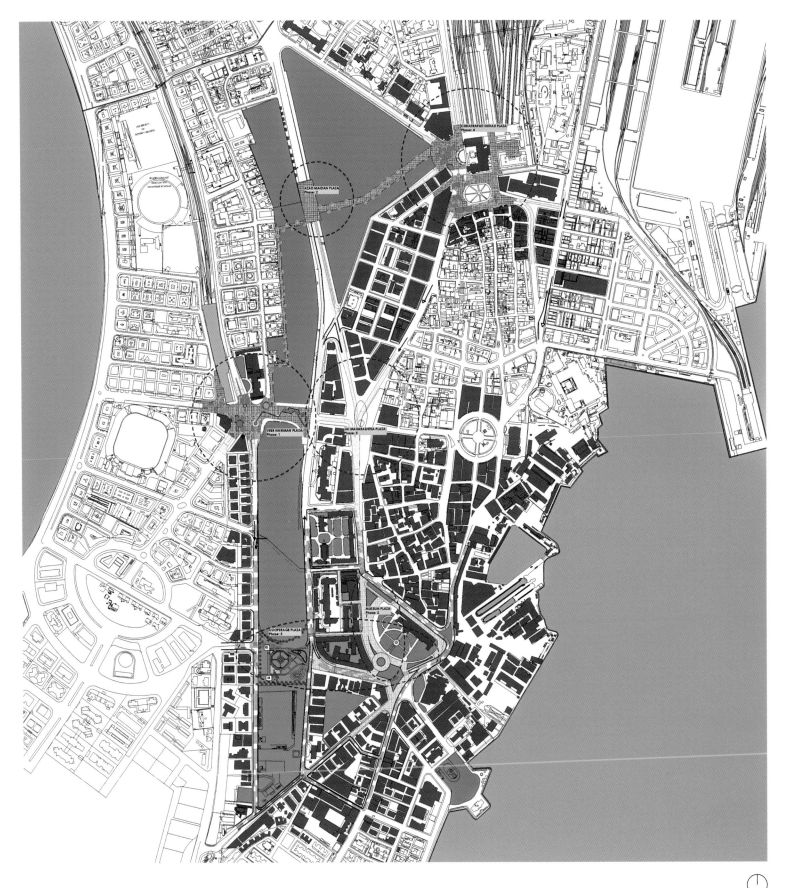

Fig 11

The Community · 209

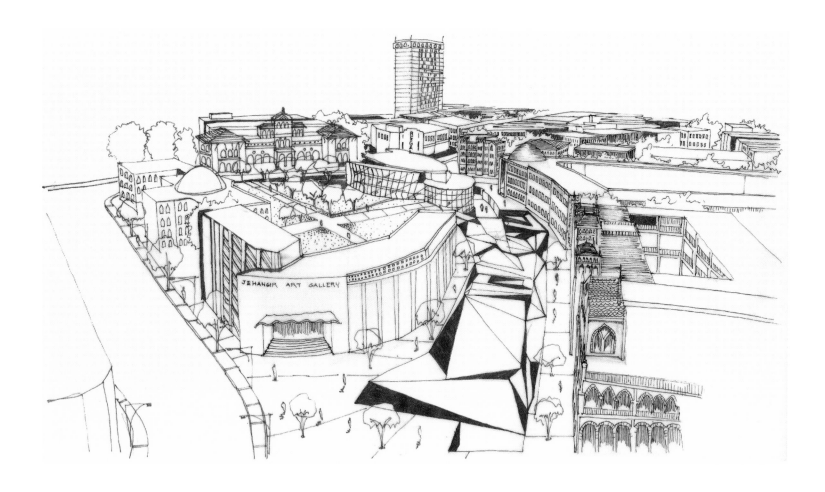

Fig 12

"The Mumbai Esplanade Project is a key intervention in the saturated Fort precinct of Mumbai. If built as proposed, it will change the 'perception' of the core Fort area in Mumbai. In an otherwise space-starved metropolis, this proposed intervention will add to the existing maidans and open spaces of Fort, in turn creating a continuous, uninterrupted pedestrian domain stretching from Colaba to CST."

—Ruturaj Parikh

Fig 12. Schematic sketch (above) and visualisation (below) of the proposed intervention.

Fig 13. Brinda Somaya at a public presentation made to the citizens of Mumbai.

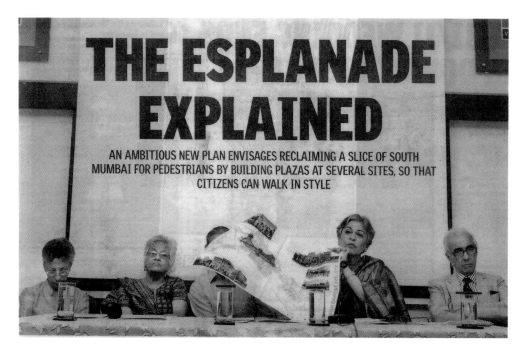

Fig 13

Many public projects develop from our continuous interest and research in issues that we think are central to the society and culture of India. This pragmatic research is a very important part of our practice. This aspect of our work has grown considerably with Nandini's enormous interest and abilities in systematic research and the analytical tools she has created in the studio that aid decision-making in design. From affordable housing to global exhibitions that we design, everything begins with a thorough process of documentation, research and analysis. The knowledge this process generates enriches the design process and creates links between the various aspects of good design. A collaborative practice for some projects is invaluable, and this model becomes more pertinent if the projects in question are in the public realm. We are a practice grounded in reality. Understanding the multiple facets, human connections and stakes in the project lie at the core of our endeavours. I do think that if as architects we are able to meaningfully contribute to society, the professional and personal fulfilment outweighs any award!

JUBILEE CHURCH
For Church of North India Trust Association

ARCHITECTURE

Navi Mumbai, India [2000–2001]

Small but well-programmed buildings that work as generators of community life are an opportunity for architects to create activity anchors in new suburban areas otherwise devoid of references.

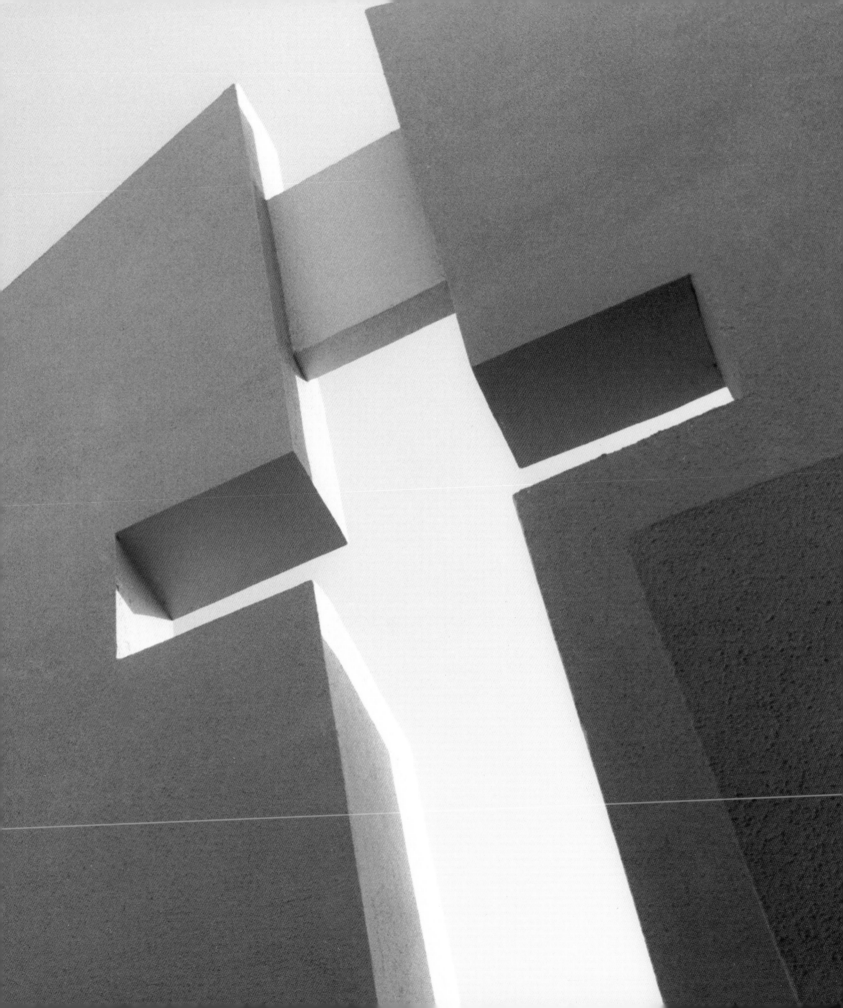

The Jubilee Church continues to stand nestled between residential buildings in Navi Mumbai. It stands as the local landmark: important, but not imposing on its surroundings. As I reviewed the archival information on the church, I could not believe that it was completed 16 years ago.

While Navi Mumbai, then New Bombay, was conceived by Charles Correa, Pravina Mehta and Shirish Patel as a network of urban centres with changing densities, the rest of Navi Mumbai developed very differently from Belapur, where one can see the potential of the original plan. I think this phenomenon is partly attributed to the fact that corporate offices, government buildings and banks that generate jobs never moved from the Fort area of South Mumbai, resulting in areas in Navi Mumbai being limited to residential sprawls. However, this has changed rapidly in the last two decades, since we built the Jubilee Church. Sanpada now has parks, lakes, bustling streets and walkways, but back then, was just a featureless suburbia with traces of infrastructure and a diminished sense of place.

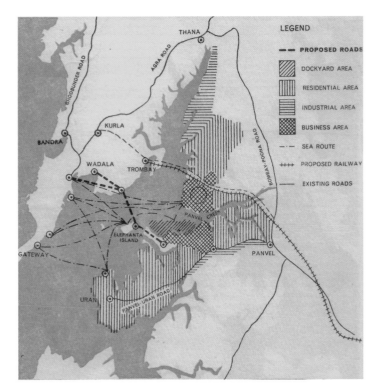

Fig 1

Fig 2

It was almost two decades ago that my journey with the church began. One of the architects working in my studio belonged to the Church of North India and brought the Trust Association to my office to discuss the vision they had for this project. They had a small piece of land measuring barely 500 sq. m, and they wanted to build a church for the community comprising of about 250 people. The land was sandwiched between dense residential plots. After several discussions with the Diocese and the individuals who ran the parish, a programme began to crystallise. Further analysis led to the development of a broader requirement not only for a religious centre but also for a community space for the people. For minority communities, a small church is a place to gather and socialise in order to connect and exchange. It had to be of a certain scale that the local community could identify with and feel extremely comfortable in. This idea evolved into the primary programme. However, it was the small size of the plot that perhaps remained the most challenging aspect of the project.

When we started designing the Jubilee Church, there were just a scattering of residential buildings in the neighbourhood that were bare and repetitive. Over time, I have had the opportunity to design and build several religious buildings, from the Nityanand Ashram near Mumbai to the historic St Thomas Cathedral in the heart of the historic precinct of South Mumbai. But this was different. There was no context we could react to. In many ways, it reinforced my belief that no two buildings can be designed with the same approach. I have seen caricaturised versions of temples and churches built today but with a disconnect to the authentic

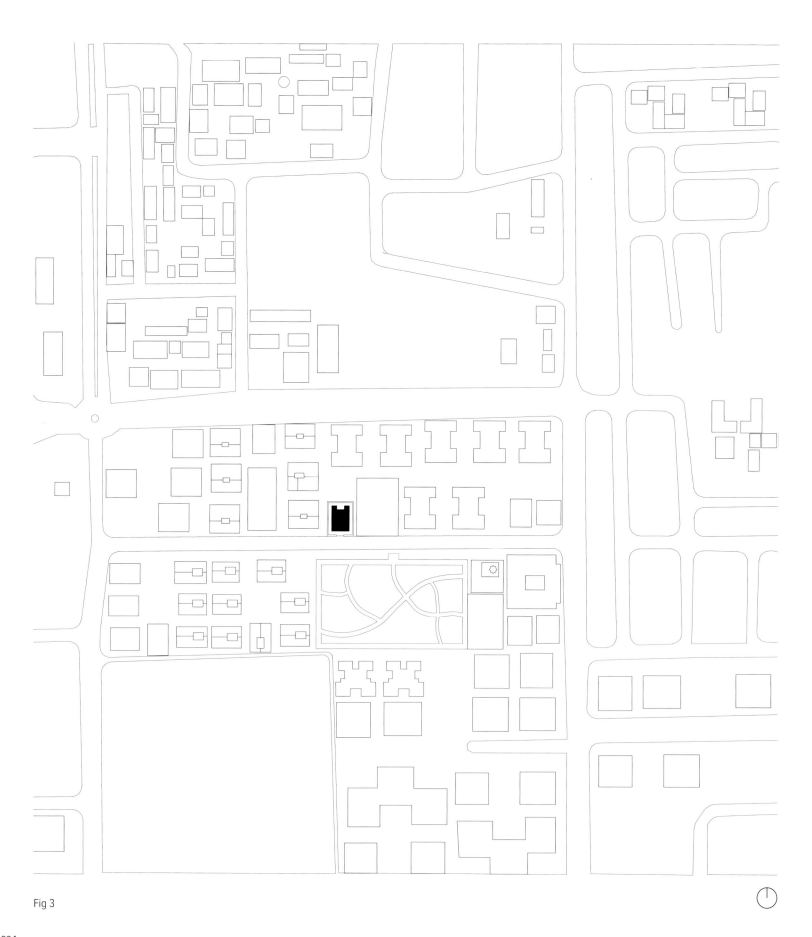

Fig 3

Fig 3. Context plan.

Fig 4. Ground, mezzanine and first floor plans of Jubilee Church.

1. Entrance
2. Vestry
3. Nave
4. Pulpit
5. Toilet
6. Altar Cross
7. Parsonage
8. Mezzanine level
9. Slit light

monuments of our history. Since we were designing in the 21st century, I realised that I had the opportunity to create a contemporary work of architecture that has an abstract and a symbolic connection to the religious space, but in a language that was mine and that responded to the aspirations of this developing community.

While one designs, many decisions are intuitive. On this limited site, the ground floor was to be used as a prayer hall with a flexible space that could adopt and act as a central community space. To accommodate 250 people on this footprint was extremely difficult. I believe that a plan is the generator of design, and in this case, it was obvious that we needed to use the maximum buildable area on the site.

This little church seats about 200 persons on the ground level and the mezzanine. On a good-weather day, the space expands to include an additional 75 people as the large doors that act as walls on the two sides slide to double up on the walls, thus opening up the structure and drawing in light and space from outside. In India, with its huge population, places of worship are usually overcrowded and rather noisy. With the number of devotees increasing, providing a tranquil atmosphere is extremely difficult. Parishioners are ready to stand for an entire service, and we as architects have to plan accordingly. As I mentioned earlier, even the terrace has now been covered and used for service. The multilingual nature of India results in numerous services being held on a single day in different languages. Hence, the peace and quiet that a worshipper can have in a cathedral like the St Thomas, which we restored, is quite different from that of the smaller new churches springing up in small towns and suburbs of Indian cities.

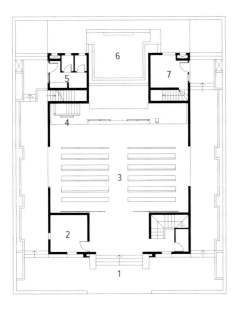
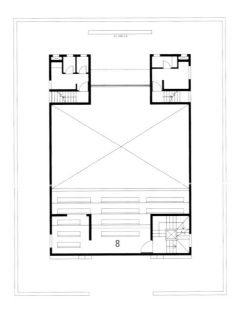
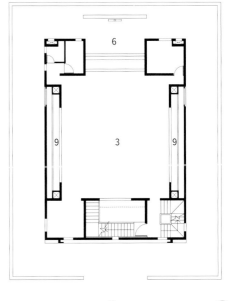

Fig 4

M
10 5 2 0

An important decision in the design of this church was to locate the Cross independent of the altar on the compound wall, which was separated from the building by a small courtyard. We were thus able to integrate the indoor and outdoor spaces right from the entrance up to the stainless-steel cross on the far wall. This facilitated the passage of natural light into the space, which rendered a sense of depth to the limited floor space we were working with. By controlling the volume of the space, larger degrees of flexibility were possible within the structure. In addition, this church, like many buildings in India, had a small budget that limited the ways in which I could deal with its architecture.

When we think of churches, we imagine them to be made up of stone and wood, apses and buttresses. Here, in this tiny plot with limited resources, how would one build? I saw this church as a small piece of sculpture. Monolithic in nature. This unbroken building, except for the cross cut-out, would thus give it its form and solidity. Even the finishing on the terrace would be white china mosaic pieces

Fig 5. North and west elevation (above) and Sections A and B (below).

Fig 6. The church construction rising upwards, ending with the terrace slab being dressed in china mosaic.

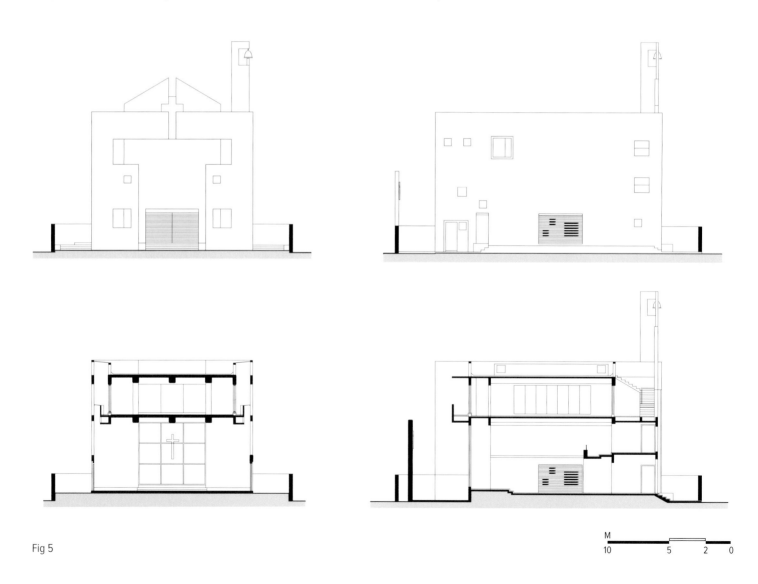

Fig 5

M
10   5   2   0

Fig 6

in pattern. The large reddish-brown doors would lend it colour and let the outside in, when required. The highly polished wooden pews and two stone-coloured podiums with the stainless-steel cross were other materials used in contrast to the simple white plastered external walls of the church. The staircase leading to the terrace worked its way around a sculptured centre, which was as chaotic in nature as the church was still. These solids and voids, perhaps metaphorically, reflected the ever-changing relationship between man and his religion.

There is a hierarchy in which one would perceive spaces in the Jubilee Church. The changing levels, quality of light, ceiling heights and sequence of volumes compose an interesting transition that takes one from the street to the cross at the altar. While the building is a public space for large congregations, it could also act as a place for reflection and solitude on a quiet day. This changing nature of the space within is a metaphor for the faith it represents and is also responsible for introducing a feeling of great depth into the building. I designed a very simple and rather elementary façade that has a certain formal and sculptural value. The roof, the bell tower and the cross cut on the façade were composed in a way that, from within, they are perceived as icons of the faith. The austere face of the building contributes to the complexity of the space within, as it allows the changing light to permeate through its volumes.

Fig 7. Archival photograph of the church in its final construction stages.

Fig 8. Views of the Jubilee Church on completion.

Fig 7

Fig 8

For this church, as for all my buildings, I aim for honesty in design. I do believe that one must interpret and respect the demands of a faith or a programme, and sometimes these demands are iconographic. I have always worked on a strong approach that is value-based and not image-oriented. I believe this line of thought enables me to create architecture that is contemporary and yet, in many ways, speaks to the people who use it.

The Jubilee Church was started with one service, but over the years, the popularity of the space in the neighbourhood led to the establishment of three consecutive services in different languages. To accommodate the expanding demand, the Diocese covered the terrace with a blue roofing sheet, and, naturally, it was not done with the sensitivity that it demands. After years, I discussed alternative design solutions within my studio. However, it was later that I learnt that the change was made in haste. There was an urgent need for the increase in space, and this had to be provided using a blistering fast solution that would also be economical. In situations like this, one must come to terms with the contradictions in which our buildings exist in a country like India. With its demanding programmes, water-tight budgets, heat, dust and rain, people take ownership of the buildings and intervene in ways that are not always in alignment with the original design or

Fig 9. The front edifice with the cross and the bell tower.

Fig 10. The inaugral service at the church.

Fig 9

intent. Sometimes, the changes are insensitive, but sometimes they discover an opportunity that I would not have thought of while designing. This is perhaps why many architects in India never re-photograph their buildings once they are in use. In an ideal world, an architect wishes to be involved with additions and alterations in the building well after the project is completed. But to me, the fact that the building is used well beyond its capacity is rewarding in itself and, in many ways, confirms the belief of my architecture.

Fig 10

Today, the Jubilee Church stands tall and proud. A public garden has developed in the land opposite the church. The Church of North India organised a wonderful consecration event and invited us all. In hindsight, I realise how open-minded they had to be to accept the kind of building I was proposing, and I believe that was based on the trust established. They knew we were concerned about their needs and a true partnership developed, as it must for a project to succeed. It stands today as a focus of many community activities, congregations, services and gatherings. In our suburban landscapes that are either rendered sterile by repetitive building formulas or cluttered by façade-architected buildings that compete to constantly dazzle us, small and considerate buildings such as the Jubilee Church provide an anchor for familiarity and a canvas for new memories to form.

RAJABAI CLOCK TOWER AND UNIVERSITY LIBRARY
For the University of Mumbai

CONSERVATION, RESTORATION AND REJUVENATION

Mumbai, India [2013–2015]

Restoration projects as opportunities in leading a discussion on shared urban heritage in a process that not only increases the longevity of an icon but also assimilates the demands of modern use.

We moved to Bombay from Calcutta when I was eight years old. We lived in a house on a wonderful old street called Cuffe Parade. It was the late fifties/early sixties, and from our home we could see all the way to Malabar Hill from the Back Bay with the "Queen's Necklace" and the Raj Bhavan at the tip of the hill. I used to take the double-decker BEST bus from Cuffe Parade to school. Our bus route would take us by the Oval Maidan where, on the eastern side of the grounds, we would drive past magnificent colonial buildings: the University of Mumbai Library, Rajabai Clock Tower and the Convocation Hall, the High Court and the Central Telegraph Office. Perhaps it was while sitting on the upper level of the double-decker bus that a connection and passion for such buildings emerged within me. Over time, I began to recognise the vast expanse of our architectural and cultural heritage in India. It is documented that the Archaeological Survey of India has over 10,000 listed monuments and sites. I believe that during the period commencing with the arrival of the East India Company and followed by being ruled by the British Empire, colonial buildings became a part of our urban heritage. This is particularly evident in the cities that the British helped develop, which include Bombay, Calcutta and Madras (now Mumbai, Kolkata and Chennai), cities that house a generous proportion of these buildings as they continue to be in use. While many of these buildings were built under British patronage, important Indian citizens contributed towards their construction and upkeep through philanthropy and civic service. The Rajabai Clock Tower is one such building.

Fig 1

Fig 1. Archival photograph of the Rajabai Clock Tower, shrouded in scaffolding, that was completed in 1878.

Fig 2. Historic map of the colonial city of Fort, Mumbai from the dockyards on the east to the magnificent Oval Maidan on the west, lined by buildings of civic significance including the Rajabai Tower.

Fig 2

At 280 ft, Rajabai Clock Tower was the tallest structure in Bombay when it was built. It is situated in a very important landscape with the tower initially facing the sea. This was prior to the development of the line of Art-Deco buildings of the 1930s on large portions of reclaimed land, known as the Marine Drive. The construction work on the Clock Tower began in 1869; the Library Building was completed in 1874 and the Clock Tower in 1878. It was designed in neo-gothic style by the eminent British architect Sir George Gilbert Scott, who, it is believed, never visited India. The funding came from a very important Indian industrialist known as the cotton-king of the time, Premchand Roychand. Known for his philanthropy, he donated Rs 4 lakh in 1869 for the University Library and the Clock Tower on the condition that the latter be named after his mother, Rajabai. The structure is built facing west with tall windows to let the sea breeze in, and it was designed with the tropical climate of India in mind. There were 16 bells in the original tower, of which only two are functional today. Lund and Blockley, a prominent London watch-making company, originally designed the Clock in the tower. The role of the J.J. College of Architecture must be emphasised at this juncture as the stone carving on the surface of the Clock Tower and the Library Building were sculpted by the students of the J.J. College of Arts under the guidance of Sir Lockwood Kipling.

Fig 3

244

Fig 3. Context plan of the present Fort city in Mumbai with the Rajabai Tower flanking the Oval.

Fig 4. Condition of the deteriorated facade of the structure prior to restoration.

The project for restoration of the Rajabai Tower and the Library Building was a public–private partnership between the University of Mumbai and Tata Consultancy Services (TCS), who provided the funding for the restoration process. The Indian Heritage Society acted as the facilitators of the project and functioned as the bridge between the University and TCS. As architects of the TCS House, the global headquarters of the company, we had already worked closely with their management on a heritage building. TCS was aware of our commitment and our sensitivity to our work, specifically when it came to historic buildings. This faith in our practice ensured that TCS chose us as the conservation architects to work on the project. It is important to speak about patronage for special projects like these, as they are only possible in an environment of genuine contribution.

There were many challenges in the project. The first was the unavailability of any drawings or documentation of the building. As we were assessing the structure, we realised the extent of deterioration; the structure had never been restored before. The stained-glass windows were repaired 20 years before our work started, by conservation architect Vikas Dilawari and Swati Chandgadkar, but apart from that, there had been no sincere effort of holistic upgrade or repair. Following a detailed condition mapping and structural analysis, we initiated the task of strengthening the building. The building and the tower were composed of four different kinds of stone: the Malad stone, the grey basalt, the Porbandar stone and the red Dhrangadhra Trivandrum stone. The Library Building had rare

Fig 4

Minton tile flooring, Burma teakwood ceilings and carved balconies. The Clock Tower housed 24 statues, each representing the different castes of western India. Apart from the structure of the building, we wanted to comprehensively upgrade the services within the building. While in our conservation work, there is much focus on the beauty of the heritage structure, the overall success and longevity of the work depends on the retrofitting and upgradation. This is especially true if the building continues to be in extensive use. In this project, we upgraded all services such as plumbing and electrical conduits, while introducing data network, Wi-Fi and CCTV systems that have become essential modern necessities.

Fig 5. Mapping of the insensitive alterations and ad hoc overlays of services in the Tower and Library building.

Fig 6. Ground floor and first floor plans.

Fig 7. West elevation of the Library and the Rajabai Tower.

Fig 8. Section A and tower plans.

Fig 5

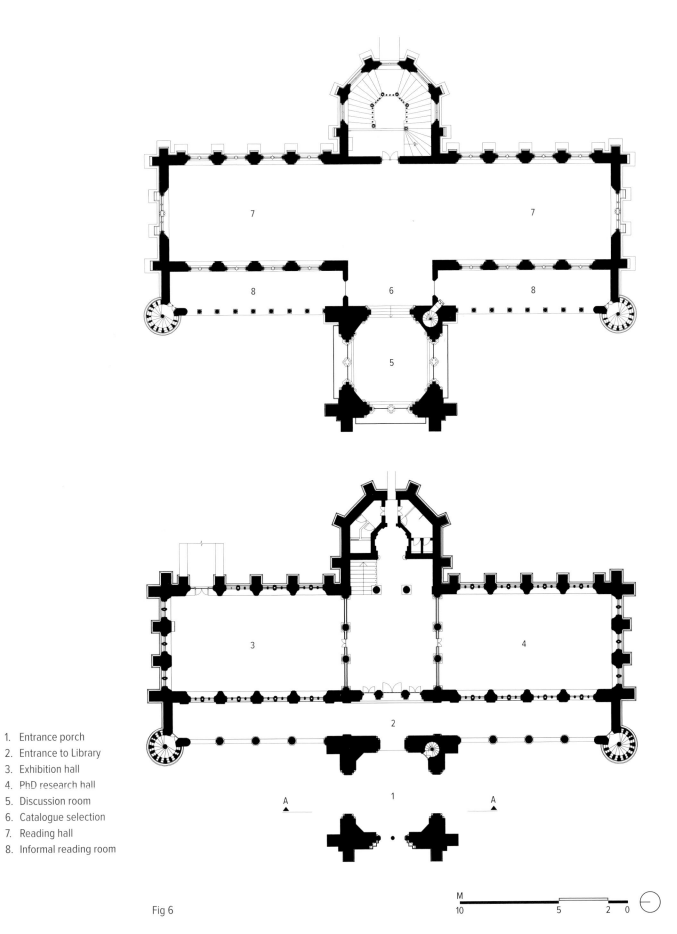

1. Entrance porch
2. Entrance to Library
3. Exhibition hall
4. PhD research hall
5. Discussion room
6. Catalogue selection
7. Reading hall
8. Informal reading room

Fig 6

M
10   5   2   0

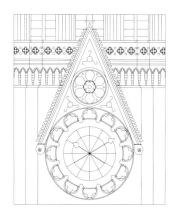

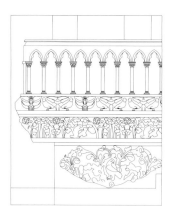

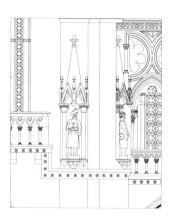

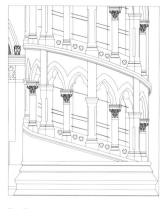

Fig 7

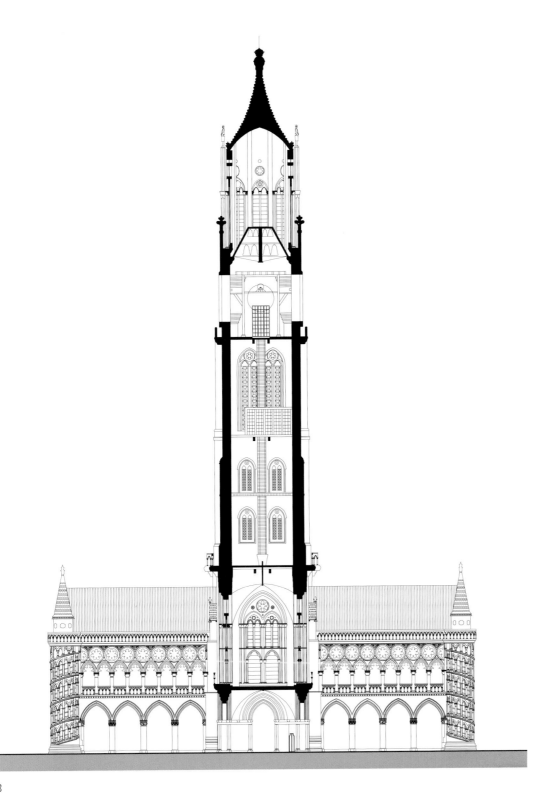

Fig 8

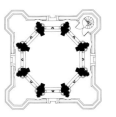

LEVEL 6

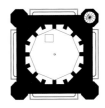

LEVEL 5

LEVEL 4

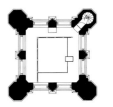

LEVEL 3

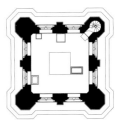

LEVEL 2

LEVEL 1

Our work began in June 2013 and the heavy Mumbai monsoon dictated the pace and pattern of work on the site. While it rained, we could primarily work only on the interior: the consolidation of masonry walls, internal re-plastering, electrical and plumbing work, flooring and restoration of the timber vault of the main hall. We initiated work on the external stone edifice, the restoration of the doors and windows, major roof repairs and structural work once the rains subsided. The restoration and repair of the timber vault was one of the most fascinating processes in the project. We had to remove the old polish and recondition the seasoned wood to take the new layer of finish, which has greater longevity. We managed to procure Minton tiles salvaged from other buildings, which were discarding them at scrap value, to recompose parts of the new floor in the original pattern. The Burma teak doors, intricately decorated with rosewood inlay, were revealed after multiple layers of paint were meticulously cleaned.

Fig 9. Restoration of the timber vault, the external facade and the Minton tile flooring.

Fig 10. The process of restoration entailed a great degree of care in dealing with the intricately ornate structure.

Fig 9

Fig 10

There are several instances during the process of a restoration where great innovation is demanded. In the Rajabai Clock Tower, two particular instances come to mind.

The first, when we began addressing the issue of conduiting and upgrade of the electrical services of the building. The original building was lit by a concealed network of gas lines. However, by the 20th century, electricity was introduced into the building and the new conduiting was introduced very insensitively. Exposed wiring ran up the walls and along the openings. We had to generate an out-of-the-box solution to secure a long-term and relatively non-invasive solution to the conduiting issue, and ensure that the new services would not damage any existing material. Upon re-examining the building details, we found the solution already built into the structure. We decided to reuse the original route of the existing gas lines for routing the new electrical conduits while carefully chasing through the lime plaster of the walls. In this way, we were able to accomplish a process in a creative way derived from the study and analysis of the innards of a building, allowing the process of restoration and conservation to go beyond just cleaning a surface.

The second instance came to light as we began work on the Clock Tower. In the tower, the only access path was a 2-foot-wide staircase, which was claustrophobic for many workers. We needed expert carpenters and artisans to access the area and work at a height of 85 m. The large louvered windows of the tower that had to be restored were located at 196 ft from the ground. In order for work to be conducted effectively at these heights by providing ample space and safety for the workmen, we decided to create a workshop in the areas directly above the bell frames at 196 ft. This novel solution ensured that workers could comfortably access a larger space and safely work with care while renovating and working on the details that could be brought to this level, restored and then reinserted at the relevant higher points of the tower.

Any conservation project is a large collaborative effort. Of late, we have seen a change in government attitude, with more funding being offered for conservation projects. However, until recently, it was often a very lonely battle. There are few good contractors who would take up a conservation project, as the parameters of what one is dealing with are very different than a conventional construction system. Savani Construction gave their personal effort and attention to this project. They exercised great restraint, care and patience as the project in many aspects demanded exploratory approach: from understanding the structure to discovering hidden details as one goes through the process. Even the drafting of the bill of quantities for the tendering process was unique, with many materials and processes being unconventional and specific to the project.

Fig 11. Views of the old juxtaposed with the new and Brinda Somaya on site.

Fig 11

Another collaboration that developed was when we were instructed by the university that we could not stop the clock. They were concerned that if the complex mechanism of the clock stopped, it would be very difficult to restart it. We were fortunate to find Venkatesh Rao, who had inherited a passion for this clockwork from his father, Narayan Swami. Swami had been maintaining the clock for years. With Venkatesh's assistance, we were able to restore the tower without any hindrance to the running of the clock. I recall standing in the workshop area, and people began looking at their watches and suggested we brace ourselves as it was time for the clock to chime. It was a soul stirring sound to hear, one that I will never forget. The clock chimed through our entire restoration process and continues to chime for the city of Mumbai long after.

Fig 12. It was ensured that the clock was functioning throughout the process of restoration. The complex mechanism was carefully worked upon by Venkatesh Rao.

Fig 12

Over time, we have worked on several conservation and restoration projects that have enabled us to articulate a process that is conceptually common and yet unique for each building. I firmly discard any notion of a superficial restoration process that deals only with the visual attributes of a building. It is my strong conviction that any building—irrespective of its age, visual attributes, historical value and significance—can be saved.

A tremendous amount of embedded energy goes into making a new building, and this energy can be saved while simultaneously enhancing ordinary buildings and nurturing them into forming legible pieces of our urban heritage. Another learning that I have derived from the process is that there are no shortcuts. The process involves understanding the history of the structure, the condition of the existing building, drawing the building and investigating details, planning and logistics of the entire construction process that often occurs in phases, which need close coordination and synergy. The time taken to understand the project, map the challenges and study the background is invested much before the process of restoration begins on site. I have worked as part of the conservation movement for many decades. My journey includes being a part of the Urban Heritage Conservation Committee in Mumbai. I recall walking from street to street listing buildings, documenting them, understanding their characteristics and trying to develop guidelines for the future development of these areas, precincts or even individual structures. Looking back, it has been a labour of love.

I believe that in the last decade, there has been significantly greater public interest in the vernacular and colonial heritage of the city of Mumbai. The designation of the Chhatrapati Shivaji Terminus, previously the Victoria Terminus, as a World Heritage site has started a public discussion on the perception of heritage, its upkeep and relevance to the collective history of the city, and the role of the government and civil society. It has thus become increasingly important to understand the value of one's past. However, to determine what is valuable is becoming increasingly difficult, and perhaps one needs to conserve and protect more than one feels is essential. I do believe that if we do not protect what has gone before, there will not remain any context left for what is going to come. Preserving icons such as the Rajabai Clock Tower is important, but as important is preservation of the "ordinary", examples of the latter being the buildings located on the Dadabhai Naoroji Road in the Fort precinct. I have campaigned many times in favour of the public to be able to walk into many of these heritage buildings, but unfortunately, they continue to have controlled access. It is crucial to realise that irrespective of ownership and patronage, these buildings must continue to render a sense of shared identity and pride for every citizen of Mumbai.

ARCHITECTURE AND CULTURE

Saryu Doshi and Brinda Somaya

Mumbai, the city of practice for Brinda Somaya and Saryu Doshi

Mumbai has been a city of living and practice for both Brinda Somaya, architect, and Saryu Doshi, curator and art historian. Somaya, as an architect, works as an orchestrator of a complex and multi-layered system that enables production of buildings, while Saryu Doshi works with artists who often claim complete authorship and work in isolation for their pieces.

While culture of the place has an undeniable influence on the work of both, does the work always contribute to the culture? What is the cultural value of architecture?

RUTURAJ PARIKH	Having spent your lives in Mumbai, it has essentially become the city of your endeavours, as both of you have contributed significantly through your disciplines. Do you think architecture contributes substantially to the culture of a place?
SARYU DOSHI	Both art and architecture articulate the aspirations of their time. In many ways, the successive phases of life of a city are recorded in its architecture which then

becomes an integral part of its ethos. Architecture lends texture and substance to the character of a city and influences its cultural currents.

BRINDA SOMAYA Architecture has always told us stories of what has gone before. Maybe that is a romantic notion as well. When we look back in time to any archaeological site or any ancient civilisations or ancient cities, we always connect the stories of the lives of those people with the architecture. So, I think the importance of that can never be negated. As far as Mumbai is concerned, you know it is nice to hear what Saryu has to say because the breadth of what she has experienced working and living here is unique.

SD Yes, I live in Mumbai and like it, despite its potholed roads, its traffic jams and its crowded living conditions. It is the typical Bombaiyya spirit of this city that is its irrepressible energy. The historic panorama of Mumbai—from its beginning as a group of seven islands to the metropolis it is today—becomes legible through the fabric of its architecture.

RP If we agree that architecture does contribute to the history or culture of a place, what is its contribution to the discipline of the arts? And how does art contribute to architecture?

SD The interface between the two has always been there. In earlier historical periods art was an adjunct to architecture, being both decorative in intent and content. A wealth of skill and effort is embedded in the creation of these architectural structures including ornamentation to enhance their surfaces. I think there is an impulse to adorn: it is in every human being and that reflects in itself in architecture.

BS I also think architecture as we practice it today is a relatively new profession. It must be hardly 200 years old. Until then, as you rightly said, building a temple was often a lifetime's work. And that is how actual passion and spirit of the people and workmen was infused into the buildings.

SD Indeed.

BS So, when it came to religious and public buildings in colonial times, it was the engineers who actually designed them. Architects were relatively unimportant. Even today, architects apparently affect only 5 per cent of the population. Everything else is built by the people themselves. So, when we talk about architecture, what are we really talking about? In a country like India, which is complex and not at all homogeneous, it is so disparate and there is a multiplicity of everything, whether it is religion, ethnicity, languages, culture or the arts. Architecture is complex.

SD   The new buildings constructed with glass and steel are modern and efficient. They are undoubtedly an expression of our times. They make a statement just as the older structures did with their profusion of ornamentation. Today's technological advances have fashioned a new aesthetic: of uncluttered surfaces and organic forms.

BS   But it is very interesting that you say how technological skills are today's adornment in some ways.

SD   That's the way I look at it. They don't need the external adornment of the olden times. Their sleekness is their adornment.

RP   In the context of aesthetics and sensibility, do you think, as an Indian architect or curator, as an observer of culture, that you read your work or the work that you see differently? Are you drawn to a different aesthetic and does that affect you being an Indian practitioner in your discipline?

BS   This is a question one always asks. I don't think I can separate India and "Indianness" from myself. I always believe that is who we are. We are a result of everything that has gone before us. And so naturally, everything that surrounds me will affect my work, but it does not have to be in an obvious way. I think a subtlety in imbibing what has gone before us is fine as far as I am concerned. I think we move on with time and with each generation. There is going to be "Indianness" in our work, which will be continuously changing and that is how it is. But it does affect us. I mean, how can it not?

SD   As Indians, we have been culturally receptive to many influences without thinking of them as 'outside' factors. We have always absorbed interesting ideas in our way of life. So, while skyscrapers mark the skyline of our cities, we do not give up our preoccupation with traditional principles of Vastu. Perhaps, in a seamless and intuitive manner we connect the present with our past.

RP   But do you find that as an art curator, a similar sort of looseness has also come into other disciplines? Like, painting or sculpture, or the kind of work that you see extensively being produced as art? Do you think there is a certain culture of casualness to how you deal with your work?

SD   Yes, I think an artist's work is primarily subjective as it either expresses the individual's concern and preoccupations or his/her point of view on a subject. The purpose of the work acts as a determining factor. An architect on the other hand has to be objective. Buildings are designed for use and occupation. Thus, in terms of pure creative expression, an artist enjoys much more freedom than an architect. Indeed, a building is a very different product of creativity. It is a large collaborative exercise and the architect has to keep the purpose of the building in mind while designing.

BS   I believe that would be unfortunate, because I think the role of an architect—while of course we are always building for others—is about fulfilling our own creativity through that process. And it would be a pity if that ever gets lost. So, I think architecture has a different type of complexity and contradiction than a sculptor or an artist would have, because there are so many different aspects to it.

RP   As an architect, do you see your work as a very creative process or do you see it more as a technical sort of generation of work? An artist might work independently, but an architect requires a large team to put together in building. So, in that context, how does the process work?

BS   I do believe that it is a creative process. And I believe that complex requirements and having to find solutions to difficult problems does not reduce the creativity involved. In fact, it enhances it. But definitely, for most architects, when one first gets a project, an excitement comes with working out the ideas and thoughts and the creativity behind what eventually becomes the building. So, I don't think you can separate the creativity from the ability to build. I don't see it as two separate aspects to the profession. I do believe that they have to work together.

SD   I personally think it has sort of seeped into art as well, because so many artists have any number of helpers. They have studios, where others come and execute their work. The idea is theirs and the way in which it has to be presented is theirs, but the actual execution or raw execution is often done by others.

BS   This has always been the case. If you go back to Michelangelo's time when everybody had helpers, whether it was painting the Sistine Chapel or whether it was sculpture, they had helpers. And perhaps that is why it is rarely known who began the works and who finished them!

SD   Yes!

BS   So, this has been there since historic times. I'm sure even in our Indian art.

SD   Where can you have temples with [only] one person doing the job? There are always people involved. I find a temple fascinating; I find an old residence like a

Chettinad house fascinating. All these have been built under certain circumstances and with certain needs in mind. And they have been able to evolve into a contextually relevant house. Each one is beautiful in its little details. Coming back to the creativity and the execution, they can be separated and can be combined.

BS   Exactly! So that's interesting because of the way you actually analyse it. It is not just in architecture, where you have more than one person working. Any work of scale is collaborative in nature, and you know that it is not possible without a large effort.

SD   To me, collaborative work is a situation in which the efforts as well as the contributions of the participants are varied. I would not use the term collaboration when someone is directing the effort according to his vision. The concept of authorship must be clearly defined, understood and accepted. So, those who aid an artist/architect in giving shape to his or her vision are to be seen as contributors and not collaborators. For instance, carpenters, welders and draftsmen working with Brinda on her project cannot be identified as collaborators.

BS   So, I think looking ahead, there are many types of collaborations in store for architects. Today, things have changed. For instance, we were recently trying for a competition where it was truly collaborative. We were many, many different partners working together, and each one brought in a particular value in a different discipline. But that's because architecture itself and the projects themselves are becoming so multidisciplinary that everyone cannot participate as an individual. But still, there has to be a "conductor".

SD   Exactly! "Conductor" is the right word.

Site meeting with (from left) Tod Williams, Billie Tsien, Brinda Somaya and Ratan Tata at TCS Banyan Park, Mumbai

RP   I want to bring into the discussion what you had once written about the panel discussions you were on, that "complex ideas do not need a difficult language". As an architect, how important is it to keep the works simple and explain like it is?

BS   Let me put it this way. I do believe that architecture is an intellectual profession. I do believe that there are layers to it. There has to be lot of thought behind conceptual design. It is very important that there is depth to the process of conceptualising. Now, depth of a process doesn't mean that the building has to end up looking complicated. You can try to analyse it in two different parts. One is the thought process that goes behind the building and then what results in the building. What I have a problem with is this analysis that goes on about this process. It is important but the theorisation that's going on today, in a language that is so difficult to understand, is a problem. Particularly in conferences where you have people who use so many difficult and complicated words and sentences that it is almost impossible to understand what they are saying unless you read it. I have a problem with that; not with the fact that all art has to have depth and thought, but that it must have a spirit behind it.

RP   That is a very important thought.

SD   Without doubt, the language one uses to frame a complex idea needs to have clarity. Communication is important, otherwise the conceptual framework that is created around a work of art or architecture may prove self-defeating. Unless the audience is familiar with different theories, the vocabulary can confuse rather than illuminate the subject. It is distressing that in India, young students have not been equipped with the knowledge to understand, leave alone evaluate, the effects of various theories in art and architecture.

BS   She is very right because it is the academicians who primarily are able to have these discourses, and that is because they are compelled to read and theorise. So much of reading happens in universities and academic situations, as opposed to, say, a situation like mine. I read, but I read what I think. . .

SD   . . . is relevant!

BS   Yes! So, I think there has to be a balance because academicians often are theorists and not necessarily practitioners. Practitioners should find the time, as she very rightly said, to also read because ultimately, every profession has to have an intellectual value to it. There's no doubt about that. You know, Saryu, this explosion of knowledge is very difficult to keep up with. I just returned from a multi-disciplinary conference involving architecture, planning, anthropology, sociology and archaeology. Everybody there was saying how impossible it was to understand. Particularly with there being verticals, "silos" as they call them now! Another new terminology! Lots of people were struggling to understand, because you can read a lot but you can't read everything!

SD   True. I want to understand and know so many aspects of different subjects but that is unrealistic.

BS   Aren't you happy you're so busy?

SD   Brinda, I am so grateful.

Brinda Somaya in conversation with Saryu Doshi in Mumbai.

Recorded on 15th April, 2016. Moderated by Ruturaj Parikh.

ST THOMAS CATHEDRAL
For St Thomas Cathedral Trust

CONSERVATION, RESTORATION AND REJUVENATION

Mumbai, India [2001–2003]

Architectural conservation that views structures
as living spaces in dynamic layers of history rather
than static monuments of the past is a collaborative
process to re-instate their role in the public realm.

As a young student in Bombay, I remember walking from the Cathedral and John Connon School buildings, through Flora Fountain (Hutatma Chowk), to the St Thomas Cathedral. Accompanied by our teachers, we would visit the cathedral for various congregations from Founder's Day of the school to celebrating Christmas. I recall one particular day, when we were walking to the cathedral, we heard about the assassination of John F. Kennedy. How shaken we all were. I remember how we prayed for him. Decades later, when I found myself executing the extraordinary task of restoring the buildings of the Cathedral school, I was asked by the trust if I would contribute to improving the environment in the immediate surroundings of the St Thomas Cathedral. I have always had a very keen interest in small-scale interventions. This had led to the improvement and upgrade of the pavements for the projects we were doing in the Fort precinct, which included the Hong Kong and Shanghai Banking Corporation (HSBC) and Banque Nationale de Paris buildings. The writer and activist Jane Jacobs in her writings talked about how "a sense of personal belonging and social cohesiveness comes from well-defined neighbourhoods and narrow, crowded, multi-use streets". Her emphasis on the importance of a pedestrianised city had a profound impact on my thoughts and design process. While the school project was underway, monsoon arrived. Heavy leakage began in the cathedral roof, and soon thereafter, T. Thomas, the Chairman of the Board of Governors of the school, approached me and asked if I could help them with repairing the leakage.

VIEW from the TOWN HALL. BOMBAY.

Fig 1

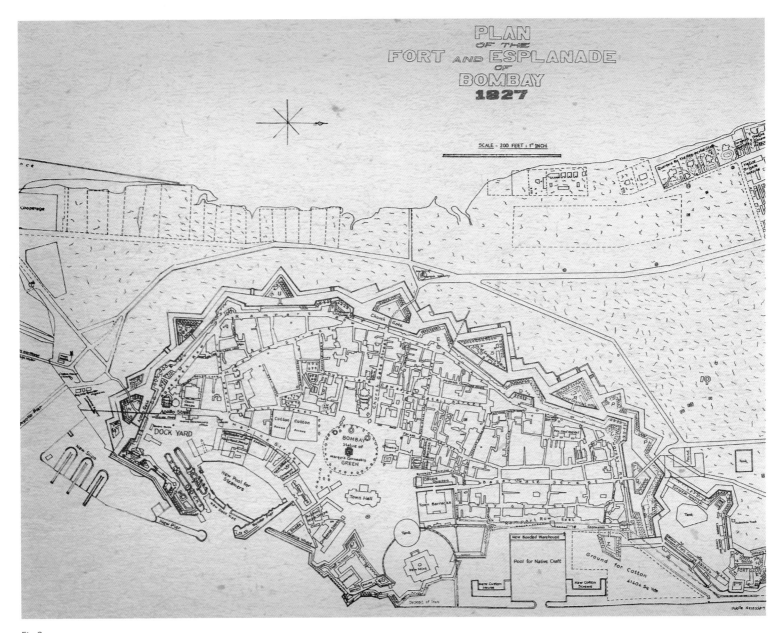

Fig 2

Fig 1. Lithograph of Bombay Green from the Town Hall showing the Cornwallis monument, the Cathedral Church of St Thomas and Churchgate by Jose M. Gonsalves c. 1830.

Fig 2. Archival plan of the Fort and Esplanade of Bombay 1827, from Maritime History Society, which reveals the old Bombay Green (present Horniman Circle) and the Churchgate street where the St Thomas Cathedral is located.

The history of the St Thomas Cathedral, the oldest Anglican church in Mumbai, is intertwined with the development of the Fort precinct of the city. The historic fort, built by the British East India Company, positioned the church on a vantage point overlooking the fort gate, thus rendering the area "Church-Gate". The cathedral is located on a significant node of the city next to the Town Hall and the "Bombay Green" (now known as the Horniman Circle). The foundation stone for the church was laid in 1676, but the construction took over 40 years and it was completed only in 1718 after Richard Cobbe, the Chaplain, took charge, opening for divine service on the Christmas Day in 1718. In July 1837, the church was consecrated as a cathedral, concurrent with the appointment of the first Bishop of Bombay, Thomas Carr. Thus, in 1838, the low belfry was replaced by a 146-inch-tall clock tower.

Fig 3

Fig 3. The old Bombay Green, created by William Johnson, c. 1855–1862 from the series *Photographs of Western India, Volume II.* Scenery, Public Buildings.

Fig 4. Context plan of the Fort, Mumbai, with the footprint of St Thomas Cathedral flanking the axis that connects Flora Fountain to Horniman Circle.

For me, the history of this cathedral is very personal as it is deeply connected with the Cathedral and John Connon School. The foundation for the Cathedral school was laid in 1860, when Bishop Harding and the Cathedral chaplain opened a grammar school and, thereafter, a choir school with the objective of providing choristers for the St Thomas Cathedral. It was during Harding's tenure that, in 1865, the cathedral underwent a major renovation to enlarge the chancel. The chancel apse was extended and built in a Victorian Gothic style with the extension made of dressed sandstone and marble, and the addition of flying buttresses that supported the chancel wall. The organ room was also covered with ribbed gothic vaulting and protective tiled sloping roofs. While the St Thomas Cathedral played a pivotal role in establishing the school initially for providing choristers to the original cathedral, today, the school has become the patron and cares for the 298-year-old structure.

At the behest of the Board of Governors, I inspected the source of the recent leak with my team. The water was primarily leaking through the concrete slab of the flat roof. At that moment, I recalled seeing a postcard belonging to Farooq Issa's collection at Phillips Antiques: a source of wonderful archived materials of the city of Mumbai. It was a film colourisation of a black-and-white image that revealed the original pitched roof of the cathedral. I took that postcard and went back to Chairman T. Thomas, sharing with him my intent. After much discussion and analysis with experts internally, my intention was to restore the cathedral's original historic slope of the roof, and the Chairman told me to proceed with it.

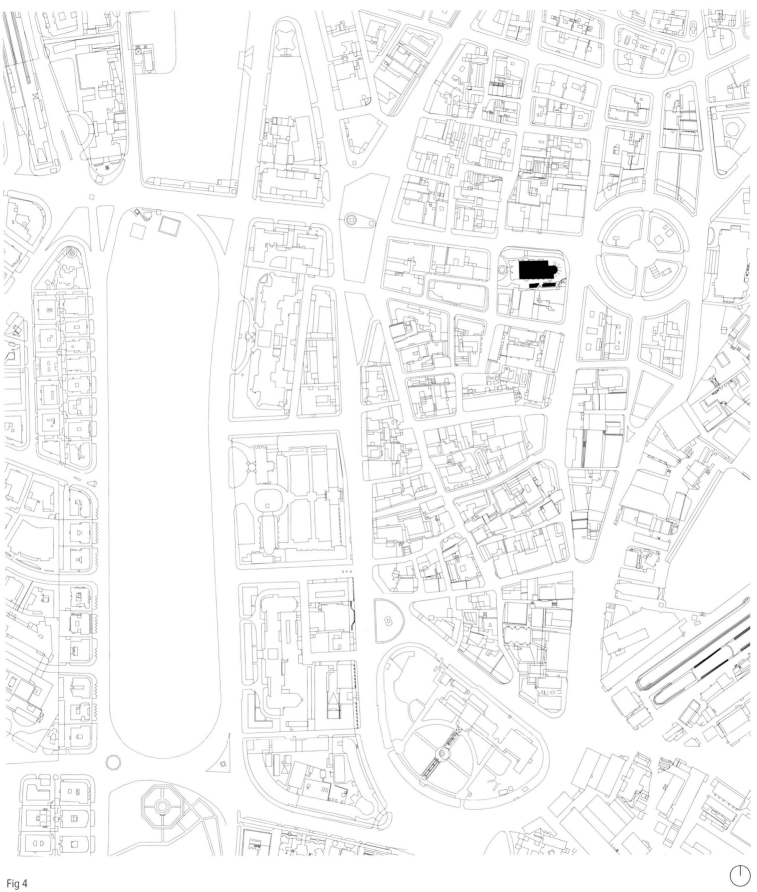

Fig 4

St Thomas Cathedral · 281

In any conservation project, there are layers that already exist on the site and within the building. There are various directives that indicate the way forward, and these include several charters. Whether the removal of the RCC roof is within the scope of the project is another debate. I was familiar with the Mumbai monsoon and knew that the church interiors were being greatly damaged with each passing year. I took the decision to go back to the pitched roofs, and that decision changed the course of the project. Several years have passed, and there has been no leakage. The cathedral is now safe.

Fig 5. The postcard found at Phillips Antiques that helped determine the original form of the roof.

Fig 6. Evolution of the plan of the cathedral over a period of time from its original form in 1718 to its restored status in 2003.

Fig 5

The approach for conservation of the St Thomas Cathedral was very different from other projects where there are major interventions of modern services. In this project, utmost sensitivity and care were required as we wanted to intervene minimally and with great restraint to restore the authentic details and elements of the cathedral. I still have vivid memories of entering this cathedral as a student, with its splendid marble monuments facing the aisles, which told a story of life and death in British Bombay. The most fascinating part was to read about each one of these people and how they lived and died in the India of their time. I recall sitting on the wooden benches surrounded by large columns, with fans mounted on decorative cast-iron brackets. The statues, the plaques and that ethereal quality of light that would filter through the wooden slats were all part of the collective memory of all that had gone before. While there are evidences from documentation and the diligent architectural process that directs the work of conservation, in the case of St Thomas Cathedral, many memories of the building that were personal to me informed my judgement as diligently.

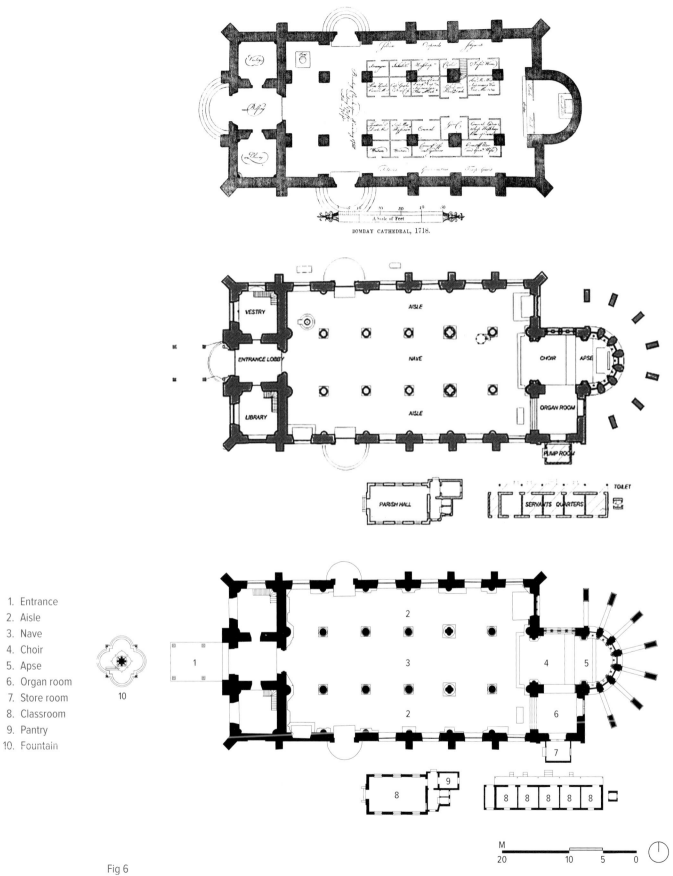

BOMBAY CATHEDRAL, 1718.

1. Entrance
2. Aisle
3. Nave
4. Choir
5. Apse
6. Organ room
7. Store room
8. Classroom
9. Pantry
10. Fountain

Fig 6

In architectural conservation, such decisions are always challenging, as you tackle multiple layers of history and interventions over a long period of time. The cathedral was a Grade-I Heritage Structure, and I worked very closely with Sandhya Sawant, a friend and a much-respected conservationist from Mumbai, to frame the strategy ahead. To identify the original spinning points and springing levels, we found a kneeler stone, which was left in position during the intervention of 1920s, when the new concrete roof was constructed. In addition, the changing weathering patterns of the stones used in the raised walls helped define the original profile of the roof. As we dismantled the RCC roof and lowered the walls that had been raised to the original level, the bitumen marks on the walls of the altar were revealed, thus conclusively establishing the profile of the original roof. We also discovered several hidden details, such as the finial pieces on the cornice coping and old stone almost fully intact, which we would later use to reconstruct what we believed to be the appropriate way forward and which would also ensure the longevity of the structure.

Fig 7. Architectural detail of the restored roof of the cathedral.

Fig 8. Section through the sanctuary and the tower.

Fig 9. Restoration of the roof from a concrete flat roof to the original pitched roof.

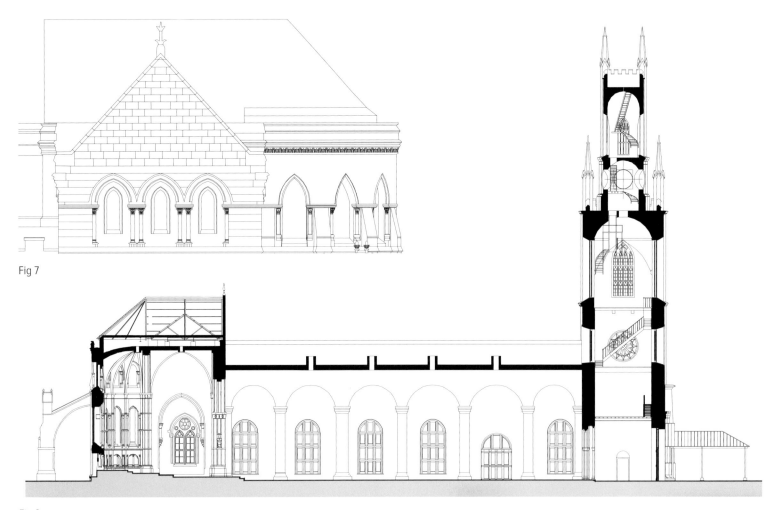

Fig 7

Fig 8

Fig 9

Due to the heavy rains and neglect, there had been an increase in water ingress causing moss growth, leakages and overgrowth of vegetation within the compound. We looked at all aspects of the cathedral, from the ambience of its interior space to its site condition, which also gave us an opportunity to think of its environs in a holistic manner. The stones were cleaned and the patina of polluting matter on them was carefully removed. There was a Victorian–Gothic fountain designed by Sir George Gilbert Scott, the famed architect of the Rajabai Clock Tower and the Mumbai University Library building, which too we later restored. The fountain had been painted many times over, and we had to clean multiple layers of paint to reveal the original red Agra stone and limestone work. We resurrected the porch that housed intricate Victorian cast-iron elements and researched on the elements of the interior space to generate a strategy to reinstate an ambience

Fig 10. Conserving the stone structure and the Victorian–Gothic fountain at the Cathedral.

Fig 11. The interior space of the Cathedral pre-restoration and post restoration (the choir singing in the apse of the restored church).

Fig 10

Fig 11

that might have prevailed in the early days of the St Thomas Cathedral. Multiple layers of paint were removed from the external walls to identify the original colour scheme, and the cathedral was repainted accordingly. Great effort was put into researching and understanding the history of the cathedral, its construction process and what needed to be done to ensure a very reverential conservation process. We collaborated with Swati Chandgadkar to restore the magnificent stained-glass panels; there were three lancet lights designed by the famous Henry Holiday.

There were two ancillary buildings—the staff quarters and the Parish Hall—that were in a dilapidated condition when we began the project. We were able to reconstruct those buildings to make them habitable. The Parish Hall was earlier used as a Sunday school and continues to be used as an activity room for the youngest students of the Cathedral School during the week and the Sunday school over weekends. The staff quarters serve as the cathedral pre-primary school. The process of restoration was done sensitively from the creation of a small shrub garden to sliding bollards that fold away when the school closes, reverting the cathedral grounds back to their original format.

While working on conservation projects, one has to often deal with the questions of authenticity. Throughout the conservation process of the St Thomas Cathedral, any incomplete or abandoned work that was a part of the original building condition was left as found. When one visits the cathedral today, they can

Fig 12. Restoration and upgradation of the staff quarters that now serves as the Cathedral & John Connon pre-primary school.

Fig 13. The pre-primary class in session.

Fig 12

Fig 13

observe this within the apse. As an architect, one must make a careful decision regarding the extent of intervention in conservation works. I strongly feel that the layers of history that have a record are more significant than the visual aspects of the work, and if the process involves a thorough understanding of this specific history, design finds ways to express and respect the past. In the years since the completion of the project, we have not found any leakage or deterioration other than natural ageing. In 2004, the cathedral project received the UNESCO Asia-Pacific Heritage Award and the jury was appreciative of the trajectory that the conservation process took.

This project taught me that there are no consistent strategies in conservation work. Each project demands its own process and much clarity comes from the documentation, research and understanding of historical evidence. As we now work on restoring the Louis I Kahn buildings at IIM Ahmedabad, many new and previously unknown aspects of the buildings are coming to light. When we visited the Kahn archives at the University of Pennsylvania, we talked to many scholars about Kahn and documented the state of the existing buildings. Much learning was also hidden in the structure itself, and as we started the process of restoration, we came to better understand the building and the issues we were dealing with.

Fig 14

Fig 14. Aerial view of the present-day Horniman Circle with the restored St Thomas Cathedral, a historic jewel in the heart of the city.

Mumbai is unique as a city as much of its colonial architectural heritage is consistently in use and very much in the public domain, be it the Victoria Terminus (now Chhatrapati Shivaji Terminus), the Old Yacht Club, the Cathedral and John Connon schools or other heritage buildings presently in use. There is a joy in working on buildings that are part of the living heritage of the city. These are not just edifices to look at in awe but places that continue to be a part of the everyday life of the people in the city. Many of my restoration and conservation projects are public buildings. The significance of restoring these buildings as living spaces takes priority over prolonging the life of these buildings as monuments. Today, we are all stakeholders of this heritage in the city of Mumbai and our history and architecture—the most public of our arts— has contributed significantly to our sense of belonging to the city. When the process of architectural conservation deals with the dynamic layers of history rather than the static state of the structure, the eventual result is richer and more authentic.

WHEN THE CASTLE EDEN TRANSPORT
WAS WRECKED
IN ENTERING THE BOMBAY HARBOUR
ON THE 1ST DAY OF JUNE A.D. 1840.

THIS TABLET
HAS BEEN ERECTED TO HIS MEMORY
BY HIS BROTHER OFFICERS
AS A MARK
OF THEIR ESTEEM FOR HIM WHILE LIVING
AND OF THEIR REGRET
FOR HIS UNTIMELY DEATH.

"THOU HAST GIVEN HIM HIS HEARTS DESIRE."

IN MEMORY OF
MAJOR SIDNEY WAUDBY H. M's 19th BOMBAY, N.I.
KILLED AT DUBRAI 16th APRIL 1880.
AND OF HIS BROTHER OFFICER
MAJOR RICHARD J. LE POER TRENCH.
KILLED IN THE SORTIE FROM KANDAHAR 16th AUGUST 1880.
THIS TABLET IS ERECTED BY THEIR FRIENDS
AS A TRIBUTE OF THEIR SINCERE ESTEEM AND AFFECTION.

"HIS HONOR IS GREAT IN THY SALVATION."

SACRED TO THE MEMORY
OF
WILLIAM MIDDLETON TENNENT
WHO DIED AT ST LEONARDS
ON THE 7th JULY 1883
AGED 38 YEARS.

THIS TABLET IS ERECTED AS A TOKEN
OF THEIR REGARD BY THE OFFICERS AND
VOLUNTEERS OF D COMPANY BOMBAY
VOLUNTEER RIFLE CORPS, WHICH THE
DECEASED COMMANDED FROM THE
INSTITUTION OF THE CORPS IN 1877
UNTIL HIS DEATH.

S. GABRIEL   S. THOMAS   S. MICHAEL

ST·THOMAS· CATH

Church of North

SUND   SERVICES

NALANDA INTERNATIONAL SCHOOL
for Nalanda Knowledge Foundation

MASTER PLANNING AND ARCHITECTURE

Vadodara, India [2003–2010]

Architecture that emphasises the environment it generates through pattern-making and design of the in-between realm deeply impacts the people who occupy it and becomes integral to their living.

I was barely eight years old and my parents, who believed in educating my sister and me by driving us to different parts of India, brought us to the ancient ruins of the famous Nalanda University in Bihar. I still recall the powerful impact the monasteries and the brick had on me. It was this site that sparked my curiosity for history and architecture. It was where it all began, in a sense.

The Nalanda connection resurfaced decades later when I received a phone call from Vadodara. This was my first encounter with Mayur Patel, a visionary individual. Over several years of working with him, I discovered a man with the depth of character, generosity of spirit and an incredible determination to enhance the quality of life of the people around him. He approached me to build a school that reflected his father's and his family's Gandhian beliefs while also creating an academic institution where students identified with their environment and felt a sense of belonging. I recall us sitting together in my small conference room in my first studio discussing the ideals upon which this school should be built. There was no programme of requirements, floor area ratio (FAR) restrictions or economic feasibility reports—only a singular idea of building something for the larger good that would evolve and succeed based on the moral and ethical principles upon which it was built.

Fig 1

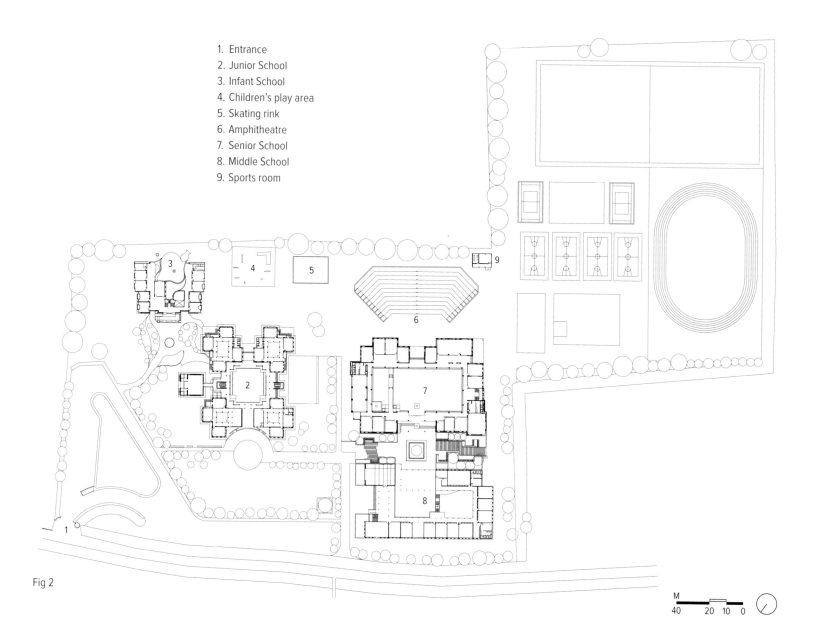

1. Entrance
2. Junior School
3. Infant School
4. Children's play area
5. Skating rink
6. Amphitheatre
7. Senior School
8. Middle School
9. Sports room

Fig 2

M
40 20 10 0

Fig 1. Brinda Somaya (centre) and the client in the carrot fields that was the proposed site for the Nalanda International School.

Fig 2. Site plan.

The school was to be built on a 12-acre piece of land: a carrot field near Vadodara in Gujarat. The land was flat, with few trees. Being on the outskirts of the city was not of concern to the client, as he was confident that it would be successful as long as a strong sense of identity was created. Both of us were aware that the architecture of the school would play a major role in this. The project broke ground in 2003 and was built over four phases. We initiated the process of design with the 40,000 sq. ft Junior School in the first phase and eventually went on to design and build the Infant School, the Middle School and the Senior School in the subsequent three phases. The final built-up area on the campus was about 2,00,000 sq. ft, with 4 acres of sports and games facilities. In the remaining 8 acres, the school buildings are woven in a series of open and permeable spaces.

Two essential aspects of Gandhian philosophy that I believed needed to be expressed in the architecture of the school were honesty and simplicity. The impact of brick from my childhood visit to the Nalanda University resurrected itself. It is a material that encompassed all the philosophical aspects we were looking to achieve. Thus, brick, in its many forms, was chosen as the primary material. Nalanda was built on a very tight budget, thereby reinforcing my decision to use brick as a structural material. From there, the idea of arches and vaults took shape. For the vaults, we had to get masons who know the craft, and the process was very engaging.

I was intensely aware of the environmental aspects of the campus. Certain elementary design approaches were outlined in the scheme, wherein the buildings were to be planned on the lay of the land, and in a way that they responded positively to the climate. The creation of different sizes of courtyards, building cavity walls, cross-shaped punctures and perforations in the walls and parapets, encouraging circulation of air, greening of the campus with trees layered against the walls, and creation of shaded breakout spaces were some important elements of the architectural vocabulary we used. These patterns manifest in the buildings in varying scales, and thus, the impact of these sustainable design elements percolates through the entire complex.

Fig 3. The double arched corridor under construction, that connected core areas of the building.

Fig 4. Integrating vernacular methodologies and materials within a contemporary architectural vocabulary.

Fig 3

Fig 4

The Infant School was interspersed with a series of smaller courts. From a young age, the children are taught to keep the courtyard and their classrooms clean, inculcating in them a sense of responsibility and dignity of labour. Simple materials were used internally, ranging from pigmented floors that created colour and pattern to patterned china mosaic on the exterior façade. The surfaces of this school are much more tactile. At this very young age, the children engage differently with their surroundings and this enhanced encounter with colour and texture stays with them. Blank walls and surfaces were intentionally left to encourage the children and teachers to add to the spaces their own artistic creativity. I do believe that it is this combination of rudimentary materials and art and craft that led to the development of the identity of the individual buildings. It also created a sense of ownership of the spaces in the users who cared for them and thereby enhanced them further. Finally, the brick piers that look into the common court connecting the Infant and Junior schools, establish the continuity that I envisioned.

Fig 5. Ground floor plan of the Infant School.

Fig 6. A vibrant colour and material palette was developed to create a dynamic and playful space for the kindergarten students.

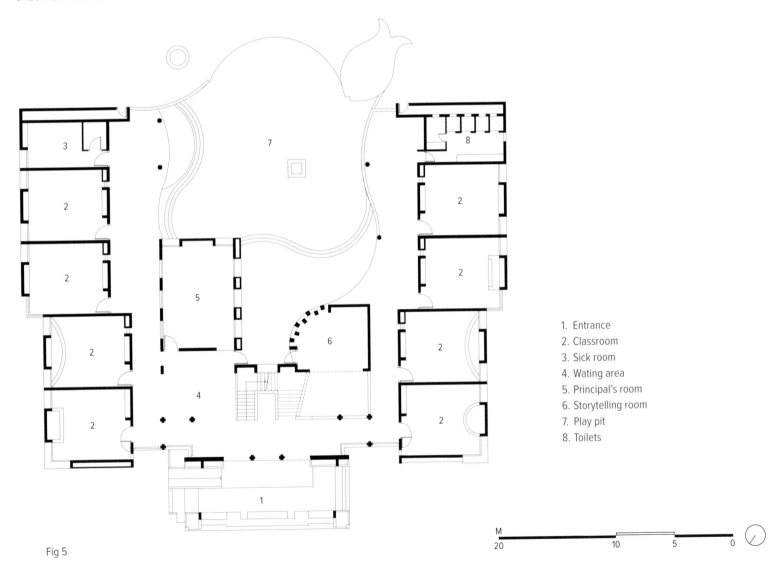

1. Entrance
2. Classroom
3. Sick room
4. Wating area
5. Principal's room
6. Storytelling room
7. Play pit
8. Toilets

Fig 5

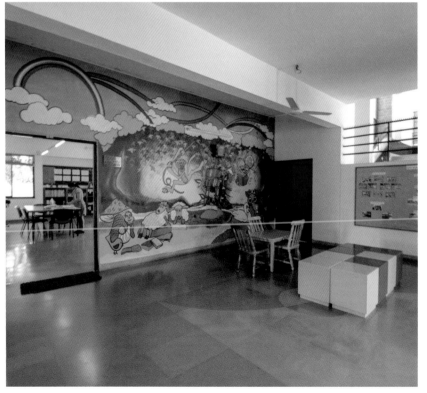

Fig 6

In the Junior School, the architectural elements remain the same but the scale differs. The courtyards are much larger, making the corridors longer. They were made larger and their form altered to cater to the need for small and large congregation spaces that the children could use. My attempt was to design a group of buildings that not only reflected the ethos of the school but enabled students to have access to spaces of peace and tranquillity. While the classrooms, laboratories and learning facilities are enclosed within; the courts, shaded corridors, pergolas, *jaali*s (screens) and the in-between spaces offer respite and retreat. The scales change dramatically, but as one moves through the campus, the buildings harmonise. The vaults were constructed using local bricks by masons from the region, who brought their understanding of traditional methods of construction to the site. Natural Kota and Jaisalmer stones were patterned and used in the flooring and connected one building to the other.

Fig 7. The courtyards and corridors go beyond circulation and transform into spaces of interaction and play.

Fig 8. Ground floor plan and east elevation of the Junior School.

Fig 7

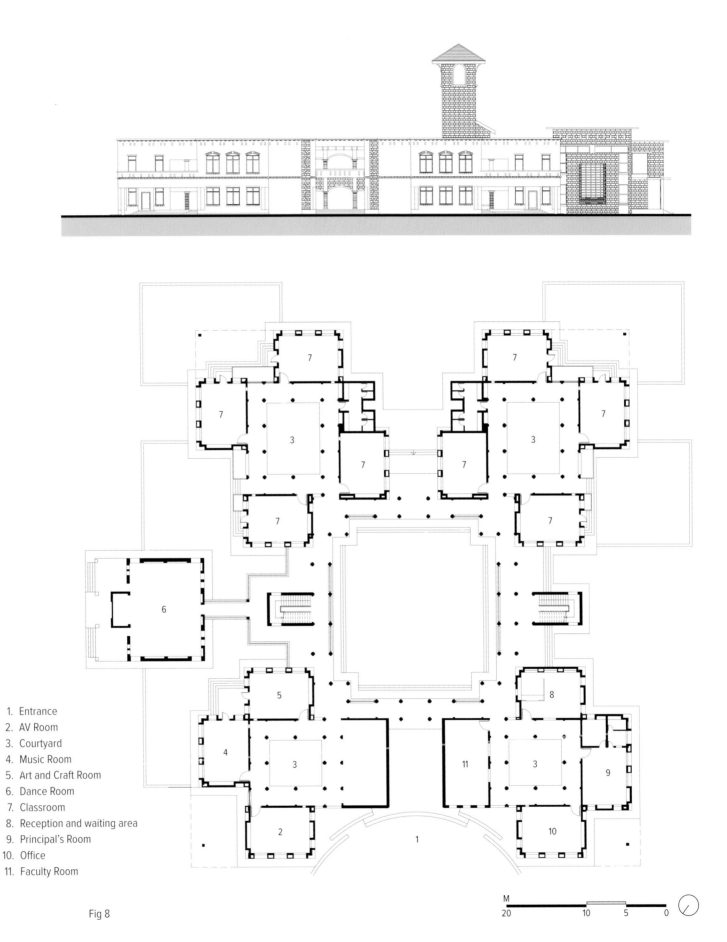

1. Entrance
2. AV Room
3. Courtyard
4. Music Room
5. Art and Craft Room
6. Dance Room
7. Classroom
8. Reception and waiting area
9. Principal's Room
10. Office
11. Faculty Room

Fig 8

M
20   10   5   0

Soon, we were commissioned the Middle School and Senior School, and this continual engagement with the clients and the project reinforced my conviction in the design process. The Middle and the Senior schools brought in a major shift of scale. The classrooms, laboratories and teachers' rooms were much larger; all bound by courtyards, extended staircases, green areas, trees that were saved and planted, and large spaces for congregation. In a way, the courtyards charted a hierarchy culminating in a large space that could hold all the students of the Nalanda International School. This large court was a massive challenge: How do we create an open space that is cohesive in scale and effect? This court was partially covered with a structure in exposed concrete and brick. Here, the concrete overtook the palette, rendering bare the structure of the canopy. This court was designed such that a major but variable part of it would always remain in shade, allowing for different patterns of use as the sun moved. Throughout the four phases, the material that bears the structure becomes the generator of the palette and there is a natural progression from structural brick to structural concrete in the campus. The organic and gradual landscape binds these related but distinct buildings. They have a common DNA but an independent identity.

Fig 9. Ground floor plan of the Middle School.

Fig 10. Ground floor plan of the Senior School.

Fig 11. Section A of Senior School.

Fig 12. Section B of Senior School.

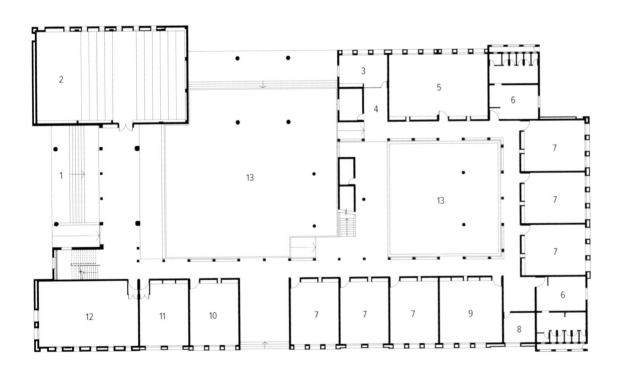

1. Entrance
2. Mini-theatre
3. Principal's room
4. Waiting area
5. Library
6. Toilets
7. Classrooms
8. Staff room
9. Faculty room
10. Services
11. Drum room
12. Wood workshop
13. Courtyard

Fig 9

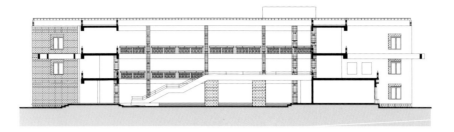

Fig 12

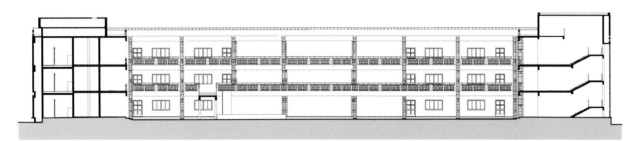

Fig 11

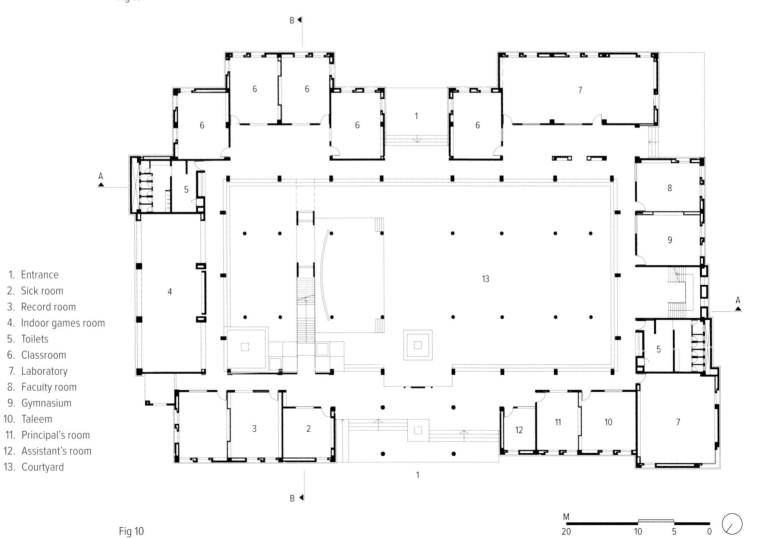

1. Entrance
2. Sick room
3. Record room
4. Indoor games room
5. Toilets
6. Classroom
7. Laboratory
8. Faculty room
9. Gymnasium
10. Taleem
11. Principal's room
12. Assistant's room
13. Courtyard

Fig 10

M
20   10   5   0

Fig 13. The design of internal and landscaped courtyards reinforces the importance of students experiencing the outdoors as much as the indoors.

Fig 14. The scale of buildings altered dramatically to respond to the requirements of the students as they progressed to higher grades.

Fig 13

Fig 14

Nalanda International School · 315

The role of light is very important. Having begun work on the restoration of Louis I Kahn's buildings at IIM Ahmedabad, I have been particularly conscious about the brilliance of Kahn in his use of light and the sciography thus created. I think back on Nalanda and believe that one can encounter several different experiences with light, in varied forms and intensities. The creation of a labyrinth of brick-vaulted connectors and perforated brick walls allowed light to filter in with a very particular texture. In the rooms for dance and music, I was not in the favour of plastering the walls. Hence, we created tessellated walls in brick resembling a screen around a court with a frangipani tree. When the students brought with them their music and dance, a sense of place unravelled. It is not just about the way the building looks; it is the way one feels while one occupies it.

The sunlight in India is strong and the shadows are sharp. I recall from my childhood the dappled light that lingered in spaces around buildings in those days. Houses would be surrounded with large trees and scatterings of leaves. This light would come through the branches of these trees, forming magnificent patterns on the walls and bringing an ethereal shimmer to the fallen leaves. That visual is so rare in today's urban India. But I do believe that I managed to recreate that environment and visual effect in Nalanda: patterns in the courtyards through shade and shadow, in the corridors through the perforated *jaali*s, geometric linear forms that move through the day from the shadow of the pergolas and streams of light with changing intensity, catching the leaves of the trees growing within and around the structures. One's experience in these spaces changes with the change of the seasons: the Indian summer, the monsoon, the Gujarat winter.

One of my most vital preoccupations in designing institutions is the porosity of the buildings. When there is a question of creating large institutional spaces, the permeability between them—from one space to another and within spaces that are enclosed, semi-open and open—generates a thread that ties all the buildings together. This porosity also creates a certain sense of comfort and ease within the spaces. Another priority is the creation of the 'special space'. These are pauses and surprises that break the monotony of a repetitive programme. There is an element of secrecy and revelation that enables students to experience a sense of delight and discovery on the campus. One can see groups of students getting together to play music, or two children talking and sharing secrets.

Creating intimacy gets more challenging when one deals with larger spaces. By changing materials and breaking down the scale, we attempted to generate an uncommon hierarchy, wherein we have primary and secondary spaces connected by a sequence of tertiary and secret spaces that are incidental to the scheme

Fig 15. The architecture allows for natural light to create dynamic patterns of shade and shadow.

Fig 15

Nalanda International School • 317

Fig 16

Fig 17

Fig 16. Mayur Patel presents a gift made by the students to Brinda Somaya.

Fig 17. The porosity of the campus allows for an ambience of stillness and introspection for the children, enabling them to engage and learn in a cohesive environment.

and unconventional to encounter as one meanders through the complex. This generates an unusual sense of order.

In many ways, the Nalanda campus reflects the core philosophy of the client. Patel believes that, beyond academics, the inculcation of value systems that students would carry with them through life is critical. If a student spends 12 years in an institution, I believe, the architecture must inspire and nurture them. I was consistently thinking of my school and how its character had a lasting impact on me. I was very fortunate to study at the Cathedral school in Mumbai, which was not just a connection of corridors and rooms but an institution that derived much of its character from the strength, history and architecture of its buildings.

And that is perhaps why I find institutions so gratifying to design. We must imagine the age and specific needs of the young minds that occupy these campuses: the way they think, the way they move, the way their memories are formed. I feel very fortunate that my work becomes a part of building these memories. I continue to get drawings, sketches and letters from the students depicting their life in the school. This has been one of the most rewarding aspects of designing the Nalanda campus.

The relationship between architecture and environment continues to be a complex interaction. While there is much value in carefully designing the buildings in drawings and detail, part of the role of architecture is to also convey and express this connection with climate, materials, people who use the spaces, nature and values that go beyond the use of these structures. In 2006, when the building won the Leading European Architects' Forum Award (LEAF) for use of traditional methods in environmental control, it was important for us to reflect that it was not simply a unique case of design. It was just as much that the values of frugality and simplicity that formed the core of the Nalanda philosophy were expressed in the architecture. Just like the ruins of Nalanda have a special place in my memory, the Nalanda school buildings will perhaps have a special place in the lives of the students who spend their formative years here. And that can only happen if the architecture of the institute is not just an object of design, but one that fuels a learning environment.

HOUSES

A narrative of continuous search for the design of houses in four decades of practice for an architecture that is appropriate and aspirational, because human interaction with space governs design.

HOUSE BY THE SEA
For Tata Electric Companies
Erangal, Mumbai, India [1981]

HOUSE BY THE HILL
For Shashikant Garware
Nashik, India [1986]

HOUSE BY THE LAKE
For Tata Electric Companies
Lonavala, Mumbai, India [1986]

THE COURTYARD HOUSE
For Saker and Mehli Mistri
Pune, India [2002]

HOUSE IN THE VALLEY
For Anita and Arun Shourie
Lavasa, India [2010]

HOUSE IN THE TREES
For Brinda and Anand Somaya
Alibaug, India [2011]

For architects, designing a house is always an important project. Many great architects, the likes of Frank Lloyd Wright, built their careers on designing houses and, in the process, finding new ways of making architecture and thinking about the human condition. There is something very special about designing a house: the human scale, the understanding of the architecture of a home and the process of space-making that prompts architects to indulge in designing houses. Whether the client is a single person or a family, the design of a house entails that you understand them in great depth, understand the way they live, the way they eat and the things they dream about. As an architect, if one really wants to build something that belongs to the people and the place, one must initiate a meaningful interaction. This combines one's personal sense of architecture and the issues of the built and the unbuilt, transition spaces, courtyards, fenestrations, light and shadow.

Houses demand a completely distinct approach compared to public buildings, campuses and other typologies. Being limited in scale, they are often very demanding in terms of programme. A multitude of functions and spaces must come together in an organised order, and yet, they must evolve into something that is unpredictable and full of wonder. My practice has designed and built many houses over the years, starting from the 1980s. I have built a house on the lake, a house by the sea, a house on the hill, a house by the temple, a house in the forest and many more. The immediate context of the house has an inseparable relationship with the house.

After I began my practice in 1975, I designed and built the first house; the Sarma House, in Pune. In fact, it was the only ongoing project back then, and my involvement with the project was absolute. It was a small project for a young couple. My collaboration with my sister Ranjini Kalappa in setting up the studio in 1975 was anchored in designing our early houses. While Ranjini receded

Fig 1. Brinda Somaya (centre) with her parents and sister at their home in Mumbai.

Fig 2. Brinda Somaya's childhood home, designed by Claude Batley, in Mumbai.

from the practice after she moved away in the early 1980s. She remained an advisor, collaborator and intellectual partner to our practice for some years, until the point SNK developed core strengths. I will always be grateful to Ranjini for her mentorship. Having grown up in a house designed by Claude Batley, our introduction to space and light were derived from an overlapping of Indian and Western influences. I still think that childhood homes, where people grow up, continue to influence people's grasp of space and light. The houses of my childhood were my grandfather's house in Bengaluru where I was born and spent many summer holidays, and the house in Mumbai where I grew up. Influences are often not immediate and they permeate into one's work through a process of slow absorption over a very long period of time.

Fig 1

Fig 2

Geometry has always played a very important role in our work. The presence of an axis is often deliberately played with. There are organisational principles and hierarchies that form the underlay for each project, and the experiential aspects become more apparent and important when one inhabits the space. While the architecture of the house is usually a reflection of preferences, it eventually becomes a connection between the static functions of a space and the dynamic experience of the same in a fine equilibrium. Over the years, my studio has designed and built houses in many parts of India for families who are very different from each other. Here, I want to discuss six houses from the four decades of my work. Each of them is very different, both in terms of the geography and the users.

House by the Sea

In 1981, we completed our first important house at Erangal Beach near Mumbai. The 'House by the Sea' sits on the Erangal beach, a very small house close to a historic church, a fishing village and Malad stone quarries. This 240-sq. m structure was designed as a series of pavilions built around courts, and connected through open-to-sky spaces and a series of walkways. The stone-clad house is placed "in between" the village and the sea in terms of its scale and continuity of landscape.

In a simple plan, the relationship between the built and the open becomes primary to the experience of the house. The in-between spaces helped us negotiate the various degrees of privacy in the house and the courts acted as spaces that enclose and are enclosed by the built. This created a constant rhythm of grandeur and intimacy: grandeur, as one experienced the luxury of the individual pitched-roof Malad stone-clad pavilions, and intimacy brought about by the continual connection between structures through walkways, courtyards and bermed landscaped mounds.

Fig 3. The courtyard space connected the built and unbuilt spaces of the Erangal House.

Fig 4. Archival drawings of the roof plan, ground floor plan and section of the Erangal House.

Fig 3

SECTION A-A

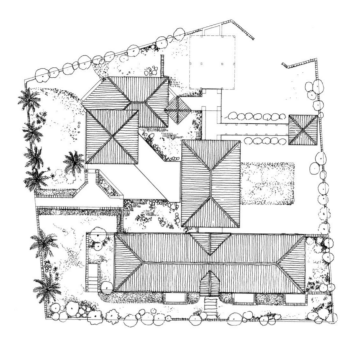

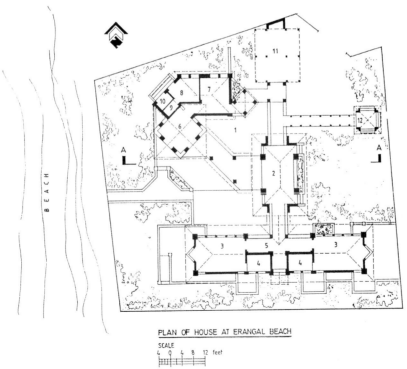

PLAN OF HOUSE AT ERANGAL BEACH

SCALE
4 0 4 8 12 feet

LEGEND

1 PAVED AREA
2 LIVING
3 BED ROOM
4 TOILET
5 CORRIDOR
6 DINING
7 KITCHEN
8 SERVANT'S ROOM
9 WASHING PLACE
10 W.C
11 OPEN GARAGE
12 PLANT SHED

Fig 4

The monolithic nature of the house helps assimilate the otherwise modern structure with the landscape, as the local stone allows the house to blend with its setting. As in many of my works, landscape becomes the unifying element. The spatial aspects of the House by the Sea define its architecture more acutely than the formal aspects of the same.

I am particularly fond of this house out of the many that we have designed as a practice, because the simple plan in this case is generative of the layered and complex spaces. The slate floors and the Malad-stone walls establish a sense of continuity with the hamlet, the church and the quarry. While from within, the house renders a sense of security and control. From the courts and its various outdoor and buffer spaces, one can experience the expanse of the sky and the sea beyond.

Fig 5. Archival photographs of the house.

Fig 6. The porosity and permeability of architecture that enables one to connect to the landscape beyond.

Fig 5

Fig 6

House by the Hill

In 1986, we received the commission for the House by the Hill, which was to be designed for a magnificent site in close proximity of the Pandav *leni* (caves) on the Mumbai–Nashik highway. The longitudinally cut caves in the rocks date back more than two millennia and are steeped in the mythological and archaeological history of the land. When we started work on the project, the land at the base of the caves had very little vegetation. The house was at the base of the hillside. It was not a very big building, but it was a big hill. We felt that the hill could absorb the building. It was after much consideration that we decided we did not want this building to merge with the contours of the hill. We decided that we wanted the house to make a statement. Thus, it was designed in stark contrast to the simple conical shape of the hill that formed the backdrop for its architecture.

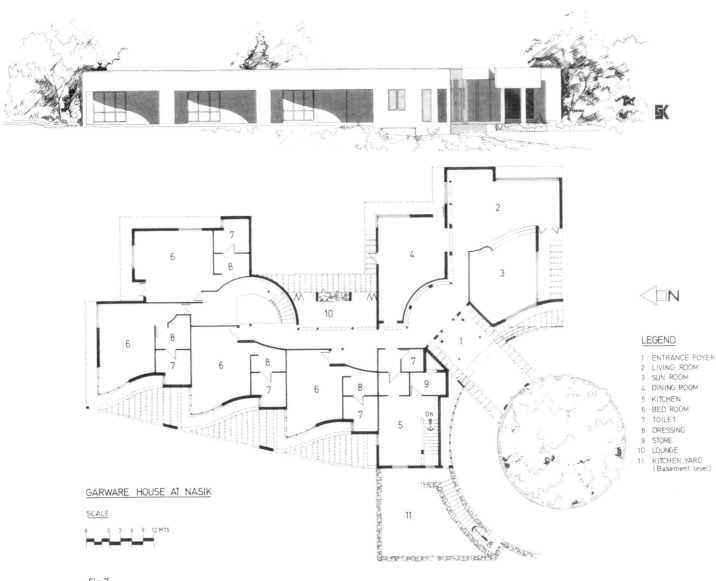

GARWARE HOUSE AT NASIK

SCALE

6 0 3 6 9 12 MTS.

LEGEND

1 ENTRANCE FOYER
2 LIVING ROOM
3 SUN ROOM
4 DINING ROOM
5 KITCHEN
6 BED ROOM
7 TOILET
8 DRESSING
9 STORE
10 LOUNGE
11 KITCHEN YARD
   (Basement level)

Fig 7

Fig 7. Archival drawings of the ground floor plan and west elevation of the House by the Hill.

Fig 8. Archival photographs of the House by the Hill under construction with the Pandav *leni* (caves) in the backdrop.

We were acutely aware of the harsh sun and the hot and dry climate of Nashik. The idea was to create a strong double wall, a series of free-standing columns with a wall behind, along a strong curve. This created a natural buffer and generated a strong geometry for framing the entrance. This double wall sets the theme for the rest of the house. The houseplan is composed of undulating faces and free-standing planes that enable patterns of light and shadow throughout the house. The skylights allow light of a very special texture to filter in, without inviting any glare. There is an incredible panoramic view and parts of the hill are framed through various spaces within the house.

Fig 8

I was very keen on the House by the Hill resisting assimilation in the landscape. I wanted the house and the landscape to be distinct. In many ways, while the work of SNK draws inspiration from the Indian landscape and its wealth, there is this strong contemporary language: a language of geometry, walls, light, water and materials that forms a consistent running thread in all my works and lends a meaning to them. Thus, buildings such as the House by the Hill and the Sanpada Church (see p. 219), built many years apart, still have much in common in terms of the architectural vocabulary. In both the cases, the design is an expression of the site and its potential.

While this white building reflects heat, the overlaying patterns of geometry in the façade of the house provide self-shading devices to counter the onslaught of the sun. To take similar approaches at different scales has always been a distinct characteristic of my work. I continue to strive to create a series of experiences through light and shade. The elements of control are the same as in the Garware house, but expressed in a very different language each time I employ them. This house continues to hold ground in front of the hill, now nestled within the dense landscape. Its geometric linearity and organic curvilinear shape continues to draw one through the green into the home.

Fig 9. Archival photographs of the completed House by the Hill.

Fig 9

House by the Lake

In 1986, the Tata Electric Companies, for whom we had designed the Erangal House, approached us to design a guest house by a beautiful lake, which was the site for their hydro-power station in a hill station near Lonavala. The Walwan Lake was breathtaking, with a large black-basalt dam running across it. The site commanded a panoramic view, and the lake had a personal connection for my sister and me. As young girls, we had spent much time around the lake, fishing and sailing, and so we had nostalgic memories of the place. This project was another collaboration between the two of us, and we were inspired by the architecture of Richard Meier.

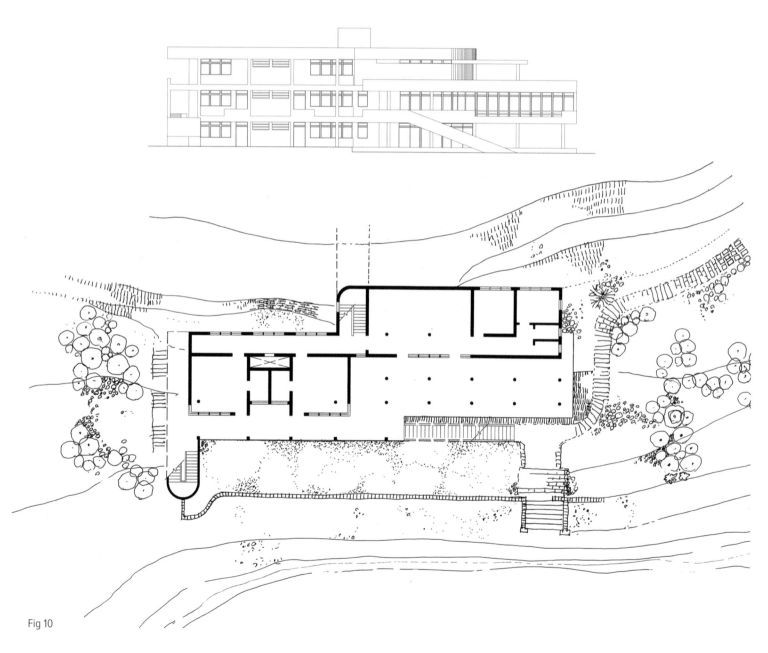

Fig 10

Fig 11

Fig 10. Archival drawings of the House by the Lake.

Fig 11. Views showing the stark geometry of the house against the backdrop of the lake.

The hot Indian sun demanded a layered building that prevented the heat from entering, while also allowing light to penetrate within. The simple plan consisted of three levels that were determined by the post-monsoon levels of the adjoining lake. A bridge provides an access to the 700-sq. m house at the middle level: the level that houses the entrance, the living and the dining areas along with two bedrooms and a kitchen. The large windows frame the views of the landscape and the expansive decks prompt sit-outs. The layered façade is also designed to resist high-velocity winds and rain in the monsoon. With its extended decks and ramps leading to water, the building resembles a ship on the verge of leaving on a voyage, making a distinct statement as it sits on the edge of a magnificent lake. While the floors are white terrazzo stone, the decks are composed of green slate. I am often fascinated by the way buildings silhouette against the sky. In this house, the contrast is intentionally stark.

The Courtyard House

The Courtyard House is a large house on a steep slope. It is designed with a series of stepped courts cascading down through interesting levels of the land from the entrance at the top to the base plane. The house is planned in two parts: the main house, which is designed around a large open to sky courtyard and the smaller guest house, that is subtly tucked into the hillside. The entrance of the house is almost hidden as it rests on the downward slope of the hill, so as one drives past, one barely notices the presence of a structure. A curved driveway leads one to the steps at the entrance of the house. A strong north-south axis connects this point to the expansive views of the hills around and beyond, as it traverses the court, the entrance hall, the living room and the deck. We also had side courts protected by pergolas on the eastern side and a very small secret walled garden off the study. There are unexpected views and vistas pervading throughout the entire home. This offers a continuous sense of surprise and delight as one wanders through this house.

We designed courtyards, enclosed gardens and terraces that work well in the tropical climate of India. The master bedroom has a private court that opens onto a deck. As one steps down to the guest room below, a tiny courtyard highlights one side of the staircase wall. The airy and spacious courts allow the daylight to filter in and effortlessly connect the outdoors with the indoors, yet providing a sense of privacy for the philanthropic and warm Mistri family.

Fig 12. The Courtyard House under construction.

Fig 13. Site plan, north and south elevation of the Courtyard House.

Fig 12

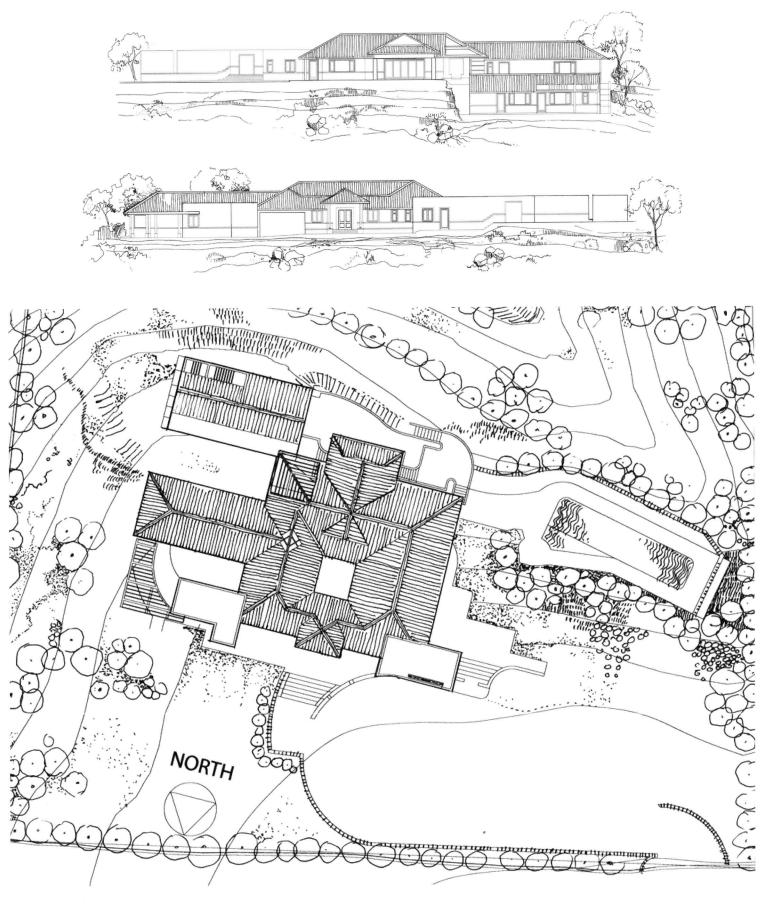

NORTH

Fig 13

The house is built using natural materials. Limestone cladding, patterned stone flooring and a collection of oriental wooden furniture, which Saker and Mehli Mistri collected as they travelled around the world, extends to the landscape and the pool beyond. The warm colour palette of the ochre floor, off-white walls and honey-hued furniture adorn the interiors. While the design vocabulary is contemporary, the way the house interacts with the site makes it universal and yet it belongs to the place where it stands.

Fig 14. The courtyard serves as the central core of the house leading to habitable spaces and beautiful vistas of the valley.

Fig 15. The landscape winds its way from the external valley to the courtyard within.

Fig 14

Fig 15

House in the Valley

The house for Arun Shourie in Lavasa was designed very differently and for very special considerations. Lavasa is a township nestled in the Western Ghats and faces extremely heavy rainfall in a hostile landscape. It thus becomes imperative to have sloping roofs and protected areas within. Arun Shourie is one of India's most respected journalists–authors and needed the house for the quietude where he could think and write. There were limitations in design owing to the special needs of his family members. This house on a steep sloping land had to be built with complete accessibility for a wheelchair.

There are two parts to the house. One part consists of a large collection of spaces where all the functions for living are clustered, and the second is a small pavilion used by Shourie as a writing retreat. The two are connected by a landscaped court. While the entire house had to be made accessible with gentle ramps, I was quite sure that the ramps would not overwhelm the design of the house. Thus, even though the ramps were obligatory, the house gains its primary character from the way it sits on the hill and the way it frames the views that surround it. The family has many personal artefacts that were collected over the years, and the house becomes a place for them to coexist with spaces that are made for comfort. This house is also a consequence of a deeper dialogue with the clients. One of the important aspects of the architecture of this house is its incorporation

Fig 16. Brinda Somaya at the site in Lavasa.

Fig 17. Site plan and east elevation of the House in the Valley.

Fig 16

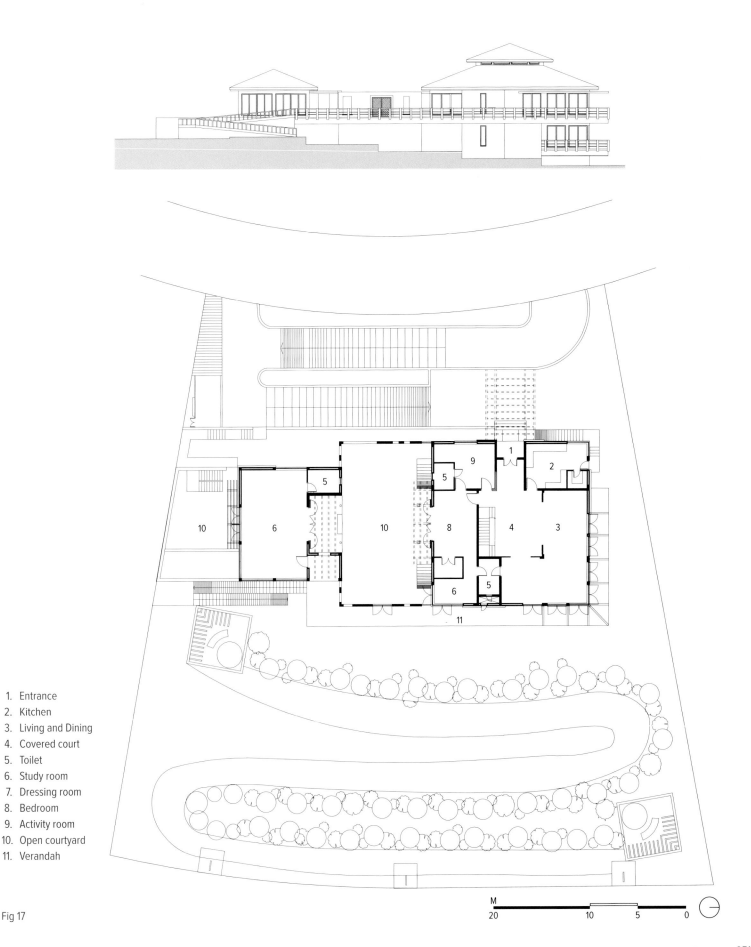

1. Entrance
2. Kitchen
3. Living and Dining
4. Covered court
5. Toilet
6. Study room
7. Dressing room
8. Bedroom
9. Activity room
10. Open courtyard
11. Verandah

Fig 17

M
20   10   5   0

of the real necessities of the people who would occupy it. The clients have always stressed on our ability as architects to be good "listeners", a trait that requires one to give time, effort and attention to the nuances of designing a private space.

Another important aspect of the Shourie house is the attention that we devoted to designing spaces for the domestic help and support staff. Built around a private courtyard, these units are occupied by people who are inseparable from the Shourie family. The attention committed to design of these spaces ensure that everyone has a connection with the home, not just the clients. Expansive scenery and uninterrupted skies form a dramatic setting for the house. The ever-changing landscape with the lake and the hills make for the view from the house, which acts as a pavilion and a vantage point for the same.

Fig 18. Views of the ramp, central courtyard and the cantilevered verandah overlooking the valley.

Fig 19. The house sits amongst the hills of the western ghats framing the panaromas of the valley.

Fig 18

Fig 19

House in the Trees

As an architect, one perhaps has the most freedom when designing one's own home. When I started thinking about our house in Awas (a small hamlet in Alibaug), I realised that there were things other than architecture that were important to me and became my primary considerations. I wanted the house to occupy the canopies of the trees and live amongst the branches and the foliage of the dense cover around. Living in the city, I longed for greenery. I designed the main floor of the house on the first level in a way that all I could see as I moved in the house are the green canopies that surround it.

The houses in the hamlet are small, vernacular stone structures with courts and sloping roofs. I decided to use the same stone inside the house. This ties up in scheme with the walls and, at places, becomes the structure. Being on the first level, one also has the freedom to secure the house with one point of exit, which only works in the rural setting of a farmland. The language of the house is very contemporary. From the first level, the double height spaces bring in the expanse of the sky into the house. The spaces are perpetually overflowing with natural light, and the generous ceiling heights accommodate a mezzanine that contains reading nooks. The balconies are oriented and extruded towards the parts of the site that I loved and wanted to emphasise. A big terrace overlooks the line of coconut trees to the north. The magnificent banyan trees can be seen from

Fig 20. The proposed site for the house had a coconut grove and two large banyan trees.

Fig 21. Site plan of the House in the Trees.

Fig 22. Ground floor plan and Section A.

Fig 23. First floor plan and north elevation.

Fig 20

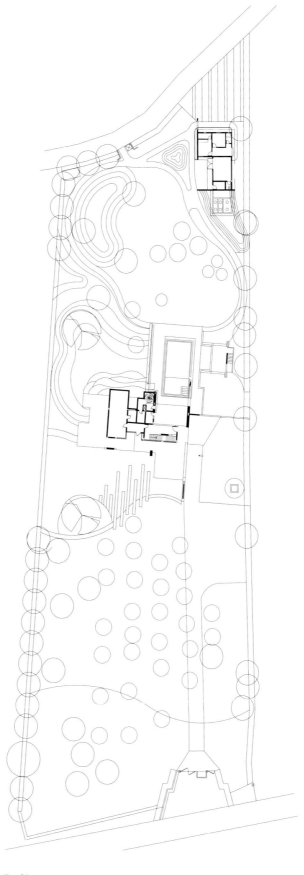

Fig 21

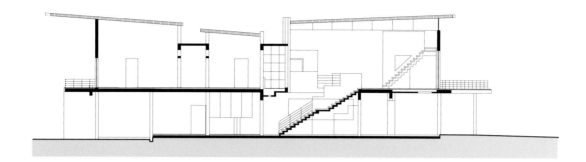

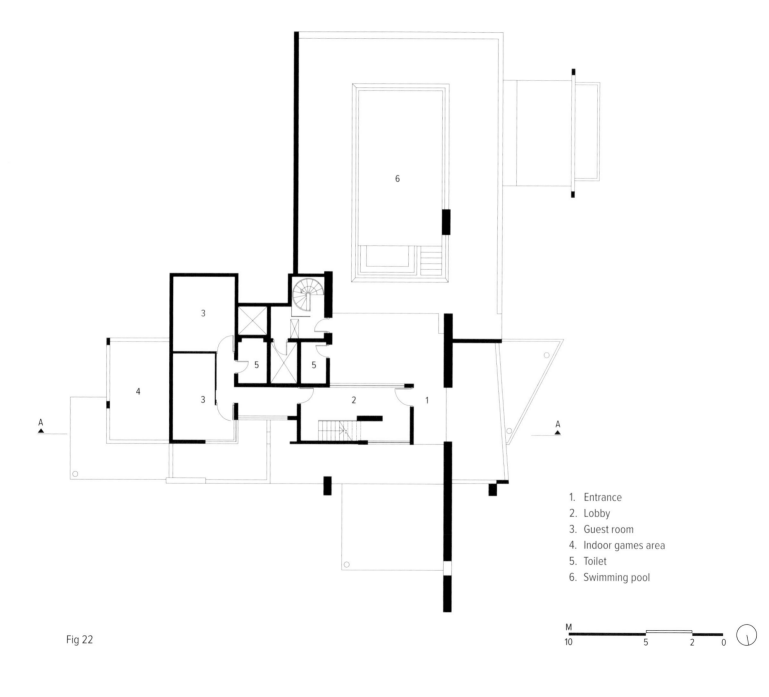

1. Entrance
2. Lobby
3. Guest room
4. Indoor games area
5. Toilet
6. Swimming pool

Fig 22

M
10   5   2   0

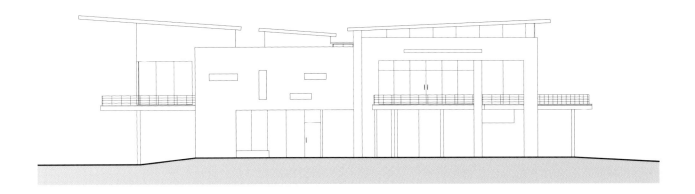

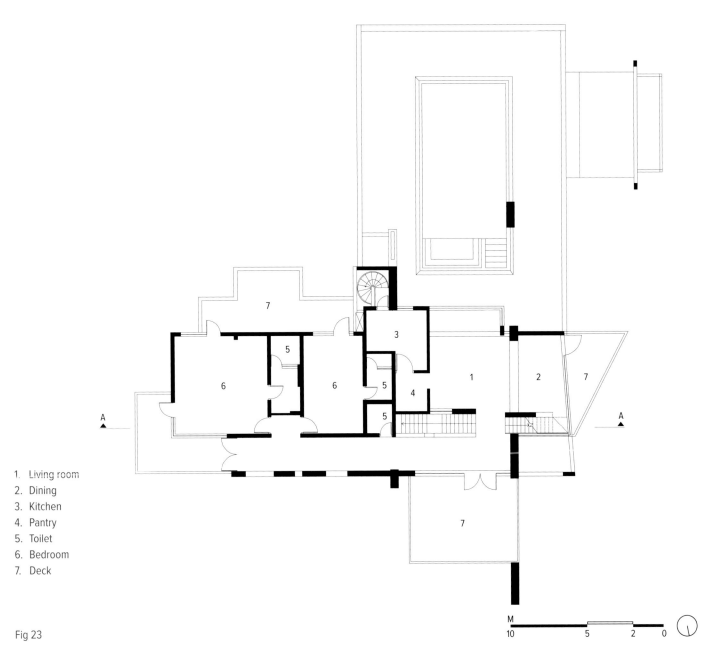

1. Living room
2. Dining
3. Kitchen
4. Pantry
5. Toilet
6. Bedroom
7. Deck

M
10 5 2 0

Fig 23

both verandahs of the master bedroom. In the west, the house opens towards the ocean and the sky and lets the sea breeze in. The wind chimes that I have collected on my travels from various parts of the world hang in the verandah here.

In the evenings, I have the privilege of listening to a symphony—bird calls from the trees mingling with the chimes—and relaxing in the salty air from the ocean. Time slows down. In that moment, I am fully submerged in my grove of trees. The plot of land used to be a *wadi*. A *wadi* references a small group of trees. The trees in my farm are old native trees and not exotic varieties brought into India over decades. Once, a historian visited the farm and told me the significance of each variety. Some were revered, some had links to ancient Indian mythology, some were planted for the flowers, some for the birds and so on. A true delight.

Fig 24. Construction of the composite structure with a light-weight roof and cantilevered terraces.

Fig 25. Views of the completed House in the Trees.

Fig 24

Fig 25

Fig 26

Fig 26. The interiors of the house are a continuation of the architecture, reflecting a contemporary design ethos.

One of the reasons I think architects are very interested in designing houses is the significance they have in a practice. Houses are a very important component in the portfolios of many firms, as many young practices often receive houses as their first commissions. While houses give an architect freedom, they can also be very demanding design projects. Preferences and requirements of each client and programme differ and are quite specific in most cases. There are also matters of taste and popular influence, personal and social preferences, interests, personal finances and varying budgets, wants and desires, and a consistent search for comfort and delight that informs the design.

Another important facet of designing houses is the way they can define one's practice and become a study in the changing approaches within the span of an architect's working career. While they are specific pieces of architecture, they can also give you the bandwidth to experiment within a controlled scale. In all the houses outlined in this piece, a singular element of the courtyard finds multiple ways to manifest. Being buildings that also solicit personal involvement of the clients in the process of design, there are many disagreements and many negotiations one has to contend with. For my practice, many clients for whom we have designed and built houses are also clients for many other projects. Thus, the dialogue extends beyond their personal preferences, which I think enriches the process of designing something unique and special for them. I have also come to realise that a house becomes a part of an individual's identity and sense of self. It ultimately evolves into one of the most collaborative of all typologies of a practice.

CLUB MAHINDRA KUMBHALGARH

For Mahindra Holidays & Resorts Ltd

MASTER PLANNING AND ARCHITECTURE

Kumbhalgarh, India [2005–2007]

Design assimilates the potential of the context—
human and natural—for an architecture that is neither
alien to the landscape nor a caricaturised version
of heritage.

One of the privileges of being an architect in India continues to be the opportunities to travel. My country is vast and beautiful, with magnificent diversity in geography, culture and tradition. All these have been my source of inspiration for design and remain one of the most fulfilling aspects of the profession. Our hotel and resort projects are often spread across several incredible locations in India and overseas including a business hotel in Tashkent, Uzbekistan, that I designed and built back in the nineties. For Club Mahindra, we have built resorts in Theog in Himachal Pradesh and Binsar in Uttarakhand, both in the foothills of the mighty Himalayas. A project was proposed in Kumbhalgarh, Rajasthan, which was on a very different terrain. The journey to Kumbhalgarh has since been etched in my mind.

We landed in Udaipur and drove a couple of hours on a rough road through the Aravalli hills. Rajasthan is often associated with a unique history deeply rooted in folklore and mythology. But there was something very different about the hills of the Aravalli. Till the last few decades of the 20th century, the country was not connected as it is today. The roads were rough, and as we drove through, it was quite deserted. The settlements were few and far between, and the combination of harsh terrain and wild vegetation was underscored by the sparsely populated areas. I recollect discussing this quality with the landscape architect travelling with me: the dry walls separating the fields, hues and patterns of stone that composed these walls, and the bushes and acacia trees. The landscape, the rural setting and the vegetation exuded a certain romanticism that is perhaps unique to this part of India. I was convinced during this journey that the landscape of the hotel could not be delicate flowers and manicured lawns; it had to respond to this wildness that is characteristic of arid Rajasthan.

Compared to the Himalayas, the gentle slopes of the Aravalli pose fewer challenges, although the gradient presents many opportunities to frame the project with specificity. The site for the resort had three small buildings with minimal architectural merit. After discussion with the clients, we took a call that we would retain them and integrate them into the masterplan. Every building has its embodied energy, and if we can make use of the building stock that exists, much energy and cost is saved. This is at the core of what being sustainable is about. One must carefully analyse the land and everything that sits on it, prior to beginning work on the project, in

Fig 1. The spectacular fort of Kumbhalgarh.

Fig 1

order to assimilate the presence of elements on the site. My very first hotel was the West End in Bengaluru, where we worked on a beautiful site in the heart of the city. It was full of ancient trees and existing structures, of which we upgraded some of the 19th-century buildings. We were faced with a similar situation in Kumbhalgarh, although there were few existing buildings compared to the West End Hotel site, and we took a decision to retain them.

Fig 2

Fig 3

The day after we arrived and completed the site inspection, we visited the heritage site of the Kumbhalgarh Fort. It is a magnificent medieval 15th-century structure with an enclosure that houses many monuments. As I walked the robust thick walls of the fort to the palace that occupies the highest point, I could feel the cool air that flowed into the rooms through a labyrinth of enclosures. From the windows of the palace, one can observe the setting—the river and the landscape beyond—and almost imagine the way in which these walls would have resisted the invasions of the past centuries. No other monument or fort in India had previously created such a powerful impact in my mind as did Kumbhalgarh. It assisted me in better understanding the spirit of the place and the cultural landscape that surrounded our land.

I believe that the masterplan must come first in the process of imagining and developing a large project. It enables me to have a bird's-eye view of the project and to inculcate many layers that are juxtaposed: the buildings, the land and the vegetation. We discovered *nullah*s (culverts) running through the site, and from our experience, we knew that one cannot change their course. We need to respect the flow of water on any site. The design of the hotel follows a contemporary architectural language. I wanted to scale the buildings carefully to make them humane and enable them to sit quietly among the hills. The design also considers the connection between the protected interiors of the building and the many transitions to the exterior.

Fig 2. The Kumbhalgarh site nestled amidst the Aravallis.

Fig 3. The existing structures on the site that were restored and retrofitted to be integrated with the new masterplan.

Fig 4. Conceptual masterplan and site elevation.

Fig 4

We studied these existing buildings on the site to understand their footprint and proportions. I had always imagined these structures quite differently. An Indian miniature painting came to mind, where the beauty of the architectural vocabulary with its intricacy and colour was often superimposed against stark and bare landscapes. The new buildings were designed with this in mind, ensuring the development of a contemporary design that was nonetheless representative of a sense of place and time. Working on a contoured site, I realised that we could create courtyards at multiple levels, enabling the landscape to work with the built form in a chequered pattern. There were groups of cottages designed around a central court and three larger linear structures with ground floors and two storeys. The rooms had balconies for people to enjoy the view of the mountains in the distance on one side; these balconies also served as the backdrop for the entire resort. Traditional details were studied and reinterpreted to create rich detailing, especially in the reception and restaurant block.

In a rural site, one must generate a balance between the standard of construction that is desired from a mechanical perspective and the available skill of the local labour. Sometimes, by allowing the human hand to make buildings, one makes allowances of time and technique. However, the amalgamation of the two is always heartening and yields surprising results. The difficulties of working on a remote site and a tough terrain are omnipresent if you work on rural sites, especially for hospitality projects that are also service-oriented. Thus, the architecture must make accommodations for the expected comfort, all the while refraining from being wasteful or indulgent.

When we started construction, we noticed several women working on the site and we began to understand their needs and sensitivities. I also realised after interacting with them that the women worked as site labourers and all the skilled labour was mostly composed of men. Even in the 21st century, the human engagement on sites in India remains exploitative and brutal. We had worked previously on our other sites for women to develop skills that would enable them to get more dignified work at par with the men and earn more to contribute better for their families. It was at Kumbhalgarh that I realised the importance of imparting skills to women beyond carrying concrete. They need to learn to be masons, painters and welders. I work with various organisations, even today, to help develop their skills. In many of our projects, we consciously use the opportunity to positively impact the people who work on them. This includes teaching skills to women labourers to organising crèches and schools for the children of migrant workers, who have no other avenue to learn. In many ways, I believe this in turn contributes to our profession, and it is therefore part of our responsibility towards the discipline.

Fig 5. Aerial view of the Club Mahindra Resort at Kumbhalgarh.

Fig 6. Masterplan and sectional elevation.

Fig 5

An important aspect of working in rural India, in contrast to working in the cities, is the conscious effort we take to involve the local people in the project. In the Indian villages, a building like a resort can be invasive and may often generate friction within the local communities. Moreover, we have always insisted that a rural project must involve the skills, crafts and human resources available in the immediate surroundings. This ensures that the building activity and subsequent project employs and generates income for the rural area that it is located in. In Kumbhalgarh, we were fortunate to interact with and recognise the inherent talent of the villagers. We engaged them in creating art and craft works for further embellishing the structure and interiors. They were also involved in the core activities of building and managing the hotel.

There is a tradition of dry masonry in Rajasthan, which we employed in the construction to create beautifully textured stone walls and to assimilate our resort in the larger backdrop of Rajasthan. In many parts of Rajasthan, there exists a culture of painting the ceiling, which was also incorporated within the interiors. We sourced ceramics and artefacts that were crafted in Rajasthan for the hotel. One of my personal favourites is a beautiful peacock created in collaboration with local artists. In some interior parts of the hotel, we worked with craftsmen who made murals with broken glass or *tikri*, wherein pieces of stained glass and mirrors are arranged in a dazzling mosaic. Even the furniture was designed to assimilate carpentry traditions. While I believe in a contemporary expression, the overall palette created for us something special that belongs to the place and is authentic and original. The building acting as a canvas for the arts. Our approach to collaborate with the local people was appreciated by the client as it naturally generated a substantial amount of goodwill for the project.

Fig 7. Women labourers on the construction site.

Fig 8. Integration of the local stone masonry into the architecture and landscape design.

Fig 9. Local artists and craftsmen were employed to highlight accent areas, thereby bringing in the vibrant traditional colours and materials of Rajasthan into the spaces.

Fig 8

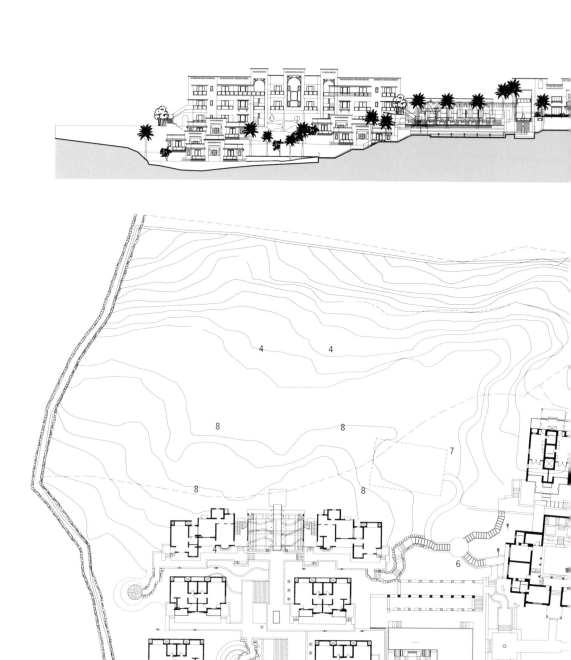

1. Entrance
2. Receptions and Restaurant above
3. Administration
4. Guest rooms
5. Banquet lawn and Conference hall below
6. Coffee shop
7. Swimming pool
8. Villas

Fig 6

3

2

M
20   10   5   0

Fig 7

Fig 9

Fig 10

In the dry and deciduous landscape, the buildings were rendered in colour. The visual impact of the changing hues of the landscape against the palette of the building colours injected a sense of dynamism and contrast with the arid landscape. I was very keen to leave the landscape organic. There were wonderful mustard plants around the site that we thought would become a part of the scenery, but there were apprehensions that a completely uncontrolled landscape would not be able to soften the terrain and may be very harsh in the even hotter summer months. We found a way to design the land by ensuring it appealed to a certain informality of objects on the site. While it does not completely connect with the farmlands and the rugged hills, it behaves like an oasis—a green relief in the barren surroundings. The buildings have large cascading terraces, and one can step out of the room into this wonderful open-to-sky space to observe the poetic landscape within and around the site.

One enters the complex through a landscaped open court; a contemporary expression of the traditional *chowk*s. From the court, one traverses many public areas: restaurants, coffee shops, gymnasium and the bridges that take one across the *nullah*s. The slope of the site enabled us to sink the large multipurpose hall and green the terrace with a lawn that keeps the hall cool and serves as a space for gatherings and celebrations. I think a common-sense approach to sustainable design is much more effective, especially in a country like India, than the many certifications one can get for an audit-based approach. As architects in India, a sense of frugality and consideration is culturally ingrained in us. This attitude to work with embedded energy to create spaces that are only essential makes our architecture much more efficient and rooted in their surroundings.

The project has left a strong visual imprint in my mind's eye. I used to take an early morning flight back from Udaipur on my site visits and invariably left Kumbhalgarh at the break of dawn, travelling in solitude through the desolate terrain. I remember seeing a full moon set behind the Aravallis and imagined the hundreds of years of history, the people and the monuments that would have witnessed this incredible setting. The Club Mahindra Kumbhalgarh resort is one of our most beloved projects. Not only has the project been well-received by the clients and the guests, it has also been a generator of employment for the locals directly and through the tourists that the resort draws. It is very crucial that in addition to the architects, their clients and the users, the people in the context too have a stake in the success and the outcome of the project. To know that this eventual impact is the consequence of my work reaffirms my faith in our architecture and practice.

CAMPUS FOR GOA INSTITUTE OF MANAGEMENT

For Goa Institute of Management

MASTER-PLANNING, ARCHITECTURE AND LANDSCAPE DESIGN

Goa, India [2009 to Present]

Greenfield projects are opportunities to respond to found topography to establish new coordinates by weaving architecture and landscape to create a cohesive, self-contained environment.

The site for the Goa Institute of Management (GIM) is a magnificent 50-acre land in Sanquelim, a village north of Panaji in Goa, nestled in the foothills of the Western Ghats. The very first time I visited the site, I remember driving up a winding road that terminated in a large plateau. The flat land had very little vegetation comprising a few bushes and shrubs. But there was the beautiful red laterite that one could almost feel through the transparent earth. You could sense it was there. The view was mesmerising: a 360-degree panorama with the enclosure of the hills. Standing on the plateau, amidst the beauty of the surroundings and the land, was where it all began. It was a unique project, being one of our first large greenfield institutions. This campus had a different set of demands. We were designing for postgraduate students of a particular age and specific aspirations. Designing this campus meant interpreting and enhancing the identity of the institution and its students through the architecture and the spirit of the spaces.

Fig 1

The Board of Trustees of GIM approached us, among several other architects for an invited architectural competition. We made a detailed presentation outlining our conceptual design and ideas. The presentation we made discussed the cultural history of Goa, the landscape, the unique topography and a tradition of colour. We also discussed the specific history that is associated with Goa's architecture. The scheme accounted for the aspirational aspects: its contemporary language and the youthfulness of the design. The clients wanted to use only 25 acre for the initial development of the 50-acre piece of land. While our masterplan accounted for 25 acre, we organised the plan in a way that would provide for future development and anticipate growth. We won the competition and were awarded the project. Over the years, I have found that while competition projects are challenging, they are also immensely fulfilling.

I have always been aware of the land in my design. I insist on walking the sites to understand the patterns of the terrain and vegetation that the design must respond to. These patterns are sometimes overwhelming, like the views that open up at the GIM site, but in other cases, they are intuitive and subtle, like the way water moves on the site or patches of earth on a rocky outcrop. By understanding these on the 50-acre site, we designed the buildings to take advantage of vantage points and respond to powerful forces of topography. The natural arid ground and the designed landscape juxtaposed to interact in a way

Fig 2

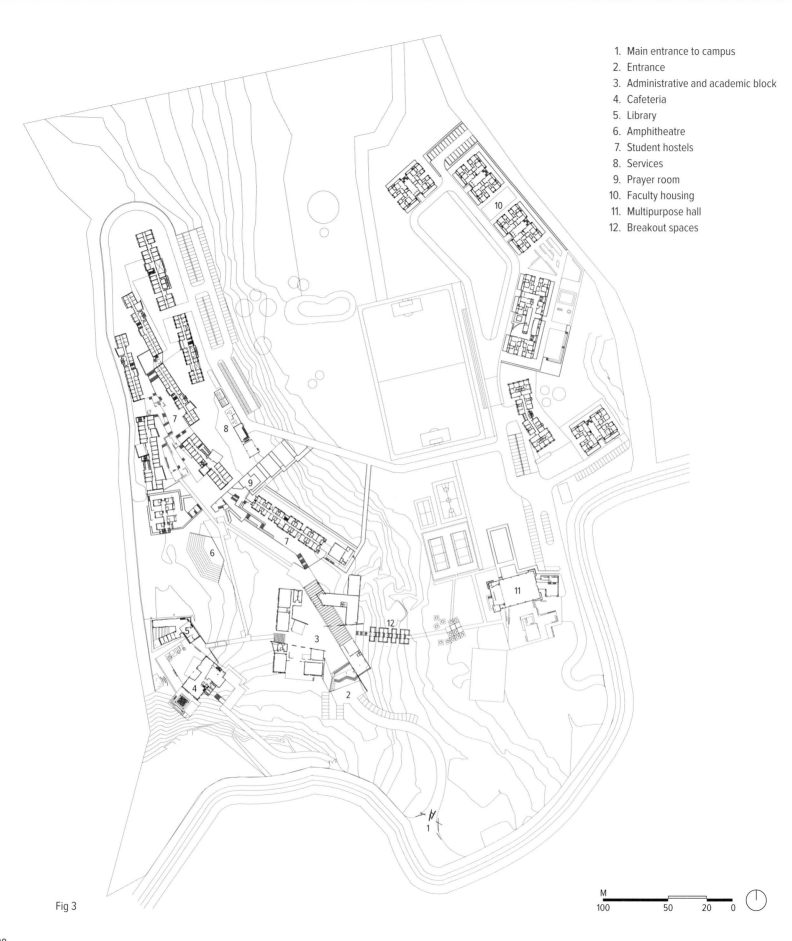

1. Main entrance to campus
2. Entrance
3. Administrative and academic block
4. Cafeteria
5. Library
6. Amphitheatre
7. Student hostels
8. Services
9. Prayer room
10. Faculty housing
11. Multipurpose hall
12. Breakout spaces

Fig 3

M
100   50   20   0

Fig 3. Site plan.

that made the experience of traversing the land comfortable and pleasurable. On the northern end of the site, the residences for the students were designed as linear strips on either side of an arcade-like space. Regular and uniform in plan, the built masses were given rhythmic openings. The tiered landscaping in the centre forms informal and intimate spaces for small and accidental gatherings, which I anticipate the students to use to their advantage to relax, meet, laugh and discuss.

The masterplan with the academic and supporting facilities was initially based on two perpendicular axes, but as we started working with the site, the apparent presence of the axes was diluted by more subtle gestures. The site had an unpredictable terrain. To accommodate the buildings naturally into the land, we decided to fragment the programme in four clusters of buildings spread across the site. These were connected using pathways and landscape. The academic and administrative areas were designed at the apparent intersection of these axes. The library and the cafeteria blocks occupied the highest point on the site with spectacular vistas framed in their architecture. We oriented the student hostels at the northern-most corner, while the recreation facilities were designed on the lowest point of the site. The corners and the core of the institution framed the site and enabled us to sense the expanse of the land. The campus is imagined as a landscape with architectural elements as gestures.

While the masterplan directs a certain development, the clusters of built forms have their independent organisation, and in many ways, they respond to the lay of the land. This enables us to resist the functional-block approach, and we could weave the architecture of the institution with its environment on the site. The built forms come together in places that are concentrations of activity. The central academic cluster is organised around a large plaza. This is a paved area designed, to contain large gatherings of people and defines the formal access to the campus. The buildings around the plaza open up into the central space while framing sweeping views of the Western Ghats on the other side. Depending on the privacy and purpose of the internal spaces, the pattern of the envelope changes in transparency, lightness and permeability. The quality, proportion and placement of fenestrations vary throughout the built form in reference to the immediate and distant context. While some elements repeat and ensure harmony, some are special inserts and help us break the monotony at places where we find an opportunity to do so. By employing differences of levels and changes in textures, we were able to distinguish spaces in a composition of vertical planes and voids. The clusters are thus dynamic intersections of spaces, volumes, surfaces and colours. Complex formal structures dissolve into simple organisational patterns. Walls intersect and overlap to create interesting spaces. The built spaces assume the presence of environmental interventions in a landscape.

While the site plan was being developed, the positioning of the various buildings became critical. I knew the administrative and academic complex had to work at the junction of the axes that I had determined. The academic block is essentially the classroom block with faculty and administrative offices. It has been designed as the heart of the campus. It would also be the first building that visitors would see as they entered the campus and drove up to the elevated part of the site. It also was positioned to capture, through its fragmented plan, the magnificent views on all sides. The entry into the court is through a high portal that leads into this open-to-sky space. Trees have been planted in very careful positions to provide shade in the courtyard from the hot Goa sun. I needed to create a secondary axis from this building to the dormitories on the north side, the library and cafeteria on the west, and the multipurpose hall and recreational facilities on the east. Therefore, the geometry worked by incorporating these cut-outs within the plan to open up these vistas. There are 12 classrooms between the ground and first floors, faculty offices and the Director's offices and conference rooms. The courtyard in the centre works as the collection space for the graduation procession as the young students work their way down towards the hall and the mountains on the east. A truly magnificent moment that they regularly capture in photographs. It becomes a memory, and the buildings around are part of that.

Fig 4. Administrative and academic block under construction.

Fig 5. Administrative and academic block ground floor plan.

Fig 6. Section A.

Fig 7. Section B.

Fig 8. Administrative and academic block first floor plan.

Fig 9. East elevation.

Fig 10. West elevation.

Fig 4

I decided to locate the cafeteria and the library near each other because I believed that the former would always attract the students so the latter would also benefit them. Today, with laptops and Wi-Fi, it is very difficult to get students into libraries. On some campuses, it is because they are one of the few air-conditioned areas that students even enter libraries. I also knew that the view from the western side was just magnificent and so the idea of creating a plaza for the students between the two buildings evolved. This plaza has sunken seating surrounded by newly planted trees, giving shade and comfort to the students as they use this open space. It is lit at night as well and so this group of three areas—the two buildings and the plaza—have become important part of the campus. Break-out spaces are very important on a campus. It is often in these spaces that ideas get created and exchanged. The days of learning being restricted to a classroom are long gone. The buildings are made up of painted surfaces and laterite walls. The roofs have steep slopes, and I often felt that the two buildings were like two birds that could take off into the beautiful Goa sunlight anytime. The interiors have double-height spaces and interesting staircases connecting the two floors. Natural materials like Kota and Jaisalmer stones have been used for the flooring. Fenestrations have been worked out carefully so that the two buildings are in a conversation with each other and the plaza below.

Fig 11. Views of the administrative and academic block in its various phases of construction.

Fig 12. The landscaped courtyard between the Library and Cafeteria becomes a cohesive binding element for the many functions of the campus.

Fig 13. Ground floor plan of Library and Cafeteria block.

Fig 14. North-east elevation.

Fig 15. Section A.

Fig 12

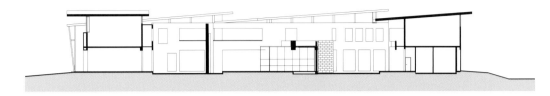

Fig 7

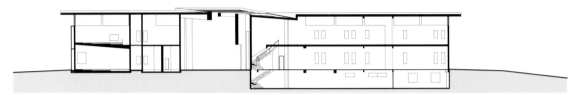

Fig 6

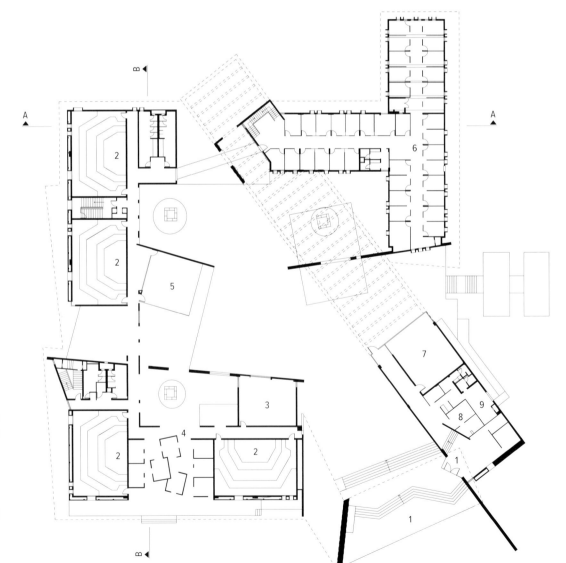

1. Entrance
2. 60-seater classroom
3. 30-seater classroom
4. Breakout space
5. Finance laboratory
6. Faculty office
7. Board room
8. Administrative office
9. Director's office

Fig 5

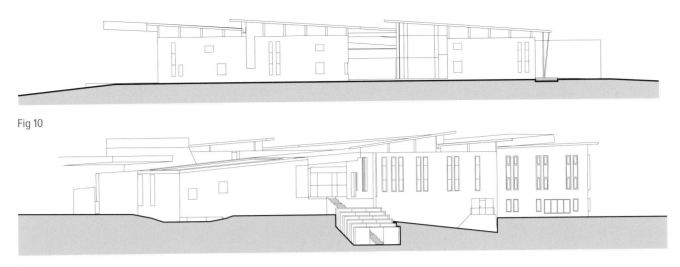

Fig 10

Fig 9

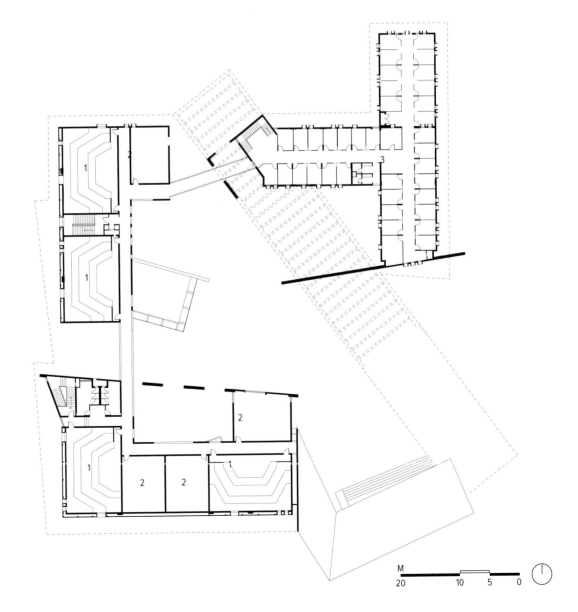

1. 60-seater classroom
2. 30-seater classroom
3. Faculty office

Fig 8

M
20   10   5   0

Fig 11

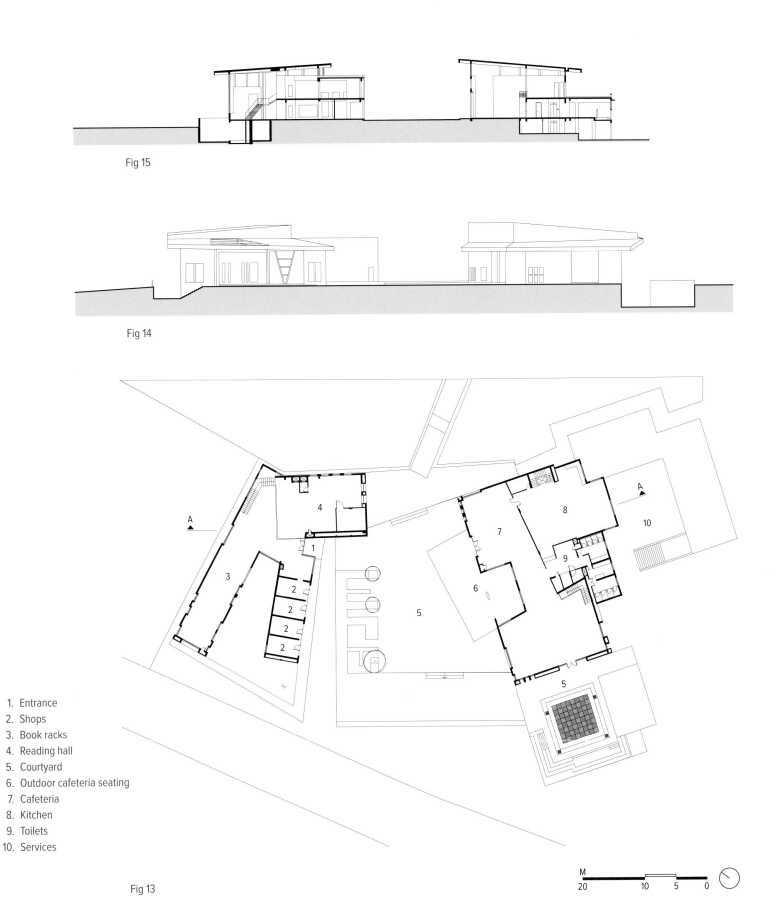

Fig 15

Fig 14

1. Entrance
2. Shops
3. Book racks
4. Reading hall
5. Courtyard
6. Outdoor cafeteria seating
7. Cafeteria
8. Kitchen
9. Toilets
10. Services

Fig 13

M
20   10   5   0

Student housing in any campus is a big challenge. In India, with its cultural traditions and extreme climate, it often becomes more complex. At GIM, I was straight-jacketed with an odd-shaped residual strip of land, and the hostels needed to be a walkable distance from the academic and cafeteria buildings. Goa has a hot summer and heavy monsoon, therefore, distances needed to be carefully calibrated. The north–south strip lent itself to a string of slim buildings that crept along the site creating a central open spine, which worked as a pedestrian walkway punctured with courts and break-out spaces at different levels due to the contours of the land. The steep gradient demanded several retaining walls, and we used the laterite from the site to do so. The linearity of these buildings defined the architectural vocabulary. The repetitive punctures for the windows were broken by angular entrances and walls, and colour was introduced to break the visual linearity. On the western face, the views from the rooms opened up to the magnificent valley and on the eastern face, the hills beyond. The repetitive nature of a particular building type on a site brings a certain strength to the masterplan and now that the construction is complete on the north–south axis, this thought seems to be confirmed.

There is a rhythm and repetition in the way the buildings enclose this street-like space and the manner in which they open into the same. This spine with the steps, podiums and porches at different levels now terminates into a lush plane on the north that we have greened.

Fig 16. Conceptual sketch of the student hostel blocks depicting an intimate streetscape within the campus.

Fig 17. Cluster plan of the student hostel blocks.

Fig 18. Plan of the hostel block 3A.

Fig 19. East elevation.

Fig 20. West elevation.

Fig 16

Two small but critical buildings are introduced here. The first is a multi-faith centre, which is a spiritual building where the students can relax and find solitude, and the second a dining hall for faculty and visiting students. These structures are interspersed between the dormitories, providing relief to the density and acting as anchors to activity and interaction. The institute felt the need for a multi-faith centre where the students could meditate and find some respite from the world outside. The original GIM campus in Ribander, near Panjim, was started by a Jesuit priest and had a space for this very purpose. Here, the client felt a centre could be built that could also be used for other connected disciplines such as yoga, prayer and meditation. The piece of land was small and wedged between the student dormitories with a view of the hills beyond. The building entry was through a small laterite courtyard, which now has a sculpture within it, and then through a sky-lit staircase going down to the centre. The room itself captured the view beyond with stone fins interspersed with glass, which brought in the special quality of light needed for prayer and quietude. The Kota and Jaisalmer stones, and the wood materials used is a combination we have employed in many of our buildings successfully.

Fig 21. Views of the student hostel blocks.

Fig 22. The multi-faith centre where students can pray, meditate and find solitude.

Fig 23. Brinda Somaya (left) and her team on site, with women construction workers.

Fig 22

1. International students hostel
2. Visiting faculty hostel
3. Students hostel A,B,C,D,E,F,G
4. Services
5. Prayer room

Fig 17

M
50   20   10   0

Fig 20

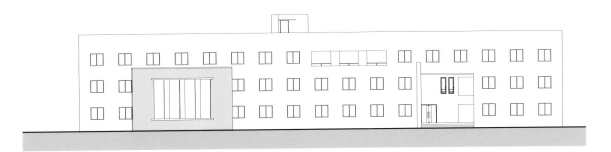

Fig 19

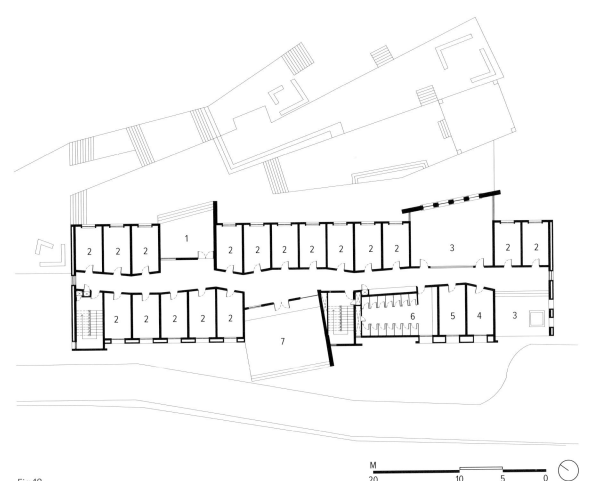

1. Entrance foyer
2. Room
3. Common room
4. Services
5. Laundry
6. Toilets
7. Deck

Fig 18

M
20 10 5 0

Fig 21

We spent much time environmentally planning the campus to harvest rainwater from recharge pits and swales. All the laterite extracted from the site was neatly stacked and used in construction, thus entrapping the embedded energy of the construction process. We designed most of the buildings with cavity walls to keep the heat out, and the deep overhangs enabled us to protect the walls and openings from the onslaught of the Goa monsoon. We also consciously fragmented the buildings, imagining that in 15 years, the landscape will take over and soften the gaps. On the eastern end of the site, there was a plan to only have the assembly hall and other recreational facilities with two blocks of faculty housing. As the demands of the campus grew, we designed the additional housing facilities. The 25-acre campus was quite successful, and while more buildings will be built, the masterplan will continue to ensure that the addition and densification follows a well-regarded scheme.

The construction labour for GIM consisted of men and women, and hence, there were also children in the labour camp. Today, fewer women are found on constructions sites because contractors do not want to be bothered with families. This is in complete contradiction to what I believe in—that women should be welders and masons and painters on these sites—but the situation is such that it has become more difficult for women labour to find jobs on construction sites. The contractor in Goa agreed, under some pressure, to organise classes for the children of the labour working on the site. The site being remote and on top of a hill with no easy access to any nearby school resulted in this cooperation. The class was made up of children of a mixed age group, but that was the best that could be managed. It was a small step in the right direction.

Fig 23

Fig 24

In many ways, the challenge of a greenfield project is to establish points of reference and context, at a site where there is little or no architectural history. The only tools to effectively reference are topography and vegetation. In projects like GIM and House in the Valley (see p. 350), the sites lent themselves to the immediate and distant context that helped frame the agenda for the architecture. Strong relationships can be established with the land and the views and architecture becomes an instrument of generating these new coordinates. This is different from the planning and design of the Zensar Technologies Campus (see p. 65) and the Nalanda International School (see p. 301). The Zensar campus is not an institute, but assumes an institutional scale. While GIM is organic, incidental and less controlled, the Zensar campus is more curated, enclosed and designed to respond to a controlled landscape. The Nalanda International School, on the other hand, are enclosures that embrace the space in a protective way for the children.

On the GIM campus, the MBA students stay for two years on a rigorous academic regime and the environs of the campus become pivotal to their life. Therefore, it is significant for the institution to be a place where life can thrive. There are instances where we come across an image shared on social media by students and faculty, expressing their affinity to this environment. This human engagement with my work is very crucial to me and is one of the central purposes of my architecture. In all my greenfield projects, I have strived to design only the essential so as to tread lightly on the ground and create an environment that is complete in itself. Each work of architecture is distinct as the unique process of design determines the eventual character of the place. It is in the making of this place that the institution is formed.

THE SIGNIFICANCE OF BRINDA SOMAYA'S WORK IN POST-INDEPENDENCE INDIA

JON LANG

In looking at the work of individual architects, it is easy to be entranced by the apparently unique creativity of the buildings they have designed and to write a laudatory essay on their work. In looking at the contribution of Brinda Somaya to architecture, it would be easy to do so. That is not the purpose of this essay. To understand an architect's contribution to their field and discipline, it is important to place their work in the context of the broader evolution of the ideas of the international and local architectural and socio-cultural realm to which they belong. The goal here is to place Somaya's work in its rightful place in post-Independence India. To do so involves looking at the long history of architecture in India, how indigenous and exotic ideas about its nature have unselfconsciously and self-consciously evolved.

India has seen waves of modern architecture brought into the country by outsiders over the centuries. The residue or aftermath of each wave was a set of building forms that matured into forms unique to the subcontinent. The first modernising architectural ideas came from elsewhere in Asia. The building and landscape forms brought with them by the Mughal conquerors ultimately merged unselfconsciously with indigenous traditions to create a diverse set of regional modern building types, structural configurations and aesthetic attitudes. The neo-classic, still referred to as modern architecture, as late as 1952, and the neo-gothic of the East India Company was an outside intrusion that self-consciously sought an Indian architecture with the development of the Indo-Saracenic.

In the early 20th century, individual British architects—such as Claude Batley of Gregson Batley King in Mumbai and Walter Sykes George in Delhi and lesser known firms such as Sudlow, Ballardie and Thompson in Calcutta—broke away from the standard historical products of Briton-headed firms in India to create modern architecture that was a departure from both indigenous and imported building forms in massing and appearance. It was responsive to the Indian climatic and colonial cultural context. They were not radical in the forms they introduced. It was these firms, but even more so their Indian colleagues and competitors, that introduced Art Deco architecture to India. Art Deco buildings, particularly in Mumbai, have stood the test of time. Many are still held in high esteem by architects and laypeople in India today.

The building forms of European rationalism, introduced by European architects and Indian architects who studied in Europe and the United States under major continental architects, came as a big shock. Their introduction coincided with Independence. This essay looks at the impact of this modernist work and the efforts of the often unsung second generation of Indian architects, to learn from the impact of that generation of modern Indian masters. It was a hard act to follow, but ultimately, being more empirical in nature, much of the work managed to merge an understanding of human needs with personal expression to form a modern Indian architecture for the ages. The contribution of each of the architects of this second generation may be unique, but some architects have been more influential than others and some should have been more influential. This essay considers the work of Brinda Somaya in this context.

THE POST-INDEPENDENCE WORLD

Political independence in 1947 brought with it a sense of optimism and the desire to identify an individual sense of place in the global world. It was also accompanied by diverse visions of a future India, which were expressed through architectural form. The two most important were Nehru's view of a modern, socialist nation and the grass-roots neo-traditional India of Gandhi. The former is manifested in the quick adoption of rationalist modernist architecture, as brought home from their studies abroad by a generation of young Indian architects, exemplified by Habib Rahman, Achyut Kanvinde and B.V. Doshi in the core geographical and professional Mumbai–Ahmedabad–Delhi axis and on the periphery by Bennett Pithavadian in Chennai. The latter was manifested in a great variety of historical revival approaches probably best exemplified on the extreme revivalist side by the modern Indian architectural efforts of Sris Chandra Chatterjee and more modernist in character in the work of Julius Vaz.

The work of architects such as Charles Correa and Joseph Allen Stein—both American educated but outside the immediate realm of influence of the continental European masters who had migrated to the United States after the Second World War and were teaching at east coast universities—while rationalist in nature, had strong empirical overtones from the outset of their practices in Mumbai and Delhi respectively. It took a while for the work of Doshi and Kanvinde to become attuned to India; their early designs reflect the ideas of the masters with whom they had studied and/or worked.

What was particularly important was that the work, bit-by-bit, followed the process of indigenisation from the 1970s onwards in much the same way that Mughal architecture became absorbed and adapted four hundred years earlier. The later work of Doshi and Kanvinde came to respect the realities of India in dealing with patterns of life and aesthetic qualities. More radical rethinking of modernist architecture paralleled their efforts.

The criticism of much modernist architecture and, particularly, urban design, led to the emergence of distinct lines of response to the first generation of Indian modernist architecture. The first two were responses to the weaknesses of modernist thought but failed to recognise its strengths. They made the same error of judgment that the modernists themselves had made, rejecting the past architecture by focusing on its problems rather than looking at what had worked well. One was the modern Indian vernacular architecture; the other was what has been called neo-traditional architecture. The first resulted in more flamboyant exterior architectural forms, the second in a looking back to the past for inspiration.

The modern Indian vernacular was an exuberant response to the simple, bold forms of modernist architecture. Two types of displays that appealed to the growing middle class of the country can be identified. They created, perhaps responded, to popular tastes. The first was a melange of past architectural forms of the sub-continent, whether it be Hindu, Islamic or colonial. The second was a parody of the work of the modern masters. It was and is highly popular because it uses elements of past forms that are readily recognised by laypeople, mixed with glass and steel to create an architecture of grandeur. It is an architecture of appearance rather than substance, but much that was built following either approach was remarkably well-executed and should not be lightly dismissed.

Neo-traditional architecture is a product of idealists looking back at patterns of past forms and reapplying them to create an architecture that is "ours". At best, it is the principles rather than the forms per se that are applied to form a new architecture. Aping past vernacular forms is insufficient, even though past forms may give visual pleasure. New ways of life, including the use of automobiles and refrigeration, have to be catered to and new technologies are available to deal with construction more expediently than past techniques. A more thoughtful response to the way modernist ideas had been interrogated by critics was to recognise what they had to offer to the modern world.

Modernist architecture—with its simplicity of forms, structural ingenuity, new materials and relationship of indoor to outdoor space—continued to provide the basis for rethinking the nature of architecture for the burgeoning middle class, their ways of life and the institutions of importance to them. The new designs were a reasoned response to local climatic conditions but also the aspirations of clients and the architects' desires to express their own identities in architectural form.

The last two decades of the 20th century and the first two of the 21st have seen a number of individual architects and architectural firms across India bring fine buildings to fruition. The work of established architects, such as B.V. Doshi, Achyut Kanvinde and Charles Correa, developed from their international modernist roots into work that was attuned both instrumentally and symbolically to the Indian climatic and cultural context. Of particular interest are the second generation of architects—such as Bimal Patel in Ahmedabad and Chandavarker and Thacker in Bengaluru who inherited architectural firms—whose principles produced fine modernist buildings. In addition, new firms emerged on the scene during the 1970s and demonstrated a broad concern not only for designing contemporary buildings but for recognising India's cultural heritage and the housing and institutional needs of the poor. Somaya and Kalappa in Mumbai is among them and, arguably, the most prominent of them. Many of these firms have shown considerable stamina, paving the way for a new generation of architects emerging in the early 21st century. What these firms have in common is a rejection of many trends of postmodern work, which brought 'Indianness' into architecture in a superficial way. In contrast, they sought a modern architecture for a modern world.

Somaya and Kalappa, established in 1975, has been a leading multi-focused architectural firm that has spanned the three generations of post-Independence architecture in India. Less well-known outside India than it should be, in the four decades since it was established, the firm, under the direction of Somaya, has taken the modernist design paradigm a step forward. While recognising the superficiality of much of first-generation modernist thinking, the firm did not fall into the trap of simultaneously rejecting what was thoughtful about it. Its work has been informed by the work of the modernist masters, but also by a close study of the Indian context, historic Indian precedents, and the strengths and weaknesses of the colonial architecture experience. It has been open to foreign influences but not taken in by them.

The firm's combination of interests makes the firm, if not entirely unique, one of a small group of outstanding practices in India. While many architects write in defence of their own work, few produce scholarly monographs. These few include the first-generation masters, Doshi and Correa. The way Somaya has integrated scholarship and practice provides a lesson for architectural practice not only in India but throughout the world. It may well reflect the intellectual richness of her graduate studies at Smith University in arts rather than architecture.

The broad range of Somaya and Kalappa's work retains the simplicity of modernist architecture but with more free-flowing lines, clearer links between inside and outside, and with greater visual richness, both in building patterns and the subtle use of colour. While often pushing the boundaries of technology, it is not an architecture of structural dexterity displaying an architect's esoteric technical skills. The inhabitants and visitors to buildings have not been forgotten while creating a thoughtful work of art. To me, this attitude seems to provide the essence of good architecture and an intellectual precedent, from which other architects can learn and have learnt.

These observations hold across building types, although the opportunities provided for spatial explorations and the constraints under which each type has to operate may differ. Like the work of other leading architects across the world, the buildings designed by the firm include industrial structures, housing, commercial building, including corporate headquarters and individual bungalows. Learning from the experience with one type informs the work on the others. While some of the buildings designed by the firm are set as "objects in space", as modernist principles decreed, others are space-making structures forming part of the urban environment. An understanding of the past has informed Somaya and Kalappa's work without inhibiting it. At the same time, studying the past has not been an independent diversion.

A number of architects have studied past regional architectural forms. Le Corbusier did, and it shaped his work. Somaya's study of the architecture of Coorg is more than a significant contribution to the understanding of the regional architectures of India. Such studies bring attention to the social and cultural practices of a society, which leads to a questioning of what we are striving to achieve today in a changing world that is much shaped by the globalisation of knowledge. Studying the past is often seen as only applicable to the designing of major cultural buildings today. It is, however, also important in understanding the broader relationships between social systems and the built environment that underlie the design of family homes and in understanding the evolving nature of commercial organisations. It also poses questions about how to deal with a country's architectural heritage.

India's heritage—Hindu, Islamic and colonial, religious and secular—is enormous and beyond the financial capacity of the central and state governments to conserve it all. Since the 19th century, the Architectural Survey of India has borne the task of preserving the country's architectural heritage, but its limited resources resulted in only a select number of important structures being preserved. INTACH (Indian National Trust for Art and Cultural Heritage) has been doing the same, and its development has paralleled the work of Somaya and Kalappa.

The concern has been for more than the physical form and materials; the symbolic geography of a place has been equally important. In cities such as Chennai, Kolkata and Mumbai, with their rich architectural histories, the authenticity of acts of restoration while dealing with the reuse of buildings, or the continued reuse by a changing organisation, are always open to challenge. Many buildings have been returned to their former glory, even though they may not be of any particular historic note nor associated with famous people or significant events. Somaya and Kalappa's respect for India's buildings has shown other architects that restoring buildings is as creative and demanding a task as designing new ones.

The firm has been, and still is, one of an influential group of practices in India (and elsewhere) responsible for the restoration of not only architecturally important buildings but also the everyday buildings that give a city its character (and are often subject to the covetous eyes of property developers). Abandoned mills may have the spatial qualities to serve new purposes as designed but as important is upgrading buildings without changing their basic instrumental function. Somaya and Kalappa's ability to show how to make them fit for contemporary ways of life, while at the same time maintaining their basic character, provides a lesson from which others can learn. The clearest example is probably the Cathedral and John Connor School in Mumbai, in which the history of the institution is reflected in the underlying symbolic quality of the restoration, while still reflecting the needs of a modern academic facility.

While this essay has concentrated on placing the work of Somaya and Kalappa into the context of Indian architecture, Somaya also provides leadership in her approach to running a substantial architectural practice. She possesses a unique and exceptional combination of administrative skills and experience through the breadth and depth of the concerns she has addressed. The firm is one of a growing number of successful architectural firms in the world headed by women. Her leadership in the architectural profession over four decades has given courage to firms not only in India but elsewhere (such as SWPlus, headed by Shymika Silva and Christine Wallbeoff in Colombo, Sri Lanka) to chart their own courses and to get their hands dirty in the hurly-burly world of a commercial architectural practice. At a time when many women graduate of architectural schools in India, to the dismay of architectural educators, have short or no professional lives, Somaya has shown a tenacity of purpose that is an encouragement to all those who hope to make their careers in a demanding profession.

CONCLUSION

In today's increasingly global world, many divergent formalistic trends are shaping architecture, as individual architects and firms seek to position themselves in the market-place for services. Their work strives for an individuality in appearance that distinguishes it from that of others. It becomes a branded product that can be bought. This is difficult for any architect.

The architect's potential role is to go beyond designing individual buildings and, through their work, bring the attention of their colleagues and the general public to issues that require discussion. Most, however, tend to focus on celebrating or defending their own works. Brinda Somaya is one of the small groups of architects who go beyond this self-examination to an open discussion of issues of modernity, heritage and sustainability, which are difficult to resolve in built form, and certainly not to everybody's satisfaction. Her work shows the importance of the integration of scholarship and design in modern buildings.

REFERENCES

Bhatia, Gautam. *Punjabi Baroque and other Memories of Architecture*. New Delhi: Penguin India, 1994.

Bhatt, Vikram and Peter Scriver. *Contemporary Architecture in India: After the Masters*. Ahmedabad: Mapin, 1990.

Correa, Charles. "Vistara: The architecture of India." *Vistara* (March 1988): 24–26.

Lang, Jon. *A Concise History of Modern Architecture in India*. New Delhi: Permanent Black, 2002.

Somaya, Brinda and Poonam Verma Mascarenhas. *Silent Sentinels – Traditional Architecture of Coorg*. Mumbai: The HECAR Foundation, 2005.

Srivastava, Amit and Peter Scriver. "Internationalism and architecture in India after Nehru." In *A Critical History of Contemporary Architecture, 1960-2010*. Elie G. Haddad and David Rivkin, eds. Farnham: Ashgate, 2014, 379–99.

HUMILITY AND FIERCE RESOLVE: THE MAKING OF A COMPLEAT ARCHITECT

PORUS OLPADWALA

A non-architect contemplating the life and work of an exemplary designer, I was reminded of the Oxbridge professor of ancient history who found himself lecturing on modern economic history. He started by saying that all contemporary investigations had to begin in the past and then spent the rest of the time talking about the fall of Rome. Fortunately, my connection to the task at hand is a little less tenuous. Four decades as an economic planner in a college of architecture, art and planning made me conversant with the pedagogies of architecture and the built environment, and about six years of leading the college had me responsible for them. It will be educational to review today's architectural instruction in light of Brinda Somaya's distinctive career.

Like all leading designers, Somaya has an extensive oeuvre in architecture as well as planning, an acute sensitivity to place, compelling contemporary designs, a concern for sustainability, substantive contributions to research, scholarship and education, and a large group of high-achieving mentees.

However, she is different in that her feeling for a place extends beyond the built environment to include not just unbuilt spaces, but open spaces[1] and rural communities as well; her contemporary aesthetic is deeply rooted in history and culture, just as her work on heritage is suffused with modernity; her designs have a clarity of purpose that do not require the "protective rhetorical coat... of essays and lectures" to be comprehended.[2] Neither do they fetishise novelty in form and materials,[3] nor is her sustainability of the common "thoughtless" type that Charles Correa criticises.[4] Somaya's contributions to research, scholarship and education are exceptional in their scope and durability.

She also is unusual in her deep social concern. To say that this is not a common attribute in designers at her level[5] would be a considerable understatement. Combined with a pragmatic idealism that functions on the principle that the perfect is the enemy of the good, this concern is manifest in every aspect of Somaya's work: in the large proportion of pro bono projects in her portfolio (20 per cent overall); her demonstrated care for the welfare of building workers on her worksites and her agitation on behalf of all construction labourers;[6] her efforts in supporting artisans and facilitating entrepreneurship in indigenous arts and crafts; and her open and genuinely participatory approach when working with clients, large and small. In each of these, she probably is one of only a handful of designers of her calibre. In uniting them, she is close to unique.

Somaya has combined these three groups of qualities to great success in building and sustaining, over four decades, a major design practice in a profession that everywhere stresses entrepreneurs and is particularly hard on women. As the contents of this book will testify, underlying and anchoring her many separate capabilities are the two central strengths of highly effective leaders: an "extreme personal humility blended paradoxically with intense professional will", or, as the author of the *Harvard Business Review* study titled his work: "The triumph of humility and fierce resolve".[7]

Asked about the formative influences on her stellar career, Somaya credited her liberal, open-minded parents—an electrical engineer and a zoologist—who had broad interests in history, archaeology, architecture, dance and music; who took her travelling the length and breadth of India when young, visiting not just cities but also towns and villages; who gave her full autonomy in deciding her own course in life, insisting only that she strive to find her true calling to enrich her life; and who instilled in her the confidence that she could achieve whatever she set out to do. Torn between archaeology and architecture, Somaya chose the latter, recalling later that "there was never any doubt in my mind from the age of 13 that I wanted to be an architect". Enrolled at India's premier school of architecture in Mumbai, she was "not inspired" by the rigid mode of education, but credits that shortcoming with forcing students to learn on their own, such that "reading became an important part" of her life.[8]

It turns out that these influences also were important in the lives of other leading architects. In a landmark study, the University of California (Berkeley) brought to campus, in 1959, 40 architects for three days of joint psychological assessment in perception, cognition, conformity, childhood, education and professional life. The purpose was to uncover "the peculiar personality profile [of] those committed to making an imprint on the world through physical changes to the built environment". Among the subjects were Philip Johnson, Louis I Kahn, Richard Nelson, Richard Neutra, I.M. Pei, and Eero Saarinen. The profile developed for these and other highly creative people included the features mentioned by Somaya: substantial autonomy accorded by parents, active independent mothers, self-directed learning, and a tendency to be bored with conventional education.[9] In addition, she shares other common attributes uncovered in the study: a healthy restlessness, profound independence expressed through work and not in general rebellion,[10] confidence in one's own artistic trajectory and destiny, a willingness to go up against the status quo in knowledge and professional culture, a childlike curiosity in all things...[11]

Somaya's life and career is a useful medium through which to reflect on some of the more important contemporary issues of architectural pedagogy. A foremost observation is the critical contribution of the liberal arts and culture to exemplary design, whether this be through formal coursework, travel, or personal study.[12] Unfortunately, this criterion, today, seems to be met only by those who study liberal arts as majors at the undergraduate level and go on to study architecture at the graduate level, or by mature (mostly graduate) students with broad life experience. Undergraduate architecture programmes, despite their length (five years), leave little time for electives, and graduate programmes in design, with an approximately three-year term, have even less time to produce "generously educated architects".[13]

Equally important is the realisation that it is of lesser consequence whether students begin the study of architecture as undergraduates or graduates, or in college at all. Some, like Somaya, know that it is their calling from a tender age; others are convinced during undergraduate or graduate study; and still others have unique reasons for entering the profession, for example, Eero Saarinen who confided in the Berkeley study that he would not have become an architect had he grown up in the US and not Finland: "[There] it is normal to follow your father in his occupation"(!).[14] Then there are the designers and builders through the ages who learnt their skill outside of academia "through apprenticeship. (Louis) Sullivan, Wright and Corb never went to architectural school. Even (Edwin) Lutyens had just six months of apprenticeship... It is naïve to think that architecture can be taught only through academic institutions."[15]

That emphatically may be so, but today's reality is that schools and universities are the main locales for the study of architecture, and the debate about the ideal time for instruction continues.[16] Correa went on to observe presciently that "academia... is an industry like any other – one which naturally pushes its own products". Historian Mary Woods has shown for the US how the divergent needs of the professoriate away from practice led to faculties who rarely got involved in professional issues, were no longer advocates for the profession, who shifted their prime allegiance away from the profession to universities and developed separate agendas for the schools. The curricular impact of this is a stress on individual creativity and competition over collaboration and interdisciplinary work; to focus on classical orders, architectural drawing and design, over technological studies, administrative skills and courses in professional practice; and to add a hefty dose of theoretical discourse that both baffles and ill-serves the needs of the larger profession.

In students, this approach instils qualities and attitudes that run counter to Somaya's example. Encouraged to venerate "star" designers, they suspend scrutiny for fear of being dismissed or castigated as philistines.[17] Taught that architecture has an autonomous aesthetic dimension separate from technology,[18] they cultivate a false superiority towards essential collaborators in their enterprise, diminishing the roles of construction,[19] "craft and detail because they might stand in the way of architectural ideas in their purest and most powerful form".[20] Recurring massive cost overruns, shoddy construction and technological fiascos, including and up to those of their idols, are dismissed or given short shrift.[21] The notion of modernism is reduced to "a single sense",[22] one that omits the key ethical and social aspect of the great modernist concern for worker housing, public health and solidarity. Students are led in word and by example to strive for novelty[23] and change[24] for their own sakes, and for the media spotlight these bring. Many leave university with a sense of accomplishment and entitlement that is not commensurate with their capabilities and have a hard time adjusting to their first professional jobs.[25]

Of course, these tendencies are not all the sole preserve of the academy. Woods has shown the strong influence of practitioners in many of these developments.[26] In addition, both professors and practitioners have to contend with the world as it is, and prepare our students to deal with it. This means working within the constraints imposed by the political economy of capital, in a world that favours private- over public-cantered decisions, does not dwell upon inequality, and where decisions about useful objects, including shelter, take a backseat to the generation of income and wealth. Thus, housing, including affordable housing, has become the preserve of developers and landlords, public health of insurance and pharmaceutical companies, nutrition programmes of the agricultural sector, etc. Regardless of the derivation, these changes and their impact on architecture pedagogy have been to direct its core away from Somaya's ethos.[27]

This is the first comprehensive documentation of Somaya's work after four decades of practice. In this, she joins the many other distinguished women designers—in Despina Stratiagos' recent *Where Are the Women Architects?* —whose contributions systematically have been overlooked. In Somaya's case, there is a telling codicil. Early in our association, I wondered aloud why there was not yet such a book on her among the many published on her peers. In reply, she recounted an incident. She was invited to an editorial board with five or six masters to advise on the publication of works of prominent Indian designers. Somaya recalled an emergency meeting of the board to decide upon a replacement subject after the one they had been working on was aborted because of a difference of opinion with the person's family (the architect was deceased). The board members assembled, went back and forth evaluating each one's potential candidacy in turn, but systematically skipped over Somaya, "as if, for this purpose, I was not there". (However, they did solicit her views as they proceeded!) So, I particularly am delighted to be able to contribute to a volume that makes right an egregious omission.

Vikramaditya Prakash has alluded to the "many existences" of architecture that have to be reconciled to produce a "construction... that simultaneously has an internal logic of its own and is created by and understood in the context in which it is situated".[28] Somaya's career is a masterclass in achieving just this, with exemplary sensitivity and a superior aesthetic. Student, teacher and practitioner will do well to inquire more deeply into this unusual designer and person.

Somaya, famously, has defined her temporal cohort as the "Bridge Generation" in Indian design. In this, she does herself and her companions some disservice. A bridge's value purely is transitional, to move material, or in this case, professional knowledge and practice, from one established point or bank to another. It does not itself contribute anything new or substantive to the journey. It does not leave anything behind. It is marked by nothing but movement.

This Bridge Generation is anything but transitional. Its great contribution has been not in moving but evolving the profession from its colonial and Western Modernist mindset at Indian Independence to the new and bold architecture of today's "Under Forties." In so doing, Somaya and her contemporaries provided fresh and lasting insights into conservation, environmental protection, and the incorporation of traditional craft. Somaya herself has been a trailblazer in the profession's notions of relations with and responsibilities towards site workers, especially women.

Every generation is a bridge generation by definition. Somaya's generation has achieved well beyond that. It has been both bridge and pier, both bridge and shore.

NOTES

1. "Lost space," in Trancik's 1986 conceptualisation.

2. Hawthorne, 2014.

3. Kanvinde questions both the cost and the purpose of such design: "Novelty does not last long... there is no reality in this... It is imposed... it becomes a false setting." Dengle, 35. Correa, in the same publication, maintains that architects "have abdicated our responsibility to create meaningful form [because]... we can indulge ourselves with any shape baecause the structural engineer will somehow make it stand... and in any material... So one's imagination turns whimsical – in short, quite meaningless". Dengle, 189.

4. Today's architect's "contribution to making a green environment is to go ahead and design a glass building anyway... but to specify low-E glass – a gesture that might get you a LEED certificate." Correa considers such behaviour part of "the most thoughtless period... in the entire history of architecture... if that is what architecture is about, I'd rather be a dentist". Dengle, 2015, 189.

5. Or indeed most other levels.

6. Her attitude brings to mind Andre Malraux' account of Le Corbusier taking him around Chandigarh, waving his hands to indicate where the Assembly would come up and where law courts "while files of men and women were climbing the inclined planes, like the bowman of Persepolis, with baskets of cement on their heads". Prakash, 150.

7. Collins, 2005.

8. Ruturaj Parikh interview in this volume.

9. Somaya's experience parallels somewhat that of Neutra: he hesitated between architecture and engineering, found architecture professors "most ineffective", "the curriculum stupid", and engaged himself in philosophy, theatre, opera, concerts, readings. Serriano, 185.

10. The study found that creative people quite often are conventional when it comes to non-work manners and actions.

11. Serriano, 2016. The other fields investigated were literature, mathematics and the physical sciences.

12. In addition to her travels within India, Somaya was privileged at a young age to make two visits to North America and to Europe.

13. A goal of early architecture education in US universities. Woods, 67.

14. Serriano, 210.

15. Correa, in Dengle, 204.

16. Debate may be too generous a term. Knowing that I was both a non-architect and a fledgling dean, at our first meeting in his Yale office, Bob Stern advised unsolicited that the best thing I could do for Cornell architecture would be to shut down our undergraduate programme and switch entirely to graduate study. When I asked why, his only answer was that I should be competing against him (Yale) and other peer institutions, all of whom had converted to graduate instruction. "When your President thinks about Cornell's competition, it is not schools like..." and here he mentioned "lesser" universities with undergraduate programmes. When I further pressed why we should terminate a highly successful undergraduate programme—one incidentally had been ranked first in the recently begun *Design Intelligence* surveys—to compete "at a disadvantage" with him and other well-established graduate programmes, he had no answer.

17. Students are not alone in this "willing suspension of scrutiny". Varma, 2010, recounts Indian Prime Minister Nehru's words at the opening of Le Corbusier's Punjab High Court: "I cannot say that I understand the true significance of every part that I see... later, I shall request Monsieur Corbusier to explain it all to me." The faith was enough; the rest would fall into place..." (118).

18. Or in Cocotas' more colourful interpretation, architecture as "a vacuum of aesthetic virtues and vague adjectives"!

19. This applies to the economics of construction as much as to engineering. A leading Indian architect, Raj Rewal pointedly has mentioned that "(T)here are enlightened builders too...", in Kanvinde, 70.

20. Architect Antonio Moreno, who oversees Eisenman's City of Culture in Santiago de Compostela, notes: "... getting the campus built has been a learning process for Eisenman and his team. They had to learn how do a wall, how to do coping." Hawthorne, 2014.

21. Mark, 1990, both enumerates and analyses leading "technological fiascos". There have been many more since then.

22. Rewal's term. He continues, "which to me is a great fallacy. Everybody is modern in their own way... If you can understand the idea of a discipline, and the sense of history, that is modern enough for me." Dengle, 72.

23. Once again, something from which even the great are not immune. "Now I have welcomed very greatly one experiment... Chandigarh... It is totally immaterial whether you like it or not. It is the biggest thing in India of its kind...

It is the biggest thing because it hits you on the head and makes you think. That is why I welcome it. You may squirm at the impact, but it makes you think and imbibe new ideas…" Prime Minister Nehru, quoted in Prakash, 2002, 19.

24. Correa maintains that "based on our current understanding of beauty, any aesthetic endeavour has to keep changing – the artist must stay on his toes, so to speak". Dengle, 186.

25. Woods notes that "practitioners feel estranged from schools [and] … complain that graduates lack technical, production and managerial skills that account for 90 per cent of a firm's time". Woods, 1999, 174.

26. For example, "with the growth of the built environment came large architecture offices who… needed people who could prepare drawings and documents for large-scale commissions. Ecole produced superb draughtsmen and served the needs of the modern office as much as it did the fine arts". 79–80.

27. That said, students and younger professionals, in particular, continue to strive after social relevance. For example, this year's Pritzker laureate Alejandro Aravena. See also Filler, 2015 on Venice-based Studio Tomassociati's work on hospitals in Sierra Leone. But as Cocotas, 2016, points out, structural impediments often derail such ambitions… the expense of training, debt, low starting salaries…"

28. Prakash, 2002. The "gap between the unconveyed aspirations and desires of the client, the secret aspirations and fascinations of the architect, and the distracted yet judgmental perceptions of the users…". 26.

REFERENCES

Collins, Jim. "Level 5 Leadership: The Triumph of Humility and Fierce Resolve." In *Harvard Business Review*, July–August 2005.

Cocotas, Alex. "Design for the One Percent." In *Jacobin*, 6 June 2016.

Dengle, Narendra, ed. *Dialogues with Indian Master Architects*., Mumbai: Marg Foundation, 2016.

Filler, Martin. "Amazing Building Adventures!" In *The New York Review of Books*, 8 November 2015.

Hawthorne, Christopher. "Coda to a Career: Eisenman's City of Culture." In *Architect*, 3 February 2014.

Mark, Robert. *Light, Wind, and Structure*. Cambridge MA: MIT Press, 1990.

Prakash, Vikramaditya. *Chandigarh's Le Corbusier: The Struggle for Modernity in Postcolonial India*. Seattle and London: University of Washington Press, 2002.

Stratigakos, Despina. *Where Are the Women Architects?* New Jersey: Princeton University Press, 2016.

Serraino, Pierluigi. *The Creative Architect*. Monacelli, 2016.

Tavris, Carol. "Breaking Out of the Box." In *The Wall Street Journal*, April 2016.

29 2016. Review of Stratigakos' *Where Are the Women Architects?*

Trancik, Roger. *Finding Lost Space: Theories of Urban Design*. New York: Van Nostrand Reinhold/ John Wiley, 1986.

Varma, Pavan K. *Becoming Indian: The Unfinished Revolution of Culture and Identity*. New Delhi: Penguin, 2010.

Woods, Mary N. *From Craft to Profession: The Practice of Architecture in Nineteenth-Century America*. Berkeley, CA: The University of California Press, 1999.

Woods, Mary N. *Women Architects in India*. London and New York: Routledge, 2016.

THE EMPATHETIC ARCHITECT

MARY N. WOODS

"*As architects, we should create space for people to speak, not to speak for them... A good architect is empathetic to the needs of her users.*"

—Neera Adarkar, 2014

THE ARCHITECT'S IMAGE

Empathy is not a quality traditionally associated with architects. In the popular imagination, they are usually associated with arrogance, wilfulness and uncompromising belief in their own design ideas. Ayn Rand cast an architect, Howard Roark, as the hero of *The Fountainhead*, her 1943 novel celebrating individualism regardless of the costs. And Frank Lloyd Wright and Richard Neutra each claimed that they had inspired Rand's fictional character. Today, the Roarks of the profession are "starchitects" like Rem Koolhaas. A master of architectural theatrics, Koolhaas once reassured a staff member, nervous about meeting a resistant client, by saying: "Don't worry, I will throw a quick tantrum, and then we will proceed as planned." In 2000, Koolhaas won the Pritzker Prize, known as architecture's Nobel Prize, for what the jury cited as his "bold, strident, thought-provoking architecture". Sixteen years later, the Pritzker jury, however, did not choose another starchitect like Koolhaas. Instead, they honoured Alejandro Aravena. The jurors now lauded the 48-year-old Chilean for epitomising "a more socially engaged architect". In response, Aravena (who pointedly used the pronoun "we" to include his partners) said: "No achievement is individual. Architecture is a collective discipline." Their practice was, he explained subsequently, "fuelled more by public service than aesthetic design". Adarkar's empathetic architect, who listens to, collaborates with, and works alongside others was now recognised at the highest levels of the Western architectural establishment. In yet another part of the global south, Brinda Somaya has quietly and steadily been building such an empathetic practice for the last four decades.

EMPATHIES OF ARCHITECTURE

Founded in 1975–76, Somaya's office is substantial in size and production. While most architects practice on their own or with a handful of assistants, her staff roster has long hovered around 75 members. Since its early days, the practice has produced a wide variety of building types and worked at different scales. Projects include not only interiors, hotels and private residences but also biscuit and electronics factories, bank and corporate headquarters, IT and IIT campuses, primary and secondary schools, and museums and exhibition galleries. Masterplanning, along with new building, is also part of the firm's brief.

Long before there were academic programmes for conservation in India, Somaya focused on older buildings. Her commissions have included such historic structures as the Rajabai Tower and modern masterpieces like Louis I Kahn's Institute of Indian Management in Ahmedabad. Such buildings are, she says, "real resources in terms of materials, energy, and labour expended", especially because "we cannot build everything anew in India". While she empathises with the past, she does not fetishise it. Somaya realises the past has no future if it cannot adapt to new purposes and functions. And this is equally true for her own work. Thus, she had many of her buildings, like the Jubilee Church at Sanpada, re-photographed for this monograph. She wanted to underscore the changes they have undergone over the decades since they were first built. The shed that the Sanpada congregants erected on the church terrace to house another worship service would horrify most architects. They would never publish or lecture about it. Yet, Somaya feels this addition demonstrates the viability of her original design and the users' ongoing engagement with it.

Empathy is about the ability to listen. It is also why architects ranging from Adarkar and Damyanti Radheshwar to James Polshek and Tod Williams and Billie Tsien have collaborated with Somaya on public and private projects. Williams told me he and Tsien could never have designed and built the Tata Consultancy Services (TCS) Banyan Park campus without her. Such collaborations always teach and challenge, Somaya emphasises, both her and her staff. Because she listened to their ideas, clients for NRK House and Nalanda International School told me they chose her to design their buildings. But Somaya also attends to those who simply use and even labour on her buildings, like the villagers of Bhadli.

The 2001 earthquake in Gujarat destroyed Bhadli's homes, dargah, temple and school. Instead of relocating the villagers to modern concrete structures elsewhere, Somaya heard what they wanted: a rehabilitation programme using traditional forms and materials (reinforced by seismic-resistant construction) on sites where the buildings had originally stood. The NGO sponsoring the project paid the villagers to construct their own buildings. Together, Somaya and the villagers also worked to rebuild identities rooted in their sense of belonging to particular places. This project, one villager told me, brought Bhadli's Hindus and Muslims together in ways that would have been impossible before the earthquake.

Yet, empathy is not simply listening to others. It is about perceiving needs and dreams that are not necessarily even recognised or articulated. Working closely with traditional artists and artisans, Somaya challenges them to think about creating designs at a larger scale for the contemporary world. Thus, her metal craftsman had never designed copper lanterns the size of those needed for the TCS Banyan Park campus before Somaya commissioned him for work there. The weavers of WomenWeave needed to have new handlooms built to create the large-scale textiles for the partitions and wall hangings at the campus. Somaya argued for a new women's resource centre alongside the rebuilt Bhadli school; this facility now attracts women from the surrounding villages as well as Bhadli.

Empathy is about advocating for the voiceless too. Thus, Somaya has long required that her building contracts include provisions for proper toilets, water, lighting, crèches and schools for workers and their children on her sites. Here they labour and live for projects lasting, she notes, two, three, five or even eight years. Compliance is never easy, she admits, and requires vigilance. She also encourages women head-loaders, who earn the least, to learn skilled trades such as welding and masonry. She stands in stark contrast to starchitects who typically remain silent about the plight of migrant workers on their building sites in Asia and the Middle East. When the late Zaha Hadid was queried in 2014 about working conditions on the construction site for her World Cup Stadium in Qatar, she said it was the government's responsibility. "I cannot do anything about it," she insisted, "because I have no power to do anything about it."

Empathy entails seeing the potential of a south Mumbai garbage dump to transform into Colaba Woods: a garden with play areas, jogging track, readers pavilion and an amphitheatre. Somaya's project was the first public–private partnership to develop an open space in Mumbai. Because it occupied a site with slum dwellers on one side and wealthy residents on the other, she had to fight to make the garden free from any admission charge. Thus, it became a truly public space accessible to both communities. Amidst global aspirations for a car-centric Mumbai of flyovers and expressways, Somaya and her young colleague Shivjit Siddhu advocated for the rights of pedestrians to the city in their Mumbai Esplanade project. Here, they envision lakhs of commuters, residents and visitors streaming into the plazas, gardens, and pathways designed to connect the *maidan*s, commercial areas, and cultural and heritage districts for all pedestrians between Churchgate and Chhatrapati Shivaji stations.

Empathy for the Indian environment entails an understanding of what kinds of forms, materials, finishes and construction methods can thrive over time in the country's remarkably varied climates. Somaya relied on traditional Indian methods such as pergolas, thick walls, water bodies, courtyards and deep window reveals to passively cool and ventilate the Zensar IT Campus in Pune. Here, she shunned the extensive glazing, aluminium cladding, and extensive air conditioning associated with such global architectures. She argues that the mechanical and technological fixes of Western-devised LEED standards, which she notes are incredibly costly just to certify, are unnecessary and inappropriate for India. The Indian designer, she has said, must be both a barefoot architect and high-tech professional.

The rebuilding of Bhadli was about more than the built environment. It also meant resurrecting the ecosystem that once supported agricultural livelihoods. Thus, rain harvesting, drip irrigation and reforestation were also essential for the rehabilitation programme. Sustainability, Somaya understands, must also be about calculating social and economic costs and values for particular communities in India. Thus, the china mosaics she has extensively used in projects such as the TCS Banyan Park campus and the Club Mahindra Kumbhalgarh Fort resort provide ongoing employment for local artisans because of the need to repair and maintain them.

DREAMING IN THE MAINSTREAM

Despite Aravena's Pritzker Prize, Adarkar's empathetic architect is still associated with practitioners working on the fringes of the profession. Called alternative architects, they are seen as limited in terms of their scale and reach. "Dreaming in the mainstream" is how architect Shimul Kadri describes the difficulties and challenges of doing good while building a sustainable practice in the contemporary world. Thus, Somaya's ability to dream in the mainstream makes her an especially important role model for architects in India and beyond. Her mother once told her that she would have to learn "how to pay... [her] rent on earth". That is, how to give back for what she would receive. Brinda Somaya has amply repaid us all as an architect, preservationist, educator and citizen.

REFERENCES

"A good architect is empathetic." KU Leuven News, 2014. www.kuleuven.be. Accessed 7 July 2016.

Pogrebin, Robin. "Pritzker Prize for Architecture is awarded to Alejandro Aravena of Chile." *The New York Times*, 13 January 2016. www.nytimes.com. Accessed 7 July 2016.

"Pritzker Architecture Prize – Alejandro Aravena." 2016. http://www.pritzkerprize.com/2000/announcement. Accessed 7 July 2016.

"Pritzker Architecture Prize – Rem Koolhaas." 2000. www.pritzkerprize.com/2000/announcement. Accessed 7 July 2016.

Saint, Andrew. *The Image of the Architect*. New Haven and London, Yale University Press, 1983.

"Zaha cuts off live BBC interview over Qatar and Tokyo stadium questions." *Dezeen Magazine*, 24 September 2014. www.dezeen.com. Accessed 7 July 2016.

Daniel Zalewski. "Intelligent design: can Rem Koolhaas kill the skyscraper? *The New Yorker*, 14 March 2005. www.newyorker.com. Accessed 7 July 2016.

BRINDA SOMAYA'S PRACTICE AND CONTEMPORARY ARCHITECTURE IN INDIA

RUTURAJ PARIKH

In a recent essay authored by Brinda Somaya, she christened her generation of architects who have practiced in India as the "Bridge Generation". This generation connects the masters who were instrumental in defining an Indian idea of modernity in an era after Independence to the contemporary practitioners who initiated their offices in the post-liberalisation economic and financial context of the 1990s. While a detailed historical analysis of this time in the discussion of Brinda Somaya's work has been made by Prof. Jon Lang in this book, the purpose of this piece is to critically evaluate the relevance and impact of the "works and continuities" of Brinda Somaya's eclectic oeuvre in the landscape of contemporary architecture in India. The change in economic policy of the state in the 1990s by the government of P.V. Narasimha Rao ushered in a new era for private entrepreneurship, which would shape the economy of India. This idea of a liberal field of operation enabled global finance to flow through India, thus fundamentally changing the nature of practice of architecture in the country. While the state was the most significant patron to the architects of the first generation, the private enterprise became the patron to the firms post-liberalisation. The bridge generation of architects in India worked through this critical change, often having to reinvent the fundamentals of practice every 15 years.

In the past two decades, India has seen three primary models of architectural practice. The first model is that of a large-scale commercial firm absorbed in the global development narrative, their agendas completely aligned to the corporate culture. Their work has limited intellectual content. While these offices are committed to new technology, materials and building systems, the architecture they produce is largely dictated by the market and is perhaps valuable to a client interested in a quick turnover.

The second model is that of a "studio" practice: media-savvy and conscious of the context of their work, these offices have largely drawn national and international attention towards contemporary architecture in India in the past two decades. Owing to their interest in discourse, they have perhaps framed the visual narrative of emerging architecture in India, but limited by scale and nature of practice, their impact in the long run, for a country with spectacular building activity, is in question.

The third model is that of an "alternative practice". Articulated as reactions to the mainstream, this set of varied studios and individuals have ventured to structure their models by strongly refusing to adhere to the rules of the game and creating, in their wake, works that seem to have greater proximity to India. Their strength is in operating in peri-urban contexts, attempting to engage with a landscape that is grossly underserved in terms of design. Nonetheless, very few of these practices have been able to scale up their operations and create financial models that do not depend on subsidy.

Somaya and Kalappa (SNK), Brinda Somaya's firm, has built a portfolio that stems from their reluctance to subscribe to either of the discussed contemporary models of practice, perhaps because of Brinda Somaya's resolve to respond to the social and cultural spheres of their work. This insistence on being involved in discussions that are larger than the practice and central to the human condition in Mumbai, where SNK is located, has enabled Brinda Somaya to stay relevant and produce works of value even as the profession is pushed to the peripheries of society. SNK is a mainstream firm where the core methods are still studio oriented, and where the growing scale of practice and projects does not change the fundamental nature of the design process. Brinda Somaya's office has been able to expand their scale and geographical spread without erosion of their foundational values.

PATRONAGE

One of the defining aspects of Brinda Somaya's work (the one that perhaps distinguishes SNK from other contemporary firms) is the diversity of its patrons and beneficiaries. Over the past four decades, SNK has rendered professional services to the government, private citizens, corporate boards, trusts and NGOs, citizens' groups, village panchayats, societies, activists and administrations of small towns. This varied clientele has in turn enabled them to initiate conversations with people from a plethora of cultural and geographical backgrounds.

Sustained dialogues with these people have enriched their work in terms of its intellectual content and its proximity to the realities of India.

SNK has also pushed the known boundaries of their professional engagement. Over the years, they have independently generated projects around pressing civic issues in Mumbai, from the redevelopment of a public park in Colaba Woods to proposing a new pedestrian realm in the form of the Mumbai Esplanade project. There has been an effort by the studio to generate a dialogue with the city, in which architecture and design becomes the citizens' voice. Today, when we have little or no representation from the fraternity in the development of our urban centres, the activist–architect approach of Brinda Somaya and the firm is critical to the profession in India.

When we discuss patronage, we must also discuss the crucial role that the office plays. In many projects, Somaya and Kalappa consciously involve craftsmen, artists and artisans with a stress on allowing them artistic independence and their ability to inform design. In the many places in India that SNK has worked, it has ventured to engage not just the local craftsmen but the skilled workers from the communities in the impactareas of the project, often making them stakeholders in a development. They convince their clients to earmark about 2 per cent of the project budget in all major developments for artworks and murals, thus extending the critical concerns of the project to include reviving traditions and encouraging contemporary art. Being built into the cost of the project, this unique transaction makes the firm's social responsibility a professional obligation.

CONTEXT

While many contemporary architecture firms have been limited by the city as their territory of operation, Brinda Somaya's work is spread across India and encompasses a spectrum of building types, scales and situations. From the densest developments in the heart of Mumbai to remote rural areas in Kutch, from the beaches in Erangal to the Himalayas, the projects include family homes, corporate campuses, schools and universities, village houses, restoration works, factories, temple precincts, luxury residential towers and exhibition design. The diversity of programmes in the studio forces SNK to engage with an exhaustive width of issues: complex and demanding problems that are either anticipated or are thrown in as surprises by India. This enforces an approach that rejects prescriptive design strategies, thus empowering people at SNK to seek new and unique ways to imagine and create architectural environments. There is a sense of collective ownership of the project, and their work establishes strong and tangible relationships with the many layers of its influence.

Brinda Somaya's buildings are approachable, and while the vocabulary is contemporary, the environments of her design are gentle and reluctant to impose their presence on those who inhabit them, unlike most contemporary work in India that is difficult to appreciate beyond the exact moment it is photographed. Her work can be located in the cultural context of India, a country of constant inspiration and reference for her. Somaya draws from many things Indian: crafts, traditions, history, landscape, colours, art, and most importantly, the people of this country and their boundless resourcefulness. Her reluctance to engage with architectural theory and her distaste for "theorising" her practice enables her to be much visceral in her ideas. Her liberal arts background has perhaps given her an opportunity to seek a different context for her work, a context that is derived from a condensed continuity of India's modern architecture and yet located on the peripheries of its dogmatic concerns. A place closer and more central to the society it serves.

LANGUAGE

"Non-stylistic", says Somaya as she talks about the visual aspects of her work. Her buildings don't intend to shock, but there are many moments of awe as one moves in and around them. They are designed environments completely conscious of the human scale and of human interaction with architecture. This dissociation of the architecture of Brinda Somaya with its photograph lends her work a certain spatial quality that the users of the buildings relate to and cherish. Each project is extremely specific, and the firm takes time to frame the core concern in each project, thus rewriting the programme many times till it becomes objectively close to the agenda of the exercise. Eventually, the landscape takes over, the boundaries diminish, and the work of design assimilates itself in its situation. Nothing is templated. This inside-out approach to architecture also gives the firm a chance to produce work in collaboration. For SNK, design is a conversation and its architecture derives its merit from the discussion each one brings to the table.

From the village of Bhadli, where the firm worked as a catalyst organisation helping people build for themselves in a process of post-disaster reconciliation, to the ongoing restoration of the IIM Ahmedabad campus where Louis I Kahn's powerful spaces are carefully studied and restored by SNK, the firm invests itself in looking minutely at the problem at hand. The process of rewriting the brief puts all projects on unique trajectories. The aesthetics and the visual language of Brinda Somaya's architecture is a consequence of this deep engagement with the critical agenda of the project.

DISCOURSE

A general lack of conscious journalism and intolerance towards quality criticism in India has created a culture of celebrating mediocre buildings. One can see this trait in the heaps of glossy magazines that flood the market today. Brinda Somaya has consistently resisted this superficial portrayal of architecture, often speaking against the "image-driven" media. Her work looks for a larger agenda. This view changes the narrative of practice at SNK as the people venture beyond their professional obligations towards their clients and propel their projects into larger societal concerns. Some of these concerns are central to practice and building: the condition of labourers on project sites, women in the construction industry, education and well-being of children of migrant workers, vocational training, investing in skill development and fairness of wages to list a few. Some questions debated at the firm are value-based: the role of the professional in the society, the relevance of working in a city, engagement with social and cultural causes, art and patronage to crafts and so on. And some issues are abstract: ethics, originality, inspiration, purposefulness and semantics.

Brinda Somaya's investment in architectural discourse is pragmatic. She is interested in thoughts and ideas that challenge real issues faced by practitioners in a country such as India. Over and above her passion for architecture, Brinda Somaya is deeply interested in society and her work is her way of conversing with it. She is concerned about the stature of the profession and apprehensive of the isolation in which architects keep speaking with other architects. A sense of diminishing value and an urgency to create a platform for discussing more pressing issues prompted her to create The HECAR Foundation, the first and one of India's few non-profit organisations whose primary agenda includes architectural discourse and stewardship of the built environment. An acronym for Heritage, Education, Conservation, Architecture and Restoration, The HECAR Foundation has initiated and supported many projects in the public realm that deal with issues that Brinda Somaya considers central and urgent to this agenda. In the year 2000, through HECAR, she curated the first conference and exhibition on women architects of India and South Asia titled *An Emancipated Place*. Since then, HECAR has spearheaded and supported publications, research initiatives and urban proposals that thrust SNK into conscious activism. As an organisation, HECAR supports professional discourse on some of the most urgent issues that concern the city of Mumbai and the discipline of architecture in India. The books that HECAR has supported as research projects and published are a testament to the critical role a professional can play: that of a trustee of the built environment.

OEUVRE

Today, the lack of civic engagement in the absence of public projects has pushed many firms to work in a few organised and predictable domains. We no longer have architects with large, mainstream offices interested in the small project of significance. The designing of streets, bus stops, temple-courtyards, orphanages, *anganwadi*s, factories, public parks and heritage precincts only interest institutions of design where the academic discourse finds itself completely disconnected from practice. Since its inception in 1975, the office of Brinda Somaya has produced exceptional works of architecture, landscape design, urban design, exhibition design, interior design, conservation and restoration. More than four decades on, Brinda Somaya's daughter and associate in practice, Nandini Somaya Sampat, represents a new generation of architects who now work in the office. The office continues to function as a large studio, with teams of architects working on independent projects of varying scales. At the core of this busy place lies a DNA, a thread and a continuity that can be traced back to the early days of practice, when Somaya used to work from a petit office with her sister Ranjini Kalappa, whose name continues to represent the practice. In this DNA, the values of a deeply ethical, reflective, intellectual and pragmatic practice can be deciphered. The exhaustive portfolio of more than 200 built projects represents their professional success: a rare large practice led by a woman architect not just in India but in the world.

Brinda Somaya often talks about clients who have continued their association with the firm for years. With very few firms in India that have a portfolio as large as SNK, there is still no formula or predetermined palette in their work. For an old practice, SNK continues to surprise observers with fresh ideas and an experimental spirit. On a recent visit to the site of restoration of Kahn's buildings at IIM Ahmedabad with Brinda Somaya, I could observe the ease and clarity with which she interacts with the contractors, masons, welders and project managers, who struggle to keep up with the pace of conversation. She does not miss a single detail, and one can sense the urgency in her tone. She is excited by the experiments on the site and has many questions for the people around, who are alert in her presence. Back in office, she has the same effect on people around her. Until the 1990s, the works of Brinda Somaya were unknown to many observers of architecture in India, but this initial isolation enabled Somaya to frame a unique model for her practice. She continues to be excited for new commissions, and in much of Brinda Somaya's efforts, the purpose of her work and its consequences are her primary motivation.

REFERENCES

Somaya, Brinda. *Architecture in India: The Bridge Generation*. ThinkMatter, 2015. www.thinkmatter.in.

Somaya, Brinda and Urvashi Mehta. *An Emancipated Place: Women in Architecture*. The HECAR Foundation, 2000.

Lang, Jon, Madhavi Desai and Miki Desai. *Architecture and Independence: The Search for Identity— India 1880 to 1980*. Oxford University Press, 1998.

Bhatt, Vikram and Peter Scriver. *Contemporary Architecture in India: After the Masters*. Mapin Publishing, 1990.

EPILOGUE

TOD WILLIAMS AND BILLIE TSIEN

I remember our first meeting with Brinda Somaya. We were driven to her office to meet our future partner in a project that, when completed, will have spanned nearly two decades. The area of Mumbai where she had her first office was called the Fort. The streets were dusty, shaded by tall sycamore trees and lined with large Victorian buildings in various states of disrepair, many seemingly abandoned. Over the years, we have seen these buildings being beautifully restored. That this has happened is primarily through Brinda's powerful championship of preservation, both through the example of her own work and through her public advocacy.

Being new both to the project and to India, everywhere we looked there was something amazing. So, when we stopped in front of a small office building that seemed a bit forlorn, we were surprised but also expectant. We were told to go up to the third floor. The wooden steps were old, slightly tipped and very shallow. It seemed that you ascended many steps without making any headway. The walls were scuffed and stained red with spittle from chewing betel leaves. We arrived at the correct floor more than a little winded and entered another world: bright and cool with quiet, purposeful people at work. Upon being led to a conference room, we were given lovely cups of sweetened tea by the two young men whose job it was to provide tea for the office. And then, in walked Brinda.

She is a beautiful and elegant woman, almost always dressed in a sari.

But what one notices first is the warmth of her eyes.

This was the beginning of a long collaboration and friendship with a remarkable woman. What we have come to know over time is that her deep warmth is matched by a quiet and immense strength and integrity, driven by a love for the sense of place. This integrity has led other architects to seek her advice and partnership on projects. Her connections are global. We feel profoundly fortunate to be recipients of both her wisdom and her friendship.

India, like all the world, seems to be rushing headlong into huge change. Architecture is, for better or worse, an agent of the change. The work of Brinda Somaya sits squarely in the present but has roots in a culture that is timeless. It is an architecture that, while absolutely contemporary, respects the work of the hand. She understands the grace that comes from more humble interventions such as tilework, embroidery, and hand-hammered copper and block-printed fabric. This is a place where craft, both simple and exquisite, still lives. The crafts of India are the identity of India. It is this love of the material culture and the sense of place that it instils that has led Brinda to create projects ranging from IT campuses to schools to housing for earthquake victims, and these always have a strong sense of appropriateness and place. They are, no matter what the scale, always deeply humane.

In the Bhadli village reconstruction project in Kutch, Brinda and her team took the time to meet and connect with the villagers who had lost their homes to a tremendous earthquake in 2001. They determined that what was needed was not architect-ordained forms, but rather a way of encouraging the villagers to rebuild their homes themselves on their original sites. Providing funds and technical expertise and a simple set of design strategies, 150 homes were reconstructed in one year. As an architect, she brought all her skill but left behind her ego. The nomination for an Aga Khan Award in 2007 was a recognition of the importance of this work.

In Mumbai, Brinda has become known as an urban conservationist. She believes in saving the bones of the city. As she has said, "If you don't save the past, there is no future." Her commitment to preservation is demonstrated in her restoration of the Rajabai Tower and the Mumbai University Library. Designed by George Gilbert Scott and constructed in 1878, this landmark needed serious infrastructural work—electrical and structural— as well as restoration. To do this kind of work invisibly, ingenuity must be fuelled by a passionate commitment.

At the opposite end of the spectrum is the Zensar Technology campus. This is a state-of-the-art facility for 2,000 people. Here, she unites the simple, strong building forms with the very architectural presence of a stone wall. The stone speaks of time and the hand. This stone-wall enclosing landscape, creating courtyards and carrying water is a beautiful expression of her architectural vision, which strives to balance the built work with the landscape. Here, unlike Bhadli village or her restoration work, her vision and ego were in full play.

These disparate projects exemplify the character of Brinda Somaya. She has a sense of responsibility to the larger world in terms of her global leadership on the issue of the preservation of both humble and exalted communities. At the same time, she has a powerful effect on the immediate world in terms of her general practice. She is one of the most powerful voices in India, a person who is greatly respected and admired. Everything she does is done with the utmost integrity. She answers to history, and she answers to the child. Our own lives have been made richer by knowing her.

The work of Brinda Somaya is informed by a deep love of people and of place.

You can see it in her eyes.

CHRONOLOGY

1970–1980

THE UNITED SERVICES CLUB, 1975, Mumbai (unbuilt)

A clubhouse comprising of cluster of smaller buildings. It was the first pro-bono project of the studio.

THE BOMBAY PRESIDENCY GOLF CLUB, 1975–1976, Mumbai

For the Bombay Presidency Golf Club. An extension to the club building that included a swimming pool and service facilities. This was the first completed work by the studio.

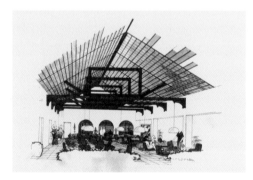

PARLE PRODUCTS FACTORY, 1976–1978, Mumbai

For Parle Products Pvt. Ltd. The addition of a time office and a wheat storage godown for the existing Parle factory in Vile Parle.

SARMA HOUSE, 1976–1977, Pune

For Suzanne and Ramu Sarma.

MAHADEVAN HOUSE, 1977–1978, Bengaluru

For Ponnie Mahadevan.

WEST END HOTEL, 1979–1981, Bengaluru

For Indian Hotels Co. Ltd. Restoration and upgradation of the existing buildings and addition of 100 rooms. The existing structures built in the fifties and sixties were renovated to harmonise with the Victorian architecture of the older buildings. Pitched roofs, the lace-like qualities of the Victorian detail in the roof fascias, the deep shaded quality of the arched and colonnaded balconies were used as a model to blend into the lush garden environment. The new buildings have a contemporised architectural vocabulary of the existing structures.

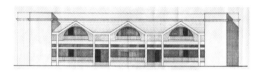

HOUSE BY THE SEA, 1979–1981, Mumbai

For Tata Electric Companies. Located on Erangal beach, this guesthouse was designed as a series of pavilions bringing in a feeling of the beach and the sea beyond. (See p. 336)

TEC STAFF HOUSING, 1980–1982, Mumbai

For Tata Electric Companies. Multistorey staff housing in a high-density suburb at Trombay.

RESORT IN COORG, 1981, Harangi, Hangala Murkal, Coorg (unbuilt)

For Department of Tourism, Government of Karnataka.

1981–1990

EXPORT SHOWROOM, 1981, Mumbai

For Madhya Pradesh Export Corporation.

HOTEL OCEANIC, 1982, Chennai (unbuilt)

For Indian Hotels Co. Ltd.

AHMED HOUSE, 1983, Chennai

For Imtiaz Ahmed. A house designed for a traditional multigenerational family.

TEC SIMULATOR AND CONTROL ROOM, 1983–1984, Mumbai

For Tata Electric Companies.

VOLTAS INDUSTRIAL PLANT, 1983–1985, Thane

For Voltas Ltd. A factory building for a hermetic motor plant. The workspace within the factory was lit by a large north light glazing bringing in a steady light.

TEC SWIMMING POOL COMPLEX, 1983–1985, Mumbai

For Tata Electric Companies. An Olympic-size swimming pool and 1,000-seater stadium.

 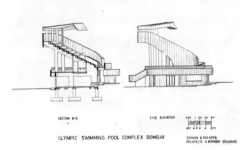

SPASTICS SOCIETY SCHOOL, 1983–1985, Bengaluru

For the Spastics Society of India. The building provided for the physical limitations of the children requiring supervision and care, whether at work, in their classrooms or at play outside. It was important that the general atmosphere of the school be bright, airy and cheerful by creating a sense of space and use of strong primary colours.

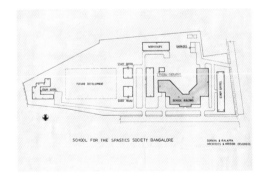 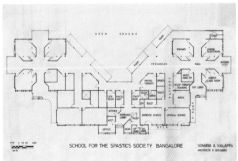

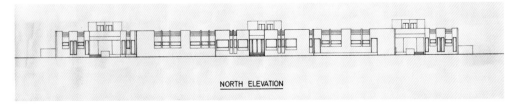

NORTH ELEVATION

HOLIDAY INN, 1983–1986, Bengaluru

For Mac Charles India Ltd. Interior design for this 200-room hotel included a stained-glass atrium that floated 70 ft above the entrance level. Public areas were designed with extensive detailing and integration of cutting-edge technology for that time that included bubble elevators.

UML GUESTHOUSE, 1984, Uttarkashi

For Usha Martin Ltd. The renovation and extension of the existing structure, along River Ganga.

VOLTAS PLANT, 1984–1986, Pune

For Voltas Ltd. A factory building for a switchgear plant.

PAREKH HOUSE, 1984, Ooty

For K.D. Parekh. Restoration and extension of a private residence.

GEC OFFICE, 1985, Mumbai

For General Electric Corporation. Interior design of an office for a multinational conglomerate.

HOUSE BY THE HILL, 1985–1986, Nashik

For Shashikant Garware. The design of this contemporary house creates a stark contrast with the hill that formed the backdrop of its architecture. (See p. 340)

TEDS FACTORY, 1985–1987, Bengaluru

For Tata Electric Companies. This factory complex was spread over 68,000 sq. ft. It was designed to create an interesting space that dispelled preconceived notions of how industrial buildings should appear.

HOUSE BY THE LAKE, 1985–1986, Lonavala

For the Tata Electric Companies. This guesthouse is located on the shores of Walwan lake. (See p. 344)

UML GUEST HOUSE, 1986, Kolkata

For Usha Martin Ltd.

MARUTI SUZUKI OFFICE, 1986, Mumbai

For Maruti Udyog Ltd.

DODSAL PVT. LTD, 1987, Bengaluru

For Dodsal Pvt. Ltd.

BEST & CROMPTON OFFICE, 1987, Mumbai

For Best & Crompton Engineering Ltd.

OBEROI COMPLEX, 1987, New Delhi (unbuilt)

For the Oberoi Group. Masterplan of an institution for hotel management studies and student housing.

SIMURG HOTEL, 1988–1992, Tashkent, USSR

For GOSKOMINTOURIST, the central tourist organisation in the USSR. A 600-room hotel designed as a T-shaped tower block of 11 floors set on a three-storeyed podium, which accommodates public facilities. In 1985, as a consequence of the Indo-Soviet Trade Protocol, tenders were floated exclusively for Indian companies for building three international-class hotels in Samarkand and Bukhara. In December 1987, the consortium led by Tata Projects Ltd., of which Somaya & Kalappa was a part, won the Simurg Hotel. The project involved working with several women engineers heading various government departments in Tashkent and was unique for that time. The inspiration for the hotel came from the distant past of the city, with its monumental gates and minarets. The design attempts to capture this spirit by striking a balance between the traditional architecture of these cities and the modern buildings with new materials, ideas and technology.

INDMAG, 1988, Bengaluru
For Dodsal Indmag Ltd.

COLABA WOODS AND SPORTS COMPLEX, 1988–1989, Mumbai
One of the earliest public–private partnerships in Mumbai that created a park for the neighbourhood. (See p. 199)

HOTEL SREE KRISHNA, 1988–1990, Hyderabad
For Hotel Sree Krishna Ltd.

WARTSILA DIESEL OFFICE, 1989, Mumbai and Delhi
For Wartsila Diesel India Ltd.

NRK HOUSE, 1989–1990, Mumbai
For Naveen Kapur. Adaptive reuse of selected ancillary buildings in the Kamala Mills compound into a contemporary office and garment showroom. (See p. 168)

UML CLUB HOUSE, 1989–1990, Ranchi
For Usha Martin Ltd.

GREEN PARK HOTEL, 1989–1991, Hyderabad
For Diana Hotels Ltd. One of the first budget hotels in Hyderabad.

GOOD RELATIONS, 1990, Mumbai
For Good Relations (India) Pvt. Ltd.

BELVEDERE COURT, 1990–1992, Bengaluru
For Tarapore Constructions Pvt. Ltd. A housing complex based on the courtyard concept, with each apartment overlooking a lush green space.

1991–2000

TEC STAFF HOUSING, 1991, Mumbai
For Tata Electric Companies. A multistorey housing complex at Sewree.

BOMBAY HOSPITAL AND MEDICAL RESEARCH CENTRE-ADMINISTRATIVE SECTION, 1991, Mumbai
For Bombay Hospital Trust.

NATIONAL INSTITUTE OF CONSTRUCTION MANAGEMENT AND RESEARCH (NICMAR), 1991, Pune (unbuilt)
For NICMAR Trust.

HSBC HEADQUARTERS, 1991–1992, Mumbai
For Hong Kong and Shanghai Banking Corporation Ltd. The façade of the Mumbai headquarters building was restored along with cleaning and repairing of the pavements around the bank, thus impacting change in the building and its immediate surroundings. The ground, mezzanine and first floor were redesigned to capture the rich heritage.

LEELA BEACH RESORT, 1992, Goa

For Hotel Leela Venture Ltd. Redesign of the existing banquet facility into a conference centre.

RAMACHANDRAN HOUSE, 1992, Bengaluru

For Anita and Kris Ramachandran.

HOLIDAY INN, 1992, Mumbai

For Ramesh Khanna. Design of the lobby and ancillary areas.

PRUDENT TOOTHPASTE FACTORY, 1992, Lonavala

For Parle Products Pvt. Ltd. An industrial project entailing the building of a toothpaste factory.

HSBC, 1992, Bengaluru

For Hong Kong & Shanghai Bank Corp. Ltd.

GARMENT EXPORT OFFICE AND SHOWROOM, 1992, Mumbai

For Boomclub Inc.

AMBROSIA INNS, 1993, Hyderabad

For Ambrosia Inns Pvt. Ltd. Interior design for a restaurant and bar complex.

PEERLESS HOTEL, 1993, Kolkata

For Peerless General Finance and Investment Co. Pvt. Ltd. The existing 'Ritz Hotel' in Kolkata was redesigned and upgraded.

THE CATHEDRAL AND JOHN CONNON MIDDLE SCHOOL, 1993–1994, Mumbai

For the Anglo Scottish Education Society. The stone building was restored to its original character and was connected visually with the new extensions to form a cohesive whole. (See p. 102)

CITICORP OFFICE, 1993–1994, Bengaluru

For Citicorp IT Industries Ltd.

WARTSILA DIESEL STAFF HOUSING, 1994, Khopoli

For Wartsila Diesel India Ltd. This project succeeds in combining openness with privacy in the same complex where people live and work. The staircase as a central core creates a vibrant and interactive space, thereby instilling a sense of community.

ING BANK, 1994, Mumbai

For Internationale Nederladen Bank. Apart from fulfilling the functional and technical requirements of the bank, it was ensured that the bank's corporate image be preserved, resulting in an elegant corporate office interior.

CEEBROS HOTELS, 1994, Chennai (unbuilt)

For C. Subba Reddy. Architecture and interior design for 108-bed hotel.

LEELA SCOTTISH LACE OFFICE, 1994, Mumbai

For the Leela Lace Pvt. Ltd. The four-storey warehouse was transformed into an office complex for the garment export group. By puncturing the floor slab and introducing skylights the departments were connected vertically to create a dramatic interior space.

SWAMI NITYANANDA ASHRAM, 1994–1995, Ganeshpuri, Thane

A project that included revitalising the area surrounding the temple which had deteriorated over time. The upgrade included careful repainting of the temple, creation of a plaza and introduction of a decorative stone pattern flooring. (See p. 202)

BNP BANK, 1995, Pune

For Banque Nationale de Paris. Interior design of a functionally efficient and sophisticated corporate office.

THE CATHEDRAL & JOHN CONNON SENIOR SCHOOL, 1995–1998, Mumbai

For the Anglo Scottish Education Society. The restoration and expansion of the senior school building. (See p. 108)

DHARAM VILLA APARTMENTS, 1995, Mumbai

For Dharam Villa Co-op Housing Society. Located amidst the high-rise buildings on Mumbai's Bhulabhai Desai Road, this residential building was designed to take advantage of the sea view.

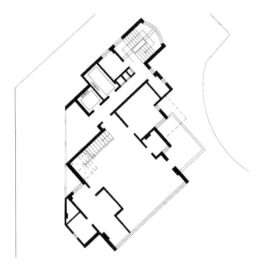 

HOUSE BY THE TEMPLE, 1996, Bhusawal

For Sree Vindhya Paper Mills. Designed along the axis of an adjoining temple, the site was flat, barren and located within a factory complex. The rooms are linked with connecting corridors forming landscaped courtyards. Screen walls with openings protect and give depth to the building from the extremely hot summers.

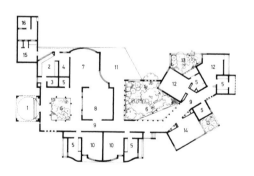 

S.B.C. WARBURG OFFICE, 1996, Mumbai

For M/s. S. B. C. Warburg Securities Asia Ltd. Interior design of a corporate office that integrated the aesthetic, branding and functionality requirements put forth.

MARG CORPORATE OFFICE, 1996, Mumbai

For Market and Research Group.

NAIR HOUSE, 1996, Mumbai

For Captain Nair. Expansion of a heritage building for multigenerational residential use. This beautiful bungalow existed within the property of the Leela Hotel in Mumbai.

GODREJ SHOWROOM, 1996, Thane and Pune

For Godrej GE Appliances.

MECKLAI FINANCIAL COMMERCIAL SERVICES, 1996, Mumbai

For Jamal Mecklai. Located on the first floor of a warehouse adjoining the historic Ballard Estate area, this 2,000 sq. ft attic served as a store of an office on the ground floor. Without touching the external walls or the roof this 'shed' was converted into a dynamic and colourful experience for an ebullient client.

UBS, 1996, Mumbai

For United Bank of Switzerland Ag. Interior design of the corporate office in collaboration with M. Moser Associates Ltd., Hong Kong.

ELBIT DIAGNOSTICS, 1996, Bengaluru

For Elbit Medical Diagnostics Ltd. Transformation of an existing non-descript building into a state-of-the-art medical diagnostic centre offering a wide range of services. The core of the design bridged the gap between aesthetics and functionalism and resulted in a building with a strong identity.

JINDAL CORPORATE OFFICE, 1996, Bengaluru

For Jindal Vijayanagar Steel Ltd. Interior design of offices located at Manipal Centre.

SATYAM CORPORATE OFFICE, 1996-1998, Hyderabad (unbuilt)

For Satyam Computers Services Ltd.

SONATA SOFTWARE OFFICE , 1996, Bengaluru
For Sonata Software Ltd.

WARTSILA DIESEL CORPORATE OFFICE, 1996, Belapur, Navi Mumbai
For Wartsila Diesel India Ltd. Interior design of a workspace.

BRADY GLADYS PLAZA, 1996–1998, Mumbai
For Naveen Kapur. This project revealed the gradual transformation of 'The Street' into a booming commercial district. This contemporary terraced structure integrated landscape spaces with offices and workshops of five different companies. (See p. 172)

APARTMENT BUILDING, 1997, Bengaluru
For Pearson Builders Pvt Ltd.

OFFICE & SHOPPING COMPLEX, 1997, Hyderabad
For Nava Bharat Ferro Alloys Ltd.

GANJAM JEWELLERY SHOWROOM, 1997, Bengaluru
For Ganjam Nagappa & Sons Pvt. Ltd. A project that entailed redesigning of the interiors of a showroom.

BNP PARIBAS, 1997, Mumbai
For Banque Nationale de Paris. An urban renewal project in the Fort area of Mumbai that created a new corporate image for the bank, apart from fulfilling the functional and technical requirements.

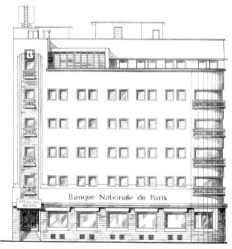

GOKALDAS IMAGES, 1997–1998, Bengaluru
For Jagdish Hinduja. The challenge lay in designing the corporate headquarters of a garment export firm in a long and narrow plot. The various functional blocks were staggered along a spine corridor creating several courtyards of varying forms and functions. Architectural elements including skylights, double heights, sculptural walls and finishing materials were employed to tie these spaces together. White columns accentuate the two-toned grit finish external walls spanning a total area of 7,000 sq. m.

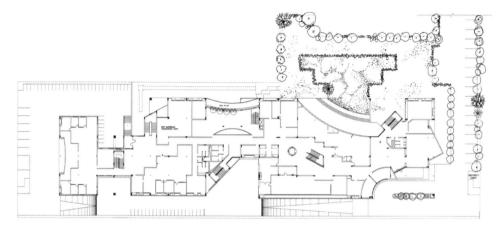

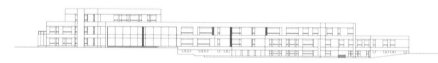

BSES MANAGEMENT TRAINING INSTITUTE, 1998–1999, Mumbai

For BSES Ltd. The institute comprises of classrooms and an auditorium.

HOME FOR THE AGED, 1998, Kodagu

A project spearheaded by a 91-year-old gentleman, who identified the need for an old peoples' home in the area. The home was designed and submitted to his social services group, who raised money to build one house at a time, ultimately resulting in a highly successful project.

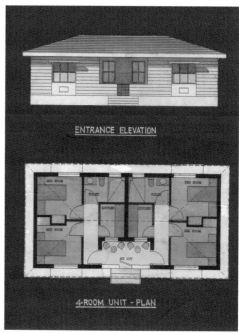

ENTRANCE ELEVATION

4-ROOM UNIT - PLAN

THE CATHEDRAL & JOHN CONNON JUNIOR SCHOOL, 1998–2001, Mumbai

For the Anglo Scottish Education Society. Restoration of the heritage building, expansion and upgradation of the later additions and the creation of a fourth floor over the entire footprint of the building. (See p. 115)

THE SHIRT COMPANY, 1999, Mumbai

For Shivanand Shetty.

JAMAAT ART GALLERY, 1999, Mumbai

For Pravina Mecklai. Conversion of an office space in an old building into a contemporary art gallery.

TATA HOUSING APARTMENT COMPLEX, 1999–2001, Chandivali, Mumbai

For the Tata Housing Development Co. Ltd. Housing complex containing a clubhouse and a swimming pool. The odd shaped plot and severe setback requirements left a long, narrow strip of usable land for the stilt plus twelve-storey building with 192 apartments.

JUBILEE CHURCH, 2000–2001, Navi Mumbai

For the Bombay Diocesan Council, Church of North India Trust Association. Designed and constructed within the spatial constraints of the plot, the church meets the needs of the community and is a contemporary place of worship. (See p. 219)

PARLE BISCUIT FACTORY, 2000–2001, Bengaluru

For Parle Products Pvt. Ltd. The factory houses the new biscuit production facility. The project's design consisted of a built-up area of 2,00,000 sq. ft that comprises of administration and production buildings.

KEM HOSPITAL CASUALTY CENTRE, 2000, Mumbai

For Pentagon Charitable Trust.

THE COURTYARD HOUSE, 2000-2002, Pune

For Saker and Mehli Mistri. A courtyard home that ensures privacy for its residents while creating interconnected intimate spaces. A curved driveway leads down the slope, an elegant entry that ensures the house cannot be seen from the road as the house is tucked in the contours of the land. (See p. 346)

CLUB MAHINDRA VALLEY VIEW RESORT, 2000-2002, Binsar

For Mahindra Holidays and Resorts India Ltd. A contextual architectural plan sensitive to the needs of holiday-makers resulted in a distinct time share resort. The plan follows two specific functions: an optimally functional architectural design that adheres to and functions around the rigid contours of the site.

EMPIRE INSTITUTE, 2000-2002, Mumbai

For Satish Malhotra. Restoration and adaptive reuse of a voluminous mill into an institutional space. Retention of north light trusses and creation of independent interior rooms aligned along a corridor that mirrored the idea of the street brought in a sense of dynamism into the space. (See P. 177)

FAIRWINDS APARTMENT, 2000-2003, Mumbai

For Great Eastern Shipping Co. Ltd.

KRISHI GRAM VIKAS KENDRA (KGVK)—RESEARCH AND TRAINING INSTITUTE, 2000, Rukka, Bihar (unbuilt)

For Usha Martin Ltd. The Vikas Kendra was designed as a society that promotes the quality of life in rural Bihar by involving villagers in an integrated system for socio-economic and health programmes. Water-shed management is one of the principal programmes undertaken by KGVK to unleash agricultural potential of the region. The training institute was designed to develop human resources, institutional infrastructure and to build specific capacities of individuals and self-help groups at the grass roots level.

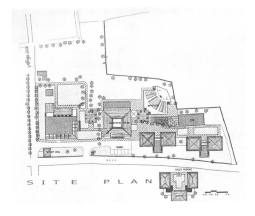

KRISHAN HOUSE, 2000, Bengaluru

For Gitanjali Krishan. Design of a private residence.

GATEWAY OF INDIA, 2000, Mumbai

A proposal for restoration.

SIEMENS CORPORATE OFFICE, 2000, Bengaluru, (Unbuilt)

For Siemens Ag.

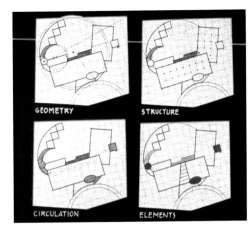

2001–2010

DR REDDY'S LABORATORIES, 2001, Hyderabad (unbuilt)

For Dr Reddy's Group. Corporate Headquarters.

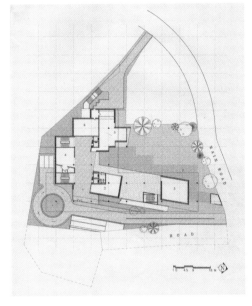

ALLIANCE FRANCAISE, 2001, New Delhi (unbuilt)

Competition entry: finalist.

BHADLI VILLAGE, 2001-2003, Bhuj

For Shrujan and Pentagon Trust. Implementation of the plan for the rehabilitation of the village, after a devastating earthquake. An integral part of the project was that as architects we would be facilitators. The help offered to the people of Bhadli was financial, material and professional expertise. Speed, safety, and sustainability were the three most important factors in this reconstruction project. (See p. 33)

CAMP SITE AT BADLAPUR, 2001, Maharashtra (unbuilt)

For Mr Kanodia. A campsite for overnight campers and day picnickers, providing a variety of entertainment, sports and educational facilities. The challenge was to create a stimulating and creative environment without using modern technology. All the structures were designed with a framework of bamboo covered with thatch. All levels and low walls for sitting were made of mud bricks. This design, although unbuilt, was an eco-friendly and inexpensive solution that provided facilities without disturbing the site.

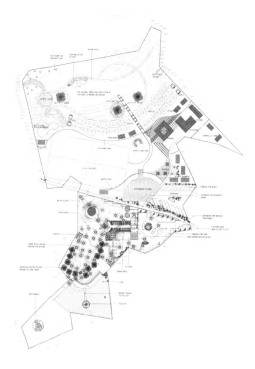

PHILLIPS ANTIQUES STORE, 2002, Mumbai
For Farooq Issa.

ELBIT DIAGNOSTICS LAB, 2002, Hyderabad
For Elbit Medical Diagnostics Ltd.

VASANT VIDYALAYA, 2002–2003, Bhadli village, Bhuj

For Pentagon Trust. A contemporary educational centre for the village of Bhadli, after the earthquake of 2001 in Gujarat. The new school centre has classrooms, meeting spaces for the villagers, a *baalwadi* (children's playschool) and a working women's area. (See p. 46)

GANJAM JEWELLERY SHOWROOM, 2002–2003, Bengaluru
For Ganjam Nagappa & Sons Pvt. Ltd.

ST THOMAS CATHEDRAL, 2002–2004, Mumbai

For St Thomas Cathedral Trust. Restoration and repair of Mumbai's oldest English building, and its first Anglican church. (See p. 275)

THE OLD YACHT CLUB, 2002–2007, Mumbai
For the Department of Atomic Energy. Restoration of the existing structure and the reconstruction of the demolished section of the building.

TCS CLUB HOUSE, 2003, Thane (unbuilt)
For Tata Consultancy Services.

ALHAMBRA APARTMENT, 2003, Mumbai
For Hindustan Lever Ltd. Reconfiguration of an apartment.

NCPA APARTMENT, 2003, Mumbai
For Chanrai Finance Company Pvt. Ltd.

APARTMENT AT CUFFE PARADE, 2003, Mumbai
For Farooq Issa.

JEEJAMATA NAGAR COMMUNITY CENTRE, 2003, Mumbai
A women's centre during the day within the Worli informal housing complex.

ANJANI KHANNA'S HOUSE, 2003, Alibaug
For Anjani Khanna.

SATYAM INSTITUTE OF E-BUSINESS, 2003, Hyderabad (unbuilt)

For Satyam Computer Services Ltd. An extensive institutional project on a plot area of 130 acres, conceptualised in collaboration with Sydness Architects, New York, USA.

INFANT & JUNIOR SCHOOL, NALANDA INTERNATIONAL SCHOOL CAMPUS, 2003–2004, Vadodara

For Nalanda Knowledge Foundation. The courtyards, corridors, classrooms and bell tower offer a seamless harmony between the buildings and its young students. (See pp. 308 and 310)

ZENSAR INFORMATION TECHNOLOGY CAMPUS, 2003–2010, Pune

For Zensar Technologies Ltd. (See p. 65)

DATA CENTRE, 2004, Thane

For Tata Consultancy Services.

HOUSE IN THE FOREST, 2004–2006, Khandala

For Mala and S. Ramadorai.

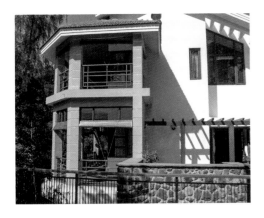

E-SERVE INTERNATIONAL OFFICE, 2004–2005, Mumbai

For Citigroup. An adaptive reuse project creating a vibrant space for young employees.

TCS CAMPUS BANYAN PARK PHASE ONE, 2004–2006, Mumbai

For Tata Consultancy Services. A project that nurtured and enhanced a 22-acre piece of lush green campus in the busy suburb of Andheri in Mumbai. The three colonial bungalows Gandavali, Sarosh and Orchid, and the one art-deco villa Lotus, formed a part of the existing fabric on the Redlands property. They were restored and upgraded to state-of-the-art executive briefing centres and an executive dining complex and guesthouses.

TCS CAMPUS BANYAN PARK PHASE TWO, 2005–Present, Mumbai (ongoing)

For Tata Consultancy Services. In collaboration with Tod Williams Billie Tsien Architects, USA. This project entailed the design of a campus that functions as corporate headquarters and operations base. The hot and humid climate of Mumbai is alleviated by shaded passageways, wide stairwells and water features. This reduces the cooling demands and energy consumption necessitated by the campus.

TCS HOUSE, 2005-2007, Mumbai

For Tata Consultancy Services. This unique retrofitting project preserved and restored the facade of the original Ralli House, while creating a cutting-edge modern office environment from within. (See p. 133)

RECREATIONAL CLUB, 2005, Navi Mumbai (unbuilt)

For Small Scale Entrepreneurs Association.

SONATA SOFTWARE OFFICES, 2005, Bengaluru

For Sonata Software Ltd.

VOICE—GIRLS' SCHOOL, 2006, Thane

For Voluntary Organisation In Community Enterprise. A residential school designed for the girl child living on the street. Two dormitory blocks with the cafeteria enclose a play area for the children, thus creating a safe space for them to learn and interact. (See p. 205)

VIRGIN F.M. RADIO STATION OFFICE, 2006, New Delhi

For Virgin Radio Station, Hindustan Times.

VIRGIN F.M. RADIO STATION OFFICE, 2006, Mumbai

For Virgin FM Radio Station, Hindustan Times.

TCS CAMPUS HINJEWADI, 2006, Pune (unbuilt)

For Tata Consultancy Services. A competition entry for their information technology campus in Pune.

KANILA BUNGALOW, 2006-2007, Mumbai

For Raj K. Chauhan. Interior design of the residence.

CLUB MAHINDRA RESORT, 2006-2007, Kumbhalgarh

For Mahindra Holidays & Resorts Ltd. A luxury resort located near the Kumbhalgarh Fort that weaves together the local crafts, architectural traditions and contemporary architectural elements.

FLAMBOYANTE, 2006-2007, Mumbai

For Amrish Arora. Interiors design of the restaurant and lounge bar located at the World Trade Center.

MIDDLE SCHOOL, NALANDA INTERNATIONAL SCHOOL CAMPUS, 2006-2007, Vadodara

For Nalanda Knowledge Foundation. As part of the campus, the design of the middle school brought in a shift in the scale of the courtyards and spaces as well as materials used within the building. (See p. 312)

ALAPATT'S JEWELLERY SHOWROOM, 2006-2007, Kochi

For Antony Francis Alapatt. A jewellery showroom that seamlessly connects the company's three categories of jewellery: antiques, contemporary and diamond ornaments.

NORMANDIE APARTMENT, 2006, Mumbai

For Gopi and Ashish Vaid.

TATA MOTORS APARTMENT, 2006-2007, Mumbai

For Tata Motors.

ANGADI SILKS SHOWROOM, 2006-2007, Bengaluru

For K. Radharaman. Showroom for traditional Angadi silk textile and sarees.

SIR DORABJI TATA TRUST OFFICE, 2006-2008, Mumbai

For Sir Dorabji Tata Trust.

TWIN HOUSES, 2006-2009, Indore

For Pravin Mittal. Residences for two brothers with common landscaped areas.

HOUSE IN THE TREES, 2006-2011, Alibaug

For Brinda and Anand Somaya. The architect's home is inspired by the magnificent banyan trees that stand as guardians of the land. In every aspect, the house is connected to its natural environment. (See p. 354)

SONATA SOFTWARE CAMPUS, 2007, Hyderabad (unbuilt)

For Sonata Software Ltd. A development centre for 1,000 engineers per floor.

VIRGIN F.M. RADIO STATION OFFICE, 2007-2008, Kolkata

For Virgin Radio Station, Hindustan Times.

THE BAI SAKARBAI DINSHAW PETIT HOSPITAL FOR ANIMALS, 2007-2009, Mumbai

For Bombay Society for the Prevention of Cruelty to Animals. A project commissioned to restore buildings built in the late 19th century on their campus. As this project was a functioning animal hospital, maintaining the utmost level of hygiene was of great importance, as well as improving and upgrading the facilities. An integral part of this project was to reuse materials to ensure sustainable building practices.

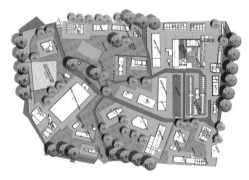

MACKINNON & MACKENZIE BUILDING, 2007-2009, Mumbai

For Adi Dubash Part restoration of a heritage building located in Ballard Estate.

MOKSHANA, 2008, Thane (unbuilt)

For Punit Agarwal. The Mokshana Wellness City is an integrated township of 300 acres providing a wide range of luxury facilities. The concept of Mokshana and that of the chakras as the wheels of life is translated into the planning of this complex.

TCS GANDHINAGAR, 2008, Gujarat (unbuilt)

For the Tata Consultancy Services. The campus was designed to facilitate walking between the corporate blocks, hostel and recreation spaces.

NATIONAL INSTITUTE OF FASHION TECHNOLOGY, 2008, Navi Mumbai (unbuilt)

A competition entry for a new campus to be designed for a modern institute building to stimulate creative minds. The design of the building was inspired by frequent revolutions of the world of fashion: a glamourous, flamboyant and transformative world along with the latest trends of donning a new skin to the buildings by changing their external fabrics. A double skin of metal fabric panels was designed to act as a thermal buffer drawing in natural air into the building.

BHARAT BIJLEE HEAD OFFICE, 2008-2009, Mumbai

For Bharat Bijlee Ltd.

SENIOR SCHOOL, NALANDA INTERNATIONAL SCHOOL CAMPUS, 2008-2010, Vadodara

For Nalanda Knowledge Foundation. As part of the campus, the design of this school was conceived as a hierarchy of spaces with a large central courtyard surrounded by secondary and tertiary courts, flanked by clusters of classrooms for the senior students of the school. (See p. 312)

HOUSE IN THE VALLEY, 2008-2010, Lavasa

For Arun Shourie. Nestled in the steep hillside of the Western Ghats, the house is designed on steep contours, while also incorporating barrier-free design and easy accessibility. (See p. 350)

FIRST INTERNATIONAL FINANCE CENTRE, 2008-2010, Mumbai

For TCG Developments India Private. Ltd. Commercial office building at Bandra Kurla Complex. This project was designed in collaboration with Kohn Pederson Fox Associates, New York, USA.

BHARAT BIJLEE LTD, 2008-2012, Kalwa, Thane

For Bharat Bijlee Ltd.

SEKSARIA HOUSE, 2008-2012, Mandwa, Alibaug

For Tarun Seksaria.

VERSOVA APARTMENT, 2008-2013, Mumbai

For Apurva and Rohan Parikh. A stilt and six-storey apartment building on an irregular plot of land. The design of the building ensures that the residences have maximum exposure to the sea view that the plot affords, yet privacy for each apartment is maintained by the use of contemporary architectural slats on the façade.

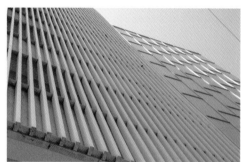

MUMBAI ARTS AND CRAFTS CENTRE, 2008-Present, Mumbai (ongoing)

For MCGM. The project is conceptualised at the Love Grove Sewage Pumping Station Complex, Worli, in the form of the *wada*, which was adopted and taken as its design principle. With a revival in ethnic traditions, a new market for the traditional arts and crafts of the state as well as the country is explored and represented through this proposal. It becomes a representative in the global market by hosting various events to promote the different arts and crafts of Maharashtra.

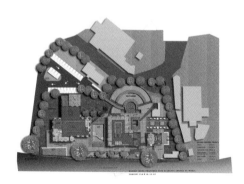
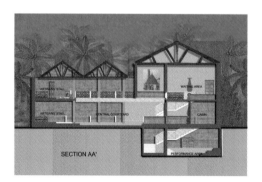

SECTION AA'

BRITISH COUNCIL, 2009, Mumbai

For the British Council.

INTEGRATED SCHOOL, 2009, Mumbai

For Sir Shapurji Billimoria Foundation. A building that will provide equity, access and quality in education for children through training of their teachers.

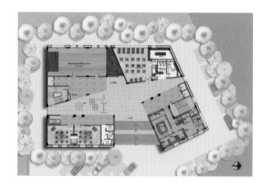

OMEGA TOWERS, 2009, Kolkata

For TCG Developments.

NCPA THEATRE, 2009, Mumbai (unbuilt)

For the NCPA Trust. The proposal for a new building for the performing arts.

VALLIAPPA'S RESIDENCE, 2009, Bengaluru

For C. Valliappa.

COFFEE TRAILS HOMESTAY, 2009, Coorg

Architecture design for homestay and residence.

GOA INSTITUTE OF MANAGEMENT CAMPUS, 2009-Present, Goa (ongoing)

For Goa Institute of Management. A new campus for the institute in Sanquelim. It is a greenfield project that entailed the design of an academic block, library, cafe, student hostels, recreational and sports facilities as well as faculty residences. It is now in its fourth phase. (See p. 397)

THE WORLD TOWERS, 2009–Present, Mumbai (ongoing)

For Lodha Group. Planned in collaboration with Pei Cobb Freed & Partners New York, USA, the complex is composed of three residential towers uniquely curvilinear in shape. (See p. 180)

HOUSES AT LAVASA, 2010, Dasve

For Lavasa Corporation. The master-planning and construction of residential bungalows as part of the 300-acre township.

DIAMOND MANAGEMENT & TECHNOLOGY CONSULTANTS, 2010, Mumbai

For Diamond Management & Technology Consultants.

INDUS CENTRE, 2010, Pune (unbuilt)

The Indus Heritage Program wanted to establish a world-class archaeological site and museum/research institute for the Indus civilisation. It was a collaboration with the Indus Heritage Trust (IHT), an India-based non-profit, the Global Heritage Fund (GHF), Deccan College and other partners.

CORPORATE OFFICE, 2010–2011, Mumbai

For Igloo Dairy Pvt. Ltd.

LODHA EXCELUS HEAD OFFICE, 2010–2011, Mumbai

For the Lodha Group.

THE FERN RESIDENCY HOTEL, 2010–2013, Mumbai

For Natvar Parikh Group. The key design element revolves around the design aesthetics of the Indian language scripts. The hotel has been designed keeping in mind the importance of this key design element, which is reflected in the exterior and interior design.

ACRON WATERFRONT RESORT, 2010–2014, Goa

For Amar Britto. Built on the edge of the river and facing the ocean, this resort was created when a motley group of buildings were converted into a boutique resort.

CLUB MAHINDRA RESORT, 2010–Present, Theog (ongoing)

Mahindra Holidays & Resorts Ltd. The resort blends seamlessly into its landscape, and the design reflects the cultural history of this region. The use of local materials, south-facing orientation of the buildings and stepped terraces ensured economical and sustainable design.

2011–PRESENT

THE EROS CINEMA TOWER, 2011, Mumbai

For the Cambata Trust. The EROS Cinema Tower, also known as the Cambata Building, is a project that involved conserving the built fabric of this 80-year-old art deco heritage structure tower and suggest a strategy for future management, including maintaining the structural authenticity and the ambience.

MUMBAI ESPLANADE PROJECT, 2011, Mumbai (unbuilt)

For the people of Mumbai. An extensive urban design project for the city in collaboration with Professor Shivjit Sidhu, Apostrophe A+uD, Mumbai. (See p. 208)

BIRLA INSTITUTE OF TECHNOLOGY & SCIENCE, 2011–2015, Rajasthan

For Birla Institute of Technology & Science. A masterplan for the conservation, expansion and redevelopment of an existing 225-acre campus of an all-India technical and private university located in Pilani. A complex phasing plan was derived to execute the masterplan, followed by the condition mapping of the existing structures, some of which were over 50 years old. The student and housing complexes have been built.

HOUSING AT AGARSURE, 2012, Alibaug (unbuilt)

For Veda Real Estate Corporation Pvt. Ltd. Housing Complex at Agarsure. Located near the coastal town of Alibaug, the Agarsure Second Homes provided a community composed of apartments and a clubhouse.

RAJABAI CLOCK TOWER & MUMBAI UNIVERSITY LIBRARY, 2012–2015, Mumbai

For the University of Mumbai. Restoring this neo-gothic style tower, once the tallest structure in Mumbai, and the adjacent library, a Grade I heritage building, was a challenging project in terms of the structural, architectural and logistical aspects. (See p. 239)

TEXTILE GALLERY AT CSMVS, 2012–2015, Mumbai

For the Chhatrapati Shivaji Maharaj Vastu Sangrahalaya Museum. The permanent collection is of particular importance in the context of Mumbai, a city whose contours have been defined by textile mills. The design vocabulary of this exhibition continually refers to the nature and creation of textiles. The rich array of colours used to dye fabric in India identifies the different sections of the collection. The dynamic way in which one experiences the collection is reflective of the warp and weft pattern that is weaved into textiles.

YUSUF MEHERALLY PLAYGROUND, 2013, Mumbai (unbuilt)

To create a partnership and upgrade a semi-abandoned open space into a safe park. The goals of this project were to create lively spaces, redefine accessibility, enhance visual connectivity, ensure security, and design a programme for all ages and economic classes.

SCHOOL OF PLANNING AND ARCHITECTURE, 2013, Vijayawada (unbuilt)

Finalist at the all-India competition for the development of an eco-friendly campus with state-of-the-art facilities.

MAHESHWARI BUNGALOW, 2013, Indore

For Ashutosh Maheshwari. This bungalow is planned with an array of covered, semi-covered and open spaces.

CLUB MAHINDRA RESORT AT YELAGIRI, 2013, Chennai (unbuilt)

THE KENSINGTON CLUB, 2013-2017, Nashik

For Kings Club Pvt. Ltd. Designed to be a retreat from city life, this sports club incorporates a wide variety of facilities. The distinction between outdoor and indoor spaces is blurred as the open restaurant offers an uninterrupted view to the river and beyond.

B.D. PETIT PARSEE GENERAL HOSPITAL, 2013-Present, Mumbai (ongoing)

For B.D. Petit Parsee General Trust. This medical facility addresses international healthcare planning principles and offers cutting-edge technology.

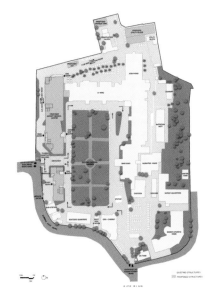

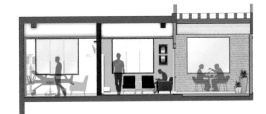

BHAU DAJI LAD MUSEUM EXTENSION, 2014, Mumbai (unbuilt)

For Dr Bhau Daji Lad Mumbai City Museum. A competition entry in collaboration with OMA (lead architects). Concept development of the north-wing extension was derived from the structure of a flower dedicated to the city. The proposed wing included galleries and a learning centre, research centre, auditorium and conference centre. A library and archive, conservation facilities, museum shop, cafe and restaurant were also integrated into the design.

TCS CAMPUS, 2014–Present, Indore (ongoing)

For Tata Consultancy Services. An IT facility located along a main arterial road connecting the city to its airport. The project includes approximately 15,000 IT and BPO seats along with the necessary common facilities such as the administration building, cafeterias, training rooms, a recruitment centre, multi-purpose hall and business centre. The conceptual planning is based on the Narmada river, and the architectural forms are derived from the physical features it creates as it winds its way down from its source and through the campus.

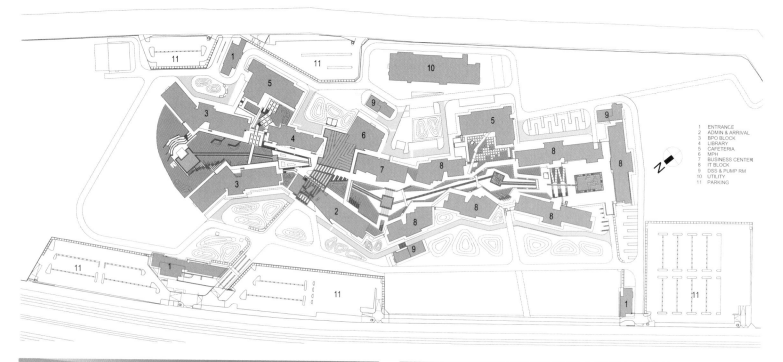

1   ENTRANCE
2   ADMIN & ARRIVAL
3   BPO BLOCK
4   LIBRARY
5   CAFETERIA
6   MPH
7   BUSINESS CENTER
8   IT BLOCK
9   DSS & PUMP RM
10 UTILITY
11 PARKING

IIM-A CAMPUS, 2014–Present, Ahmedabad (ongoing)

For Indian Institute of Management. An ongoing preservation and restoration project of conserving the built fabric of the iconic 20th-century heritage structures designed by Louis I Kahn. These include Dormitories 1–18 and the main complex building that includes four faculty blocks, classroom complex and the Vikram Sarabhai Library building. The project entails conservation survey works, building condition mapping and assessments, preparation and execution of a detailed conservation plan and strategies for restoration, retrofitting, upgrade and reusability of the built fabric along with its spatial expression.

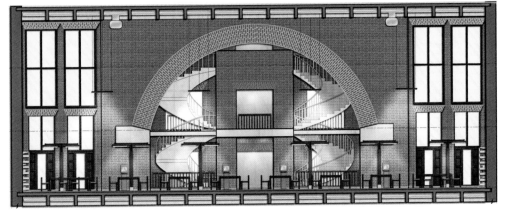

GANDHI HOUSE, 2014, Lonavala

A private residence involving restoration, upgradation and interior design for an existing colonial bungalow.

DAYANAND SAGAR UNIVERSITY, 2014, Bengaluru (unbuilt)

A competition entry for a sustainable campus integrating academic programming with landscape, infrastructure, built form and place-making objectives. The open plazas and green spaces complement the built forms and become places for recreation, athletics, community enjoyment and ecological restoration.

AMBEDKAR MEMORIAL, 2014, Mumbai (unbuilt)

A competition entry, AMTABHAN, was a proposal conceptualised in collaboration with James Polshek, Damyanti Radheshwar and team. AMTABHAN develops a memorable and inspiring experience, as well as a visual, intellectual and physical journey of Dr Babasaheb Ambedkar. It was designed to be a national venue for millions of people that visit Chaitya Bhoomi during Ambedkar Jayanti and a permanent venue for Mumbaikars who deserve a vibrant public space in the form of a plaza.

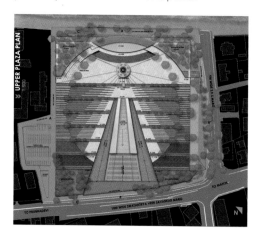

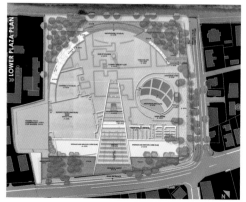

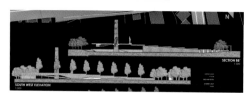

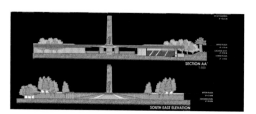

DR PUNAMIYA'S CLINIC, 2014-2015, Mumbai

For Dr Kirti Punamiya

NANDA HOUSE, 2015-2017, Tungi

For Neeru and Arun Nanda. This bungalow was designed to create a seamless relationship between the built form and nature. The house is composed of two separate blocks and the pool. The site is a flat plateau overlooking a lake on one side and a steep mountain on the other. These two natural features form the axis for the house connecting indoor and outdoor spaces. The zinc roof contrasts with the local Nevasa stone cladding and the Kota stone flooring.

PROJECT INDIGO, 2015, Dubai (unbuilt)

For Amea Ventures Ltd., United Arab Emirates. The competition entailed the design of a large complex in Dubai that was primarily for the Indian community. Community facilities, such as clubs, sports facilities and a youth centre, allow like-minded people to interact and relax. Several strategies were employed for passive cooling, groundwater recharge and rainwater harvesting, which aid in developing a built environment that conforms to the traditional architecture of the Arabian Gulf and responds to its harsh climate.

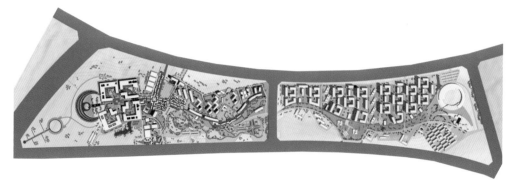

IIT-BOMBAY MASTERPLAN & RESIDENTIAL BUILDINGS, 2015–Present, Mumbai (ongoing)

Proposed faculty housing for the IIT-B campus. The cruciform-shaped building core and staircases have been planned to receive maximum natural light and ventilation. The proposed building has been planned with a minimum intervention to the existing vegetation.

IIT-BOMBAY MASTERPLAN & ACADEMIC BUILDINGS, 2015–Present, Mumbai (ongoing)

The programme includes the master planning of 16 acres of land and the detailed design of four academic buildings. The buildings are unified through the landscape and a series of plazas that are to be used by pedestrians to channelise student movement and provide spaces that encourage student interaction. They are oriented to take advantage of natural light and allow contextual connectivity.

GODREJ HOUSE, 2015–Present, Coonoor (ongoing)

For Pheroza and Jamshyd Godrej. Located on a hill overlooking the valley, the house moulds into the landscape as the hierarchy of spaces, which cascade along the slope. A wooden screen roof that covers a corridor, which connects all the blocks forms the axis.

D V ASSOCIATES, 2016, Mumbai

For Dhaval Vussonji. This project entailed design of a corporate space for a law firm.

MALHI HOUSE, 2016, Chandigarh (unbuilt)

For Kamal Malhi. A house designed around a sky-lit Zen garden creating an experiential circulation for the spaces.

MAHARASHTRA NATURE PARK, 2016, Mumbai (unbuilt)

A design competition with a consortium of architects including Cecil Balmond Studio (London), ADF Consultores (Portugal), Mathur/Da Cunha (Philadelphia), Junya Ishigami+associates (Tokyo), Matias Echanove and Rahul Srivastava—URBZ, Sunjoy Monga, Prashanta Bhat, and Damyanti Radheshwar with Somaya & Kalappa Consultants as the lead architects. The project sensitively integrated the MNP and New Bridge among the BKC, Dharavi and Milthi River, enabling the exploration of the natural environment.

INDIA AND THE WORLD: A HISTORY IN NINE STORIES, 2016-2017, Mumbai

For Chhatrapati Shivaji Maharaj Vastu Sangrahalaya Museum. Concept and design for a landmark exhibition in collaboration with Chhatrapati Shivaji Maharaj Vastu Sangrahalaya, Mumbai, the British Museum, London, and National Museum, New Delhi.

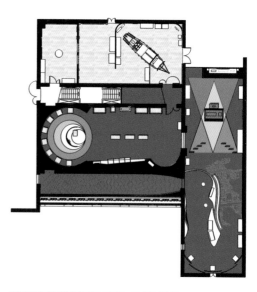

WAR MEMORIAL AND MUSEUM, 2016, Delhi (unbuilt)

A competition entry for the Ministry of Defence, Government of India. The memorial is conceptualised as a quiet and respectful landscape that not only honours the memory of the nation's heroes but also informs and inspires future generations. The layout of the war museum was developed by seven cubes along an existing spine creating a singular powerful form. The seven cubes represent the seven metals of India (brass, copper, gold, zinc, silver, iron and steel) and the courage, strength and power associated with the armed forces.

KODAK HOUSE IB SCHOOL, 2016–Present, Mumbai (ongoing)

For the Anglo Scottish Education Society. This project involves the conservation, adaptive reuse and retrofitting of a 110-year-old neo-classical building in the heart of the Fort precinct of South Mumbai. The existing bank building will be converted into the International Baccalaureate School for the Cathedral & John Connon School.

ANGADI HERITAGE, 2017–Present, Bengaluru (ongoing)

For K. Radharaman. This retail showroom reflects the legacy of Angadi Heritage with an aim to introduce visitors to the history, textiles and various products.

SAI MAA ASHRAM, 2017, Varanasi

This project entails the interior design of an existing ashram.

BOMBAY SCOTTISH SCHOOL, 2017–Present, Mumbai (ongoing)

For the Bombay Scottish Orphanage Society. Conservation of Bombay Scottish School in Mahim.

BAKORI AFFORDABLE HOUSING PROJECT, 2017–Present, Pune (ongoing)

For Konark Karia Builders. Bakori affordable housing project is set on a 20-acre contoured site near Pune. The objective of the development is to create standard living conditions with basic amenities for all and provide a respectable quality of life.

MIXED-USE DEVELOPMENT, 2017–Present, Pune (ongoing)

For PRA Realty in collaboration with Steven Harris Architects LLP, New York, USA.

BOMBAY HOUSE, 2017–Present, Mumbai (ongoing)

For Tata Sons Ltd. Refurbishment and upgradation of the international headquarters for the TATA Group.

POULTRY FARM, 2017–Present, Mulshi (ongoing)

For Lantern Greenfields Pvt. Ltd. Planning and design of poultry sheds with ancillary buildings.

PARLE PRODUCTS FACTORY, 2017–Present, Mumbai (ongoing)

For Parle Products Pvt. Ltd. Master planning and adaptive reuse of the existing Parle Products Factory. The project entails the restoration, retrofitting, upgrade and expansion of the buildings on site into a fully functional information technology complex along with recreational areas. It is a full circle from one of our earliest projects where we had designed some of the buildings ourselves.

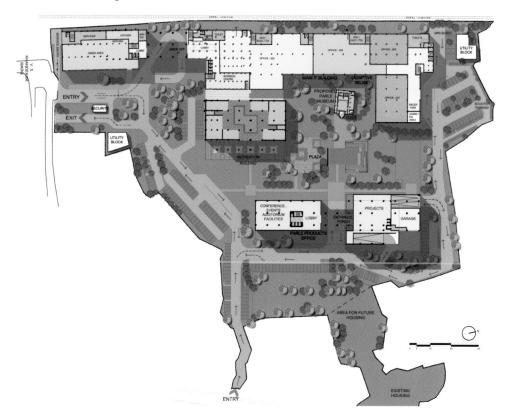

"I am an Indian and all what I am comes from my heritage. It is an intrinsic part of my being and will naturally reflect in my work in many ways. The architect's role is that of a guardian, he or she is the conscience of the built and the unbuilt environment."

BIODATA

1949 Born in Bangalore.

1958 **Loreto House School**, Calcutta.

1959–65 **The Cathedral & John Connon School**, Bombay.

1965–66 **Sir. J.J. School of Architecture, University of Bombay**, Bombay.

1966–67 **American Field Service scholarship**, USA.
American High School Diploma, Lee H. Edwards High School, Asheville, North Carolina, USA.

1967–71 **Bachelor of Architecture**, Sir. J.J. School of Architecture, Bombay University, Bombay.

1971–73 **Master of Arts**, Smith College, Massachusetts, USA.

1972 **Summer Programme**, Cornell University, New York, USA.

1974 **Associate Member**, The Indian Institute of Interior Designers, India.

1975 **Founder and Principal Architect**, Somaya and Kalappa Consultants, Bombay.

1984 **Member**, Council of Architecture, India.

1987 **Fellow**, Indian Institute of Architects, India.

1999 **Founder Trustee**, The HECAR Foundation, India.

2000 **Chairperson and Curator**, Women in Architecture 2000 Plus—Conference & Exhibition on the works of the South Asian Women Architects, India.

2012 **Honorary Doctorate Recipient**, Smith College, Massachusetts, USA.

2014 **Indian Institute of Architects' Baburao Mhatre Gold Medal** for Lifetime Contribution to the Field of Architecture.

2016–21 **Chairperson**, Board of Governors, School of Planning and Architecture, Vijayawada, India.

2017 **Member**, Board of the LafargeHolcim Foundation for Sustainable Construction, Zurich, Switzerland.

2017 **Member**, Council of Architecture Committee to Review the Profession and Education of Architecture in India.

2017–23 **A.D. White Professor-at-Large**, Cornell University, New York, USA.

PROFESSIONAL AFFILIATIONS & COMMITTEES

1988–93: **Trustee**, Spastic Society of India, India.
1989–99: **Member**, Managing Committee of the Colaba Woods & Sports Complex, Mumbai, India.
1993: **Fellow**, India Society of Engineers, India.
1996: **Member**, High Power Committee, University of Bombay, India.
1996: **Member**, Selection Committee for the Post of Principal, Sir. J.J. College of Architecture, Mumbai.
1993–95: **Member**, Urban Heritage Conservation Committee, Mumbai.
1996–99: **Member**, Urban Heritage Conservation Committee, Mumbai.
1999: **Member**, Mumbai's Initiative for the Protection and Improvement of Streets and Public Spaces, Mumbai.
2000–03: **Member**, IAWA Board of Advisers (International Archive of Women in Architecture), Virginia Tech, Blacksburg, USA.
2001: **Trustee**, Friends of JJ School of Art Trust, Mumbai.
2005: **Member**, Committee of Oval as the Nominee of the Navajbai Ratan Tata Trust, Mumbai.
2006–08: **Member**, Committee of Environmental Impact Assessment of New Construction Projects & New Industrial Estates for Ministry of Environment & Forests, Government of India, India
2007: **Member**, INTBAU (International Network for Traditional Building, Architecture & Urbanism) India Committee of Honour (IICoH), Delhi.
2008: **Member**, Editorial Board for MARG Architectural Books, Mumbai.
2014–17: **Member**, National Advisory Board of NCSHS (National Centre for Safety of Heritage Structures) under the Aegis of the Ministry of Human Resources Development (Government of India) IIT–Madras, Chennai.
2015: Honoured as **Distinguished Professor**, Indian Education Society's College of Architecture, (IES) Mumbai.

AWARDS AND HONOURS – INTERNATIONAL

1999: **Award for Best Practice**, Commonwealth Association of Architects–Indian Institute of Architects, International Conference on Urbanization and Housing–II.

2004: **Culture Heritage Conservation Award of Merit**, UNESCO Asia-Pacific Heritage Awards, for St. Thomas's Cathedral, Mumbai.

2006: **ABB LEAF Award**, Leading European Architects Forum, for Nalanda International School, Vadodara, India.

2007: Nomination, The Aga Khan Award for Architecture for Nalanda International School, Vadodara, India.

2007: Nomination, The Aga Khan Award for Architecture for the Rehabilitation of Bhadli village and school, Kutch, India.

2008: **The Phaidon Atlas of 21st Century World Architecture: All the Greatest Buildings of the 21st Century** for Bhadli village school, Kutch, India.

2008: **Vassilis Sgoutas Prize** for Poverty Alleviation, International Union of Architects, for the Rehabilitation of Bhadli village, Kutch, India.

2011: **Honorable Mention**, Structures for Inclusion–11, Social Economic Environmental Design (SEED), for the Rehabilitation of Bhadli village, Bhuj, India.

2012: PUBLIC INTEREST DESIGN, Global 100, Persons working at the Intersection of design and service globally.

2014: Nominated for **arcVISION Prize—Women and Architecture**, Italcementi Group.

2015: **Finalist**, Concept Design and Masterplan for Amea Ventures Limited, Project Indigo, Dubai.

2017: **Honourable Mention**, Arcasia Awards, for the Restoration and Preservation of Rajabai Clock Tower and University Library Building, Mumbai.

AWARDS AND HONOURS – NATIONAL

1989: **Urban Heritage Award**, Indian Heritage Society, for The Colaba Woods & Sports Complex, Mumbai.

1990: **Urban Heritage Award**, Indian Heritage Society, for "Progressive Conservation" for the NRK House, Mumbai.

1994: **Journal of Indian Institute of Architects Award**, Shelter category, for Garware House Nashik.

1994: **Indian Institute of Architects Award** for Excellence in Architecture for the Garware House, Nashik.

1994: **Kitply Award**–Conservation, Indian Institute of Architects, for The Cathedral and John Connon Middle School, Mumbai.

1998: **Kitply Award**–Conservation, Indian Institute of Architects, for The Cathedral & John Connon Senior School, Mumbai.

1999: **Designer of the Year**, Interiors and Lifestyle India: Millennium Edition.

2001: **Women Achievers Award**, Women Graduates Union (Indian Federation of University Women).

2002: J. K. Cements **AYA Award**, Indian State Architecture Awards, for the Jubilee Church at Sanpada, Navi Mumbai.

2002: **Architect of the Year Award**, Commendation for the Jubilee Church, Navi Mumbai.

2003: **Society Interiors Award** for Outstanding Contribution towards Interior Architecture.

2003: **Urban Heritage Award**, Indian Heritage Society, for St. Thomas's Cathedral, Mumbai.

2004: **Finalist**, Architecture+ Awards—Preservation and Conservation, for Bhadli village, Bhuj.

2007: **Urban Heritage Award**, Indian Heritage Society, for Banyan Park campus, TCS, Mumbai.

2007: **Wienerberger Golden Architect Award**, Architecture+Design & Spectrum Foundation Architecture Awards, for Lifetime Achievement.

2008: **VM & RD Retail Design Award**, for Alapatt Heritage, Kochi.

2010: **CSI Architecture and Design Excellence Award**, for Alapatt Heritage, Kochi.

2011: **Second Prize** for Campus Design and Development of School of Planning and Architecture, Vijayawada.

2011: **Felicitation and Honour for Being an Achiever and an Icon among Women**, Institute of Indian Interior Designers.

2015: **Honourable Mention**, IIA Award for Excellence in Architecture, Indian Institute of Architects, for Restoration and Preservation of Rajabai Clock Tower, Mumbai.

2016: **Estrade Real Estate Award**—Heritage Category for TCS House, Mumbai.

2017: **Commendation**, Institute of Indian Interior Designers—Design Excellence Award, for Textile Gallery at Chhatrapati Shivaji Maharaj Vastu Sangrahalaya, Mumbai.

2017: **Grohe NDTV Design and Architecture Award** for Outstanding Industry Contribution.

ACADEMIC AFFILIATIONS

1991: **Jury Member**, "A Critical Analysis Of A Recent Architectural Project" at the National Association of Students of Architecture, India.

1991: **Jury Member**, Indian Institute of Architects' Kitply Award 1991 for Conservation, India.

1991: **Jury Member**, "Revitalization/Adaptive Reuse and infill for Heritage Buildings," G. Sen Trophy for National Association of Students of Architecture, India.

1992: **Judge**, Interior Design Project Competition, SNDT University, Mumbai.

1996: **Judge**, Building and Landscape Design for the development of the temple complex at pilgrim centre, Shri Saibaba Mandir Complex Development, India.

1997: **Jury Member**, National Association of Students of Architecture—Nari Gandhi Trophy on "A Critical Analysis of a Recent Architectural Project," India.

1998: **Judge**, "INSITES" for an Interior Design Project Competition at SNDT University, Mumbai.

2002: **Jury Member**, A+D and Spectrum Foundation Architecture Awards—Apartment Planning, India.

2003: **Jury Member**, University of Mumbai, Ratnagiri Campus, Mumbai.

2005: **Jury Member**, Inside Outside "Designer of the year 2005," Residential Architecture, Mumbai.

2007: **Jury Member**, A+D and Spectrum Foundation Architecture Awards, The Habitat Award for a Single Residence Design & The Institutional Architecture Award for Design Development of Institutional/ Office Buildings, India.

2011: **Jury Member**, Selection of the IITJ Campus Master Plan, Indian Institute of Technology, Jodhpur, India.

2012: **Jury Member**, Selection of Architect, Indian Institute of Technology, Gandhinagar, India.

2012: **Jury Member**, Selection of Master Planner & Architect, Indian Institute of Management, Udaipur, India.

2012: **Jury Member**, Thesis Awards Programme at The National Institute of Advanced Studies in Architecture, Academic Unit of ouncil of Architecture, Bhubaneshwar, India.

2014: **Jury Member**, All India Stone Architectural Awards (AISAA), Centre for Development of Stones (CDOS), Jaipur, India.

2014: **Jury Member**, Innovative Approaches To Sustainable Construction, Holcim Awards—Asia Pacific 2014, Beijing.

2015: **Jury Member**, Sustainable Housing, Saint-Gobain 350 Shaping the Future Housing Innovation Challenge, Mumbai.

2015: **Jury Member**, "Transit Shelters for Construction Workers" for The IGBC Green Design Competition, Mumbai.

2015: **Chairperson**, Maharaja Sayajirao University of Baroda—Selection of Architect for Maharaja Ranjitsinh Gaekwad Institute of Design.

2017: **Jury Member**, Best Student Design Dissertation, Charles Correa Gold Medal, Mumbai.

2017: **Jury Member**, Limited Architectural Design Competition, Maharashtra National Law University, Nagpur, India.

TALKS – INTERNATIONAL

1995. "**Recent Projects.**" Department of Architecture, University of Moratuwa, Sri Lanka.

1998. "**Conserving the Old, Building the New.**" Department of Architecture, University of Edinburgh, UK.

2000. "**Conserving the Old, Building the New.**" Virginia Tech, Virginia, USA.

2001. "**Heritage, Urban Space and Identity: Conservation in Urban India.**" Karavan Karachi Festival, Karachi, Pakistan.

2001. "**Village Earthquake Rehabilitation and Urban Architectural Issues in India.**" Virginia Tech, Virginia, USA.

2002. "**Recent Projects 2001–2002.**" University of Technology, Sydney, Australia.

2002. "**Recent Projects 2001–2002.**" University of New South Wales, Sydney, Australia.

2002. "**Recent Projects 2001–2002.**" Royal Australian Institute of Architects (RAIA), Melbourne, Australia.

2004. "**Urban Space and Identity.**" United Nations Asia-Pacific Leadership Forum, Hong Kong, SAR China.

2005. "**The Art of Architecture.**" Sri Lanka Institute of Architects, Sri Lanka.

2008. "**India, My Architectural Canvas.**" Cornell University, New York, USA.

2009. "**Sense of Place Not Solely Space: Context vs. Global Design Identity.**" IFI Dubai Congress, Dubai, United Arab Emirates.

2010. "**India's Changing Landscape Buildings and Beyond.**" Catholic University of America (CUA) with the Embassy of India, Washington DC, USA.

2011. "**India's Changing Landscape.**" Jugaad Urbanism, Center for Architecture: AIA New York Chapter, New York, USA.

2011. "**India's Changing Landscape Buildings and Beyond.**" Barnard College, Columbia University, New York, USA.

2012. "**Our Next Train Stop.**" Society of Indo-American Engineers and Architects, New York, USA.

2013. George Anselevicius Memorial Lecture on "**India, My Architectural Canvas.**" School of Architecture and Planning, The University of New Mexico, New Mexico, USA.

2013. "**Four Projects.**" Chicago Architectural Club, Illinois, USA.

2013. "**Architecture as Resource.**" American University of Beirut, Lebanon.

2013. "**Architecture as Resource.**" Academie Libanaise des Beaux Arts, Universite De Balamand, Lebanon.

2015. "**Building Storeys: An Architect's Journey through the Indian Landscape.**" Graduate School of Architecture, Planning, and Preservation, Columbia University, New York, USA.

2015. "**Building Storeys: An Architect's Journey through the Indian Landscape.**" South Asia Institute, Harvard University, Massachusetts, USA.

2016. "**Building Storeys: An Architect's Journey through the Indian Landscape.**" RIBA Members, Sri Lanka.

2016. "Building Storeys: An Architect's Journey through the Indian Landscape." Crossover, Balmond Studio, UK.

2016. Keynote Speech, "Threads and Continuities." Thomas Memorial Symposium, AAP, Cornell University, New York, USA.

TALKS – NATIONAL

1990. "The Indian Architect—Our Changing Role in the '90s." Mavlankar Memorial Lecture, Indian Institute of Architects, Bangalore.

1991. "Woman as Architect." Women & Architecture, Indian Institute of Architects, Bangalore.

1994. "Continuity and Change." Indian Institute of Architects, Bangalore.

1995. "Future of Interior Design." Indian Institute of Interior Designers, Bangalore.

1995. "Economic Viability of Listed Heritage Buildings & their Re-adaptability." CAA/WSE/AA ASIA Conference, Trivandrum.

1996. "Altering the Original—Restoration, Renovation and Reuse." Centre for Environmental Planning and Technology (CEPT), Ahmedabad.

1997. "Guardian or Broker." Department of Architecture, Maharaja Sayajirao University, Vadodara.

1997. "Corporate Interiors." 2nd National Convention, Indian Institute of Interior Designers, Pune.

1998. "Conservation in Urban India: Challenges and Responsibilities." UIA–Indian Institute of Architects International Meet on 'Architectural Heritage,' Aurangabad.

1998. "Conserving the Old, Building the New—Challenges and Responsibilities." Goa College of Architecture, Goa.

1998. "Conserving the Urban Heritage—The Experience of Bombay." Indian National Trust for Art and Cultural Heritage and B.M Birla Science Centre, Hyderabad.

1998. Lecture series on "Conserving the Old, Building the New—A Journey in Time and Space." Urban Design Research Institute, Max Mueller Bhavan, Mumbai.

1998. "Poor Countries Need Good Design." Indian Institute of Interior Designers 3rd National Convention, Vadodara.

1999. "A Sense of Place: Building the New–Conserving the Old." MK India, Mumbai

2000. Inaugural address on "Women in Architecture." South Asia Women in Architecture 2000 Plus, Mumbai.

2000. "Architectural Education." Indian Institute of Interior Designers & Indian Institute of Architects, Surat.

2000. "Places of Public Congregation." IES College of Architecture, Mumbai.

2001. "Design as a Process." Forum for Exchange and Excellence in Design, Pune.

2002. "The Restoration & Expansion of the Three Cathedral School Buildings." Indian Institute of Architects Western Zone Regional Conference, Goa.

2002. "A School and a Church: Continuity & Change." Goa Heritage Festival, Goa.

2003. "Recent Projects 2001–2002." Indian Institute of Architects, Thrissur.

2003. "Archi-Tech." Inside Outside Mega Show, Mumbai.

2005. "Architecture of Sensibilities Buildings & Beyond." Indian Architect and Builder–AEC, Mumbai.

2007. "Bhadli village, Gujarat." Traditional Architecture & Urbanism in India. INTBAU, New Delhi.

2008. "The Changing Landscape." TATA Steel Design Knowledge Series, Hyderabad.

2008. "TCS House." Rachana Sansad's Project Management Institute, Mumbai.

2008. "The Changing Architectural Landscape of India." Smt. Manoramabai Mundle Department of Architecture, LAD College, and Smt. R. P. College for Women, Nagpur.

2008. "The Changing Architectural Landscape of India." Indian Institute of Interior Designers, Vadodara Chapter.

2009. "Indian Architecture: Our Next Train Stop." Indian Institute of Interior Designers, Nashik Chapter.

2009. "The Art of Green Design Ancient & Contemporary." Confederation of Indian Industry, Indian Green Building Congress, Hyderabad.

2009. "Striving for Excellence, Yearning for Innovation." Panel. Confederation of Indian Industry, 8th Manufacturing Summit, Mumbai.

2010. "Architecture of Sensibilities Buildings and Beyond." Indian Institute of Interior Designers, Ahmedabad Chapter.

2011. "A Journey in Time and Space—India's Design Legacy." Indian Institute of Interior Designers—National Convention, Jaipur.

2011. "Weaving Architecture." Conserving the Old, Building the New. Modern Interventions in Historic Areas, Kamla Raheja Vidyanidhi Institute for Architecture and Environmental Studies, Mumbai.

2011. "India's Changing Landscape Buildings and Beyond." Indian Institute of Interior Designers, DRC International Seminar, New Delhi.

2012. "Our Next Train Stop." Columbia University Symposium, Mumbai.

2012. "Women Changing India." Panel. Barnard College Global Symposium, Mumbai.

2013. Keynote speech on "India, My Architectural Canvas." Indian Institute of Architects–Council of Architecture National Conference on Women in Architecture, Pune.

2013. Keynote speech on "India, My Architectural Canvas." 55th Annual NASA Convention, Gateway College of Architecture and Design, New Delhi.

2013. "Weaving Architecture: Conserving the Old, Building the New." ARTISANS, Kala Ghoda Festival, Mumbai.

2013. Keynote speech on "Weaving Architecture." Kanvinde Memorial Lecture Series, BNCA, Pune.

2013. "Mumbai Esplanade Project." India Design ID, New Delhi.

2013. Keynote speech on "Architecture as Resource." 4th International Holcim Forum for Sustainable Construction, Mumbai.

2013. "Weaving Architecture: Conserving the Old, Building the New." KIT Thomas Memorial Oration, Chennai.

2013. "Architecture as Resource: Rendezvous with the Legends—Indian Institute of Architects." Indian Institute of Architects, Indore.

2014. "Our Next Train Stop." University of Edinburgh Symposium, Mumbai.

2014. "Architecture as Resource." Architecture+Design: Shaping Architecture, New Delhi.

2014. "Architecture as Resource." 5th Annual Sustainability in Design and Construction India Summit, Nispana, Bangalore.

2015. Keynote speech at Women's Education Society, Smt. Manoramabai Mundle College of Architecture, Nagpur.

2015. "Architecture as Resource." 17th International Conference for Humane Habitat 2015, IAHH and Rizvi College of Architecture, Mumbai.

2015. "Architecture as Resource." Workshop on Recent Trends in Architectural Practice, School of Architecture MSRIT, Bangalore.

2015. "From Bombay to Mumbai." The Z-Axis Conference on Architecture and the City, Goa.

2015. Keynote speech on "Building Storeys." Royal School of Architecture, Guwahati.

2015. "Mumbai's Timeless Heritage." CSMVS and the Museum Society of Bombay, Mumbai.

2015. "Building Storeys: An Architect's Journey through the Indian Landscape." Jnanapravaha, Mumbai.

2015. "Building Storeys." Institute of Indian Interior Designers, Bhopal Regional Centre.

2015. "Mumbai's Timeless Heritage." Association of Medical Consultants, (AMCON) Mumbai.

2016. "State of Practice." The State of Architecture: Practices & Processes in India (SOA), Exhibition & Conference, Mumbai.

2016. Keynote speech on "Building Storeys." The State of Architecture: Practices & Processes in India (SOA), National Gallery of Modern Art, Mumbai.

2017. "Threads and Continuities." HP Design Summit, A+D and HP, Pune.

2017. "The Future of Heritage Conservation: What the City Requires." Panel, Museum Society of Mumbai and CSMVS, Mumbai.

2017. "Threads and Continuities." CoA-TTP: Women in Architecture, Rizvi College of Architecture, Mumbai.

EXHIBITIONS – SELECTED

1999. *50 Years of Indian Architecture Retrospective Exhibition*, School of Planning and Architecture, New Delhi, India.

2000. *Women in Architecture 2000 Plus— An Emancipated Place*, Mumbai, India.

2001. *Permanent Exhibition International Archives of Women Architects*, Virginia Tech, USA.

2001. *Un-built India Vision*, New Delhi, India.

2002. *Exhibitions*, Tokyo, Japan.

2013. *Design as Social Capital*, New Delhi, India.

2016. *State of Practice—The State of Architecture: Practices & Processes in India (SOA)*, Exhibition, Mumbai, India.

2016. *Preston Thomas Memorial Symposium*, AAP, Cornell University, New York, USA.

PUBLICATIONS – BOOKS

Bahga, Sarbjit and Surinder Bahga, 1993, *Modern Architecture in India: Post Independence Perspective*, New Delhi: Galgotia Publishing Company.

Lang, Jon T, Madhavi Desai, and Miki Desai, 1997, *Architecture and Independence: The Search for Identity, India 1880–1980*, UK: Oxford University Press.

Somaya, Brinda and Urvashi Mehta, 2001, *An Emancipated Place: Women in Architecture 2000 Plus*, Mumbai: The HECAR Foundation.

Lang, Jon T, 2002, *A Concise History of Modern Architecture in India*, New Delhi: Permanent Black.

Sangghvi, Malavika, 2004, *Spirited Souls: Winning Women of Mumbai*, India.

UNESCO, 2004, *Asia Conserved: Lessons learned from the UNESCO Asia-Pacific Awards for Cultural Heritage Conservation (2005–2009)*, Lanham, Maryland: Bernan Assoc Publisher.

Gupchup, Vijaya V., 2005, *St. Thomas's Cathedral Mumbai: A Witness to History*, Mumbai: Eminence Designs.

Somaya, Brinda, Poonam Verma Mascarenhas, Kuppanda Ganapathy Premnath, and N. N. Dyan Belliappa, 2006, *Silent Sentinels: Architecture on Coorg*, Mumbai: The HECAR Foundation.

Phaidon Press, 2008, *Phaidon Atlas of 20th Century World Architecture*, London: Phaidon Press.

Prashad, Deependra and Saswati Chetia, ed., 2008, *New Architecture and Urbanism Development of Indian Tradition*, Newcastle upon Tyne: Cambridge Scholars Publishing.

Rossl, Stefania, 2009, *Architettura Contemporanea India (Contemporary Indian Architecture)*, Italy: Motta Architettura.

Maluste, Mridula and Viral Doshi, 2010, *The Cathedral and John Connon School—An Undefiled Heritage*, Mumbai: The Anglo-Scottish Education Society, 316–327.

Mukadam, Nitin, 2010, *GreenBuild—Green Architecture in India*, Mumbai: Asian Industry Information & Services Pvt. Ltd..

Simoes, Gita and Brinda Somaya, 2010, *The Cathedral School Portfolio*, Mumbai: The HECAR Foundation, India.

Singh, Nanni, 2010, *The Secret Abode of Fireflies: Loving and Losing Spaces of Nature in the City*, New Delhi: Youthreach.

Chaturvedi, Abha and Anil Chaturvedi, 2012, *Trusted by Generations Tested by Time: 75 years in the Life of ACC Limited*, New Delhi: Penguin Group.

Poiesz, Pelle, Gert Jan Scholte and Sanne Vanderkaaij Gandhi, 2013, *Learning from Mumbai: Practising Architecture in Urban India*, Ahmedabad: Mapin Publishing.

Wiszniewski, Dorian, 2016, *Bombay City Wise: Para-situation Mumbai*, Edinburgh: University of Edinburgh.

Chhatrapati Shivaji Maharaj Vastu Sangrahalaya, 2017, *The Museum Annual Review: 2015–2016*, Mumbai.

Bose Dutta, Apurva, 2017, *Architectural Voices of India: A Blend of Contemporary and Traditional Ethos*, Newcastle upon Tyne: Cambridge Scholars Publishing.

Desai, Madhavi, 2017, *Women Architects and Modernism in India*, New Delhi: Routledge.

Jain, Kulbhushan, 2017, *Conserving Architecture*, Ahmedabad: AADI Centre.

Woods, Mary N., 2017, *Women Architects in India: Histories of Practice in Mumbai and Delhi*, Oxford: Routledge.

SELECT JOURNALS – INTERNATIONAL

Raman, P. G. 1998. "Il Prezioso Lavoro di Brinda Somaya (On the Precious Work of Brinda Somaya)." *Spazio e Società* (February): pp. 86–91.

2002, February. "India: Brinda Somaya." *Interiors*: pp. 186–189.

Karunaratne, Kirthi Sri. 2005. "Styles in the City." *Explore Sri Lanka* (March): p. 50.

2005. "Form Enhances Function: The Aesthetics of Geometry." *Journal of the Sri Lanka Inst. of Architects*.

2006. "Brinda Somaya." *Abitare*: pp. 132–134 (July).

2008. "A Sense of Place: Stylish New Home of TCS." *World Architecture News* (January).

2009. "The Inclusive Practice of Brinda Somaya." *Journal of the South African Inst. of Architects* (July), South Africa: p. 60–61.

SELECT JOURNALS – NATIONAL

1987. "A Blueprint for Success." *Eve's Weekly* (February): p. 48–56.

Premji, Yasmeen. 1987. "Making it in a Man's World." *Inside Outside* (August): p. 28–51.

Ahuja, Sarayu. 1987. "Counterpoint." *Indian Architect and Builder* (October): p. 78–85.

Banerji, Ranjona. 1990. "Giving the Past a Future." *Bombay: The City Magazine* (August): pp. 38–44.

1991. "The Pearl of Parel." *Bombay: The City Magazine* (January): p. 51.

1991. "From Peeling Walls to Gleaming Paint." *Journal of India Inst. of Architects* (April): p. 13–24.

1991. "Architecture with Reason." *The Fountainhead* (September): p. 12–16.

1991. "NRK House Bombay." *Architecture & Design Interiors* (October): pp. 78–80.

Singh, Riva K. 1991. "A Complete Makeover." *Inside Outside* (October): pp. 171–189.

Tindall, Gillian. 1992. "Designscape Magic." *Interiors India*: p. 129–135.

1994. "J.I.I. A Award 1994: Project: Shelter." *Journal of India Inst. of Architects* (July): p. 3–4.

1994. "Coming of Age." *Inside Outside* (December): p. 61–82.

1995. "Continuity and Change." *Journal of India Inst. of Architects* (March): p. 34–38.

1996. "Rewinding the Existing: The Cathedral and John Connon Schools." *Architecture & Design* (January): pp. 71–77.

1996. "Economic Viability of Listed Heritage Buildings and Their Re-adaptability." *Design Ideas* (June): pp. 62–65.

1997. "Elevating Design Standards." *The Fountainhead* (July): pp. 28–33.

Paradkar, Shalaka. 1997. "Beyond the Blueprint." *Indian Architect and Builder* (August): pp. 33–70.

1999. "Designer of the Year Award: Somaya and Kalappa Consultants." *Inside Outside* (July): pp. 110–117.

1999. "Brinda Somaya: In Love with the City." *Construction World* (September): pp. 10–11.

Maluste, Mridula. 2000. "Through Time and Space: Journey of an Architect." *Interiors and Lifestyle India* (January): pp. 89–104.

Sharma, Namrata. 2000. "Buildings and Beyond." *Afternoon Dispatch and Courier* (March): p. 7.

2001. "Profile: Somaya and Kalappa Consultants." *Indian Architect and Builder* (April).

Guha, Nilima. 2002. "Inspiring Interiors." *Inside Outside* (January): pp. 126–139.

2002. "The Past is Still Passing By." *Design Today* (August).

Mugve, Sandhya. 2002. "JK Commendation Awards 2002: SNK." *Indian Architect and Builder* (October): pp. 70–71.

2002. "Constructing Life: Somaya and Kalappa Consultants Revitalise Bhadli Village." *Indian Architect and Builder*: p. 59–71.

2003. "Balancing Act." *Times Journal of Construction and Design* (April): pp. 38–40.

2004. "Relevant Architecture." *Architecture & Design* (September): pp. 42–48.

2004. "Hurrah for Heritage." *TimeOut Mumbai* (September): p. 9.

Mittal, Tapan and Kruti Garg. 2005. "Evolution, Not Preservation." *Architecture: Time, Space, and People* (February): pp. 28–36.

Mahoney, Pervin. 2005. "Three Campuses and the Champa Tree." *Inside Outside* (July).

Shah, Sonal. 2005. "Decor Heritage: St. Thomas's Cathedral." *Elle Decor* (December): pp. 68–71.

2005. "Contemporary Women Architects: Brinda Somaya." *Architecture & Design* (December): pp. 68–76.

Hira, Savitha. 2006. "The Historical Blend." *Home Review* (November): pp. 74–80.

2006. "The Art of Living." *Journal of India Inst. of Architects* (November): pp. 31–32.

Baruah, Teena. 2007. "Building Heritage." *Harmony* (March): pp. 18–22.

2007. "A Sense of Place." *Journal of India Inst. of Architects* (August): pp. 21–22.

Luthra, Kanika. 2008. "Symbolic Architecture." *Inside Outside* (March): p. 90–106.

2008. "Rubble to Renewal and Beyond...." *Journal of India Inst. of Architects* (July): p. 11–12.

Sabnis Pinge, Roopa. 2008. "The Art of Adaptation." *Better Interiors* (August): pp. 83–87.

Madhavdas, Priya. 2009. "In Conversation with a Courtyard." *Design and Interiors* (February): pp. 30–37.

2009. "Women in Construction—Revisited." *Construction Week* (November).

2010. "Master Series: Brinda Somaya." *Architect and Interiors India* (April): pp. 58–64.

Luthra, Kanika. 2010. "A House for All Seasons." *Inside Outside* (May): pp. 78–93.

2010. "Profile: T.C.S House, Mumbai." *Journal of India Inst. of Architects* (June): pp. 6–8.

2010. *Icons and Reflections of Architecture*, Hettich.

Somaya, Brinda. 2010. "Architecture of Sensibilities." SPARC Ahmedabad 7 (July).

2011. "Preserving the Past." *Insite* (February): pp. 14–15.

2011. "Ethos." *Indian Architect and Builder* (September): pp. 62–73.

Sunavala, Nergish. 2011. "Around Town: Under the Oval." *TimeOut Mumbai* (November): p. 64.

2011. "The Conscientious: Brinda Somaya." *Architect and Interiors India, Special Edition: A Tribute to 15 Green Architects*: pp. 11–19.

2012. "Mumbai Awaits." *A.C.E Update* (January).

2012. "Mumbai Esplanade." Ar. Aamcher, *Design Matrix* (March): pp. 32–33.

2012. "Doctor of Fine Arts: Brinda Somaya." *Indian Architect and Builder* (June): p. 34.

2012. "Gestures in a Landscape." *Indian Architect and Builder* (August): pp. 52–77.

Jayakar, Devyani. 2012. "Lasting Impressions." *Inside Outside* (October): pp. 82–100.

2013. "Designing Stories Through Decades." *Architecture & Design* (January): pp. 80–88.

2013. "Building Blocks of Education." *Green Construction and Design* (April): pp. 24–28.

2013. "Environment Response Forms." *Architecture & Design* (May): pp. 37–43.

2013. "Heritage Conservation: Restoring St. Thomas's Cathedral." *Journal of India Inst. of Architects India* (June): pp. 6–12.

2013. "Profile: Goa Inst. of Management." *Green Construction and Design* (August): p. 26.

Bhamgara, Fardeen. 2013. "Heritage Hotels." *Index Furniture Journal* (September).

2013. "What Might Have Been: the Mumbai Esplanade Project." *Index Furniture Journal* (November).

2014. "Architects Behind the Big Projects: Brinda Somaya." *Modern Green Structure & Architecture, India* (April): pp. 48–53.

2014. "Profile: Brinda Somaya." *Vogue India* (July): p. 165.

2014. "IIM-A Appoints Master Architect for Restoration of its Campus." *Architecture Update* (September).

Mishra, Divya. 2014. "Icon: Restoring Confidence." *Architectural Digest* (November): pp. 117–120.

2015. "Love Affair Between Architects and Lights." *India Mondo Arch*: pp. 64–66.

2016. "The Grand Masters of Design." *Society Interiors* (January).

2016. "Indian Institute of Architects Award 2015, Commendation Award: Conservation Projects." *Journal of India Inst. of Architects* (July): pp. 72–76.

Chikte, Nida. 2016. "Resurrecting Antiquity." *Architecture Update* (July).

2016. "The Mumbai Esplanade." *FuturArc* (July): pp. 44–45.

2016. "Nestled in the Foothills." *Architecture & Design* (July): pp. 101–105.

2016. "Profile: Brinda Somaya." *iDecorama* (August): pp. 80–81.

Chikte, Nida. 2016. "90s to Present: Journey of Women in Architecture." *Architecture Update* (October): pp. 16–23.

Padman, Gayathri. 2016. "Annealing the Links." *Design Detail* (November): pp. 23–34.

Nambiar, Shruti. 2017. "Shelf Life: A Book Honors India's Female Architects." *Insidetrack Newsletter* (January).

Somaya, Brinda. 2017. "Forging a Strong Foundation for Success." *INSITE Magazine* (January): pp. 23–25.

2017. "The Green, the Bad, and the Ugly." *Home and Design Trends* (February): pp. 54–55.

Joshi, Sheetal. 2017. "A True Stalwart." *The Tiles of India* (February): pp. 32–36.

2017. "The Visionaries The Big Idea." *Elle Décor* (February): p. 74.

2017. "50+ Architects–One Agenda–Greening India." *Modern Green Structures & Architecture,* India (April): p. 15.

2017. "The Influencers." *Realty Plus* (April).

Somaya, Brinda. 2017. "Power House—5 Women Who Transformed Indian Design." *India Today HOME* (May): p. 41.

Somaya, Brinda and Nandini Sampat. 2017. "100 reasons to celebrate." *Architect and Interiors* (July).

PUBLICATIONS – NEWSPAPERS

1987. "Woman Architects on the Rise." *Deccan Herald*, January 12.

1989. "This is a Technical Profession." *The Times of India*, May 1.

1997. "There Goes the Architectress." *The Times of India*, June 1.

Devidayal, Namita. 1998. "Nuturer, not Middleman." *The Sunday Times of India*, February 8.

2000. "Buildings and Beyond." *Afternoon Despatch & Courier*, March 2.

2000. "Women's Day." *The Times of India*, March 24.

Jain, Reshma. 2001. "Architect With A Mission." *Deccan Chronicle*, March 4, Hyderabad edition.

Andrade, Carol. 2001. "In Search of Roots." *The Times of India*, March 10.

Advani, Aditya P. 2001. "Past Perfect." Sunday Review, *The Times of India*, April 22.

2002. "$2000 Down and No More to Pay: A Place to Live after the Storm." *The New York Times*, May 2, New York edition.

2004. "Heritage Reclaims the Streets in the City." *The Sunday Times of India*, September 5.

2006. "Rajabai Tower Gets a Face-lift." *DNA*, December 16, p. 8.

Pant Zachariah, Mini. 2006 "Building Blocks." *Sunday Hindustan Times*, October 8.

Gupta, Preeti. 2007. "Tower Library Computerisation Set to Kick-Start." *Bombay Times*, April 27.

Zachariah, Reeba. 2007. "At Last, TCS Gets its HQ." *The Times of India*, August 17, p. 7.

Shirodkar, Hemant. 2007. "Shell Theory Gives Old Building New Lease of Life." *The Times of India*, August 20, p. 8.

Deshmukh, Smita. 2007. "TCS House: Historical Facade, Plush Interiors." *DNA India*, August 17, p. 6.

Sharma, Aabhas. 2007. "Reserve and Keep." *Business Standard*, September 22.

2007. Gianani Kareena N. and Radhika Raj. "Gothic Revival." *DNA*, August 26.

Baliga, Linah. 2007. "BMC Plans to Go Solo for Art's Sake." *DNA India*, September 26.

2008. "Eco-sensitivity Starts at the Design Board." *DNA*, August 2.

Udas Mankikar, Sayli. 2008. "Worli Arts and Crafts Centre Gets State's Nod." *Hindustan Times*, April 11, p. 8.

2008. "Art Centre for Mumbai." *The Times of India*, March 21, p. 3.

Vyas, Sharad. 2008. "A New Haat for Mumbai." *The Times of India*, March 16, Mumbai edition.

Paul, Gem. 2008. "Mumbai's Very Own Cultural Enclave." *The Times of India*, May 15.

2008. "BMC's Dilli Haat-like Park Gets State's Nod." *Mumbai Mirror*, April 12, p. 3.

Basu, Sudipta. 2008. "Wada-Project!" *Mumbai Mirror*, May 22, p. 8.

Baliga, Linah. 2008. "Mumbai is a Place Where Art Can Shine." *DNA*, April 25.

Shenolikar, Aasawari. 2008. "Buildings and Beyond." *The Hitavada Realty*, March 14.

2009. "Restored Pride." *The Hindu* group, October 23.

Tahseen, Ismat. 2010. "Mumbai's Going Desi." *DNA*, May 23.

Prashanth, Bindu. "Build to Sustain." 2010. Times Property, *The Times of India*, February 28.

2011. "Green. What Does That Mean?" *The Times of India*, July 15.

Udas Mankikar, Sayli. 2011. "Will This SoBo Walking Plan Work?" *Hindustan Times*, November 16.

2012. "Lego Lady." *Mumbai Mirror*, September 16.

Jaisinghani, Bella. 2012. "Rajabai Restoration Plan Ready." *The Times of India*, May 10, Mumbai edition.

Ramaswamy, Radhika. 2012. "Rajabai Tower to Undergo Restoration After 6 Year Wait." *Mumbai Mirror*, January 3, p. 10.

2012. "Love Grove's New Affair." *Mumbai Mirror*, January 26.

Ashar, Hemal. 2012. "Going Under the Knife: The Restoration of Rajabai Tower." *MidDay*, January 1.

2014. "Celebrating Without Complacency." *DNA*, March 8.

Iyer, Aishwarya. 2015. "MU's Heart Starts Ticking Once More." *Hindustan Times*, May 13.

2015. "After a Nip and Tuck, Rajabai Tower Regains its Original Look." *The Times of India*, May 12, Mumbai edition, p. 10.

2015. "Insider's Guide to Rajabai Tower." *Hindustan Times*, November 20.

Jaisinghani, Bella. 2015. "Fixed and Polished: Tick-tock Tick-tock Merrily Sing City's Tallest Tower." *Mumbai Mirror*, May 13, p. 6.

2015. "Tower of Pride." *Mumbai Mirror*, May, p. 8.

Sunavala, Nergish. 2016. "School Gets Architect to Save a Chapter of Their Own History." *The Times of India*, June 19.

Varghese, Shiny. 2017. "Rooms of Their Own." *The Sunday Express*, March 5.

Dore, Bhavya. 2017. "Changing Room." *Mumbai Mirror*, April 23.

Pawar, Nivedita Jayaram. 2017. "Build It Like Brinda." *The Asian Age*, May 14.

Gehi, Reema. 2017. "The Making of the Museum's Magnum Opus." *Mumbai Mirror*, October 29.

2017. "For the 1st Time, Bombay House to Shut A Year for Renovation." *The Sunday Times of India*, August 6.

INTERVIEWS – PRINT

1987. "Woman Architects on the Rise." *Deccan Herald* (January 12): p. 3.

Bhagwat, Sharmila. 1991. "Invasion of a Male Province." *The Sunday Panorama* (August): pp. 1–2.

1994. "Focus: Somaya and Kalappa Consultants." *Design Ideas*.

1999. "The Woods are Lovely." *Society Interiors*: pp. 101–103.

2000. "Of Lines and Figures." *Femina*: pp. 180–181.

2002. "Bombay: A City that Once Was." *Housecalls*: pp. 30–35.

2004. "Recipe for Success." *Winning Women in India*.

2005. "A Road to Revival." *Times Journal of Construction and Design* (April): 36–37.

2007. "Woman of Steel." *New Woman* (September): pp. 66–70.

2007. Business Class column, *Bombay Times*, May 8, p. 6.

2008. "Profile of Brinda Somaya." *Better Interiors* (May): pp. 137–141.

2009. "Earth Bound." *The Ideal Home & Gardens* (November).

2010. "Profile: Brinda Somaya." *Icons & Reflections of Architecture*: pp. 12–25.

2010. "Brinda Somaya on the Journey So Far and the Way Froward at SNK." *Design Matrix* (November).

2011. "Architecture–In Harmony with Precision." *A.C.E Update* (January): pp. 18–20.

2011. "Profiling Architects." *Society Interiors* (March): pp. 109–118.

2012. "The Architectural Altruism." *Built Expressions* (September): pp. 100–105.

2013. "Visionary Wonder." *Society Interiors* (August): pp. 136–142.

2013. "Local Thinking." *Holcim Forum* (January).

2013. "The Architect as a Guardian of the Public Realm." *Learning from Mumbai*: pp. 150–157.

2013. "Profile: Brinda Somaya." *Indian Architect and Builder* (July): pp. 54–57.

2013. "A Blueprint for Socially Sensitive Architecture." *Buildotech* (July): pp. 24–30.

2014. "Interview with Brinda Somaya." *Construction and Architecture Update* (January): pp. 54–56.

2014. "Architects are Guardians of the Built & Unbuilt Environment: Brinda Somaya." *A.C.E Update* (June): pp. 16–18.

2014. "My Life in Design: Brinda Somaya." *Kyoorius* (November): pp. 23–30.

2015. "Interview with Brinda Somaya." *Construction and Architecture Update* (July): pp. 36–38.

2015. "Gender Bender." *Architect and Interiors in India* (March): pp. 38–43.

2016. "Brinda Somaya, SNK." *Modern Green Structures & Architecture* (April): pp. 26–28.

2016. "Every Project is a Journey." *Architecture in India*: pp. 54–55.

2016. "7 Wonders: Brinda Somaya." *Architect and Interiors in India* (March): p. 18.

2016. "Multi-disciplinary Architecture and Design Practitioner." *Urban Vaastu* (October): pp. 14–19.

INTERVIEWS – ONLINE, RADIO AND TV

2000. "An Interview with Brinda Somaya on the Restoration of NRK House." *CNN: Style South Asia*, January 27.

2006. "An Interview with the Architect at the TCS Campus, Andheri." *In the House of Style*, August 17.

2008. "An Interview with Brinda Somaya." *Swadesh*, June.

2009. "An Interview with Brinda Somaya." *A.C.E World Expo*, October 4.

2011. "A Discussion on Design Philosophy." *VOICE* (Voluntary Organisation in Community Enterprise).

2015. "Architects on Architecture." *Think Matter*, June 30.

2015. "The Design Story of Acron Waterfront Resort by Brinda Somaya." *Acron Waterfront Resort*, July 6.

2016. "Webinar: The Contemporary Context of Architecture in India." *Investigating Design*, July 23.

CONTRIBUTORS

Ruturaj Parikh   Curator
Ruturaj Parikh is a partner with MATTER: an architecture, design and publishing studio based in Goa, which he founded in 2014 with Maanasi Hattangadi. He is the former Director of the Charles Correa Foundation where he led urban and public projects and research in human settlements. He has been involved in social projects that include listing and grading heritage buildings, redevelopment of backward and informal settlements and low-cost housing. From 2010 till 2014, Parikh was editor at *Indian Architect & Builder* magazine.

Nandini Somaya Sampat   Editor
Nandini Somaya Sampat is currently a director at SNK and, with Brinda Somaya, she continues to lead this multidisciplinary design and architecture firm. Upon completion of her Bachelor of Arts in Political Science from Smith College, USA, Sampat qualified as a solicitor from the College of Law, London. After working in India as a corporate lawyer, she decided to change professions and pursue design. Sampat holds a Bachelor of Architecture degree from Rizvi College of Architecture, Mumbai. She completed her Postgraduate Diploma in Architectural Interior Design from the Inchbald School of Design, London. Upon returning to Mumbai, she joined Somaya & Kalappa Consultants.

ESSAYS
James Stewart Polshek, designer, public advocate and educator, is in the sixth decade of his architectural career. In all three of these areas, Polshek has structured an inspirational template for generations of architects. In 1963, he founded James Stewart Polshek Architects, which ultimately became the internationally recognised Polshek Partnership Architects. In 2010, the partners renamed the firm Ennead Architects; Polshek is Design Counsel to Ennead Architects. He served as the dean of Columbia University's Graduate School of Architecture, Planning and Preservation from 1972 to 1987. Polshek is the recipient of the 2018 American Institute of Architects (AIA) Gold Medal.

Jon Lang is an emeritus professor at the University of New South Wales where he headed the School of Architecture and taught in the Masters of Urban Development and Design program. He is the director for urban design at ERG/Environmental Research Group Inc. in Philadelphia, Pennsylvania. He has authored books on urban design, on architectural theory and modern architecture in India.

Porus Olpadwala is Professor Emeritus of City and Regional Planning, and Dean Emeritus of the College of Architecture, Art and Planning at Cornell University, USA. His professional research domains are political economy, comparative social and economic development, and urban and environmental issues. Presently, he is consulting and writing on higher education issues and is an adjunct professor in the College of Architecture and Planning at the University of New Mexico.

Mary N. Woods is professor of architectural history at Cornell University. Her work spans film, photography, and urban and built environments in the United States and India. She is the author of *From Craft to Profession* (1999), a history of architectural education and practice in the United States, and *Beyond the Architect's Eye* (2009 and 2014), an account of photography and the American built environment. Her *Women Architects in India: Histories of Practice in Mumbai and Delhi* was published by Ashgate Press in spring 2016.

Tod Williams and Billie Tsien founded their architectural practice in 1986. Their studio, Tod Williams Billie Tsien Architects, is located in New York City and focuses on work for institutions, museums and schools amongst other typologies. They work with non-profits and organisations that value issues of aspiration and meaning, timelessness and beauty and have been chosen as architects for the Obama Presidential Library. Tod and Billie are active academicians and have lectured worldwide.

CRITICAL DIALOGUES
Arun Shourie is an Indian economist, journalist, author and politician. He has worked as an economist with the World Bank, a consultant to the Planning Commission of India, editor of *The Indian Express* and *The Times of India* and a minister in the Government of India (1998–2004). He was awarded the Ramon Magsaysay Award in 1982 and the Padma Bhushan in 1990. Shourie is the author of many books and is a shrewd observer and commentator on Indian culture and politics.

Kamu Iyer graduated in architecture from the Sir J.J. School of Art, Bombay, in 1957. As a practitioner since 1960 with Architects' Combine, a firm in which he is a partner, Iyer has built extensively in Mumbai and other parts of India. His practice covers a wide range of projects like low-income housing, educational and institutional buildings and campuses and research facilities. Iyer has authored *Buildings That Shaped Bombay: Works of G B Mhatre* and co-authored *Four from the Fifties: Emerging Modern Architecture in Bombay* as well as *Build A Safe House With Confined Masonry*.

Saryu Doshi is an Indian art scholar, art historian, academic and curator. She received the fellowship from the Rockefeller Foundation and pursued research on Indian miniature art and Jain art, for which she received a doctoral degree (PhD). She is the founder director of the National Gallery of Modern Art, Mumbai, and a former *pro tem* chairman of the Lalit Kala Akademi, New Delhi. Doshi is the author of several books, including *Masterpieces of Jain Painting*, a monograph on selected Jain art pieces. The Government of India awarded her the fourth highest civilian award, the Padma Shri, in 1999.

CONSULTANTS

COLLABORATIONS

Belt Collins And Associates, Landscape Architects USA Alan Gilbert & Associates Interior Designers, Hong Kong; Tashzniiep Institute, Architects & Service Consultants, V/O. "Sojuzvneshstrojimport" Tashkent, Uzbekistan; M. Moser Associates Ltd., Hong Kong; Tod Williams Billie Tsien Architects LLP, USA Phases II And III, TCS Banyan Park, Mumbai, India; Kohn Pederson Fox Associates, USA; Pei Cobb Freed & Partners, USA.

STRUCTURAL CONSULTANTS

Shishir Kulkarni & Associates; Cruthi Consultant Consortium Pvt. Ltd; Ghadiali & Raval; Shilp Consulting Engineers; Sterling Engineering Consultancy Services; Shashank Mehendale & Associates; Devang Sutaria; Facet Construction Engineering; Kuvelkar Salkar Associates; Pendanekar & Associates; Associated Consultants; Paresh Gaitonde; Semac Consultants Pvt. Ltd; VMS Consultants Pvt. Ltd; Leslie E. Robertson Associates; Integrated Building Services; Design Brevity; Façade India Testing Inc.

CONSERVATION CONSULTANTS

Indian Institute of Technology, Chennai; Sheetal Gandhi & Associates; Sandhya Sawant.

MEP CONSULTANTS

Vikas Doshi & Associates; MEP Consulting Engineers; Epsilon Design Consultancy Pvt. Ltd; Design Cell; Jhaveri Associates; Chander Ramchandani; Yash Consultant; Aecom India Pvt. Ltd; Sunil Services; Ramchandra G. Deo; Hydro Mechanical Consultant; Dnyanesh Bhave; HVAC Consultants Services; Dnyanesh Bhave: Eros Cinema; D. R. Bellare; Viraj Building Engineering Services P. Ltd; Castellino Engineering Consultants. Pvt. Ltd; Engineering Creation Public Health Consultancy. Pvt. Ltd.

LANDSCAPE CONSULTANTS

AMS Consultants: TCG, BKC. Vaishanvi Landscape; Ravi & Varsha Gavandi; Arun Kumar Landscape Architect. SAMA Landscape Architect; Landscape Design & Development; The Landscape Company; Integrated Design; Green Angle.

CREDITS

TRANSCRIPTION
Helen Starr and Mabel D'souza

DIGITAL ARCHIVES
Somaya and Kalappa Consultants

DRAWINGS
While many people were involved, the following made a significant contribution. Base drawings were drawn by: Ajay Harchekar, Isha Raundal, Aneesh Devi, Vanshica Chugh, Nikita Sharma, Katherine Milne and Pooja Sharma. Hadrian Lobo and Anthea Fernandes oversaw drawing production in order to express the architectural intent.

PHOTOGRAPHS
Most of the illustrations have been reproduced from Brinda Somaya's archive. All the projects featured have been revisited and photographed during the process of the book with efforts by Ishita Parikh, Sagar Shinde and Poorvi Wadehra.

Every effort has been made to identify the photographers of specific images, and where this has been possible they have been credited below:

Apostrophe A+ud pp. 200, 210; **Dr Bhau Daji Lad Museum** pp. 137, 276–277; **British Library, London, UK© British Library Board** pp. 278, 242, 283; **Sameer Chawda** p. 479; **Club Mahindra Resorts** pp. 380, 386, 392–393; **Subhabrata Das** pp. 164–165; **Dinodia Photo LLP** pp. 239, 240–241, 290, 292–293; **Noshir Gobhai** pp. 78 (top left), 112 (below right), 114 (top left), 119 (top right and below), 128–129, 148–150, 179 (top right and below), 190–191, 230, 232–233, 234, 237, 253, 258–259, 260–261, 309–310; **Haseler, A.R. (fl.1930) British Library** pp. 96–97; **Hulton-Deutsch Collection** p. 25; **Farooq Issa, Phillips Antiques** pp. 280, 282; Kamu Iyer p. 159; **LMS Bruce Private Collection–Viral Doshi** pp. 98 (below left), 99 (below right); **Ajay Lotlikar** p. 423 (top); **Maritime History Society** p. 279; **Suleiman Merchant** p. 187 (below); **Ruturaj Parikh** pp. 352, 414 (below left), 422; **Shirish Patel** p. 222; **Pei Cobb Freed & Partners** p. 181; **Fram Petit** p. 142 (below left); **Rallis Publishing House** p. 136; **Jehangir Sorabjee** p. 139; **Robert Stephens** p. 267; *The Sunday Times of India* p. 120; **Wikimedia Commons (source:http://homepages.rootsweb.ancestry.com/~poyntz/India/maps. html#area) fl.1893, Constable's 1893 Hand Atlas** p. 243.

TEAM AT SNK
Abhijeet Patki, Arvind Khanvalkar, Ashish Puradkar, Asware Pandurang, Balkrishna Vairagale, Bharat Iste, Bharat Shetty, Chandrika Sahay, Christopher Gomes, Dashrath Raut, Dhairyasheel Powar, Dhara Desai, Dipanjan Das, Dnyaneshwar Chakor, Giriyappa C., Hadrian Lobo, Hemant Kamrekar, Homeyar Goiporia, Jatin Asher, Jayant Ambekar, Jeenal Rathod, Kashinath Karelkar, Kasim Pediwala, Mani Megali, Margaret Arockiaswamy, Mary Margaret, Meenakshi Chauhan, Mehul Kapadia, Mohan Raj, Morris Pinto, Mustakim Kirkire, Nicolas Antoine, Nikhil Vichare, Nishith Kothari, Prabhakar Harwande, Prajakta Bhurke, Prashant Nalavade, Prashant Phatak, Rahul Nair, Rajan Subhedar, Rajeshwari Gopinathan, Rashmi Pookkottil, Ravindra Jadhav, Ritika Jharia, Rupal Yardi, Sabyasachi Roy Choudhury, Saiprasad Mestri, Sandeep Gore, Sandeep Pawar, Santosh Pawar, Sayed Mohiuddin, Selva Kumar, Shanthi Esakkimuthu, Sinora Penkar, Snehal Solanki, Sonali Desai, Suji Kim, Sunshine Lobo, Swapna Rikame, Swati Bambulkar, Swati Ray, Sweta Gandhi, Tryambak Date, Vikas Haldankar, Vinay Thakurdwarkar, Vinay Thambe and many many more.

The editors have attempted to acknowledge all sources of images used in this publication and apologise for any errors or omissions.